DRUGS

DRUGS

Cultures, Controls and Everyday Life

edited by
NIGEL SOUTH

SAGE Publications
London • Thousand Oaks • New Delhi

SAGE Publications Ltd
6 Bonhill Street
London EC2A 4PU

SAGE Publications Inc
2455 Teller Road
Thousand Oaks, California 91320

SAGE Publications India Pvt Ltd
32, M-Block Market
Greater Kailash – I
New Delhi 110 048

British Library Cataloguing in Publication data

A catalogue record for this book is
available from the British Library

ISBN 0 7619 5234 9
ISBN 0 7619 5235 7 (pbk)

Library of Congress catalog card number 98-61541

Typeset by Photoprint, Torquay, Devon
Printed in Great Britain by Athenaeum Press, Gateshead

For
Mike Collison

CONTENTS

NOTES ON CONTRIBUTORS

Ross Coomber is Principal Lecturer in Sociology at the University of Greenwich, London. Recent publications have centred upon concerns about the adulteration of illicit drugs, the activities of drug dealers, the rationality of drug control policies and media representations of drugs and drug users. His most recent, edited, book is *The Control of Drugs and Drug Users: Reason or Reaction* (1998).

Nicholas Dorn has published on the development of the European Union's policies on crime in the broader contexts of policies on the single market and on justice and home affairs. His publications include *European Drug Policies and Enforcement* (co-edited with Jepsen and Savona, 1996), 'Beyond pillars and passerelle debates: the EU's emerging crime prevention space' (with White, *Legal Issues of European Integration*, 1997); and *Regulating European Drug Problems: Administrative Measures and Civil Law in the Control of Drug Trafficking, Nuisance and Use* (1998). Dr Dorn is Director of Research and Development at ISDD, the Institute for the Study of Drug Dependence. ISDD is Britain's drug information service and the UK 'focal point' for the European Monitoring Centre on Drugs and Drug Addiction, Lisbon. E-mail: nicholas@isdd.co.uk or ecru@dial.pipex.com

Sheila Henderson has been involved in youth policy- and practice-related research for the last twelve years, focusing particularly on gender, sexuality and drug issues. She has run an independent research consultancy for the last seven years, conducting contract research for government departments, local and national policy bodies and charities in many parts of Britain. She has published widely on social and cultural aspects of illegal drug use and has recently conducted studies which explore rural/urban contrasts in youth lifestyles. Her most recent key publications are *Working With Young People in Rural Areas: An Evaluation Report* (London, Home Office Drugs Prevention Initiative, 1998), *Ecstasy: Case Unsolved* (1997), ' "E" types and dance divas: some implications for research and prevention', in T. Rhodes and R. Hartnoll (eds), *HIV Prevention in the Community: Perspectives on Individual, Community and*

Political Action (1996), and *Young People's Drug Use in Salford: Drug Pathways through Today's Youth Culture* (1995).

Maggy Lee is a Lecturer in the Department of Sociology at the University of Essex. She was formerly a Researcher at the Institute for the Study of Drug Dependence and Lecturer in Criminology at Birkbeck College. She has a B.Soc.Sc. (1986) and M.Phil. (1991) from Hong Kong University, and M.Phil. (1990) and Ph.D. (1993) from Cambridge University. Her publications include *Youth, Crime and Police Work* (1998) and many articles on drugs and policing.

Susanne MacGregor is Professor of Social Policy at Middlesex University, London. Her most recent publication is *Social Issues and Party Politics* (co-edited with H. Jones, 1998). She has researched widely on drugs policy and practice. Publications include *Tackling Drugs Locally* (with Karen Duke, 1997) and 'Reluctant partners: trends in approaches to urban drug-taking in contemporary Britain', *Journal of Drug Issues*, 28 (1), 1998: 191–204.

Karim Murji is a Senior Lecturer in Social Policy and Sociology at Roehampton Institute, London. He is author of *Policing Drugs* and co-author of *Traffickers: Drug Markets and Law Enforcement*, as well as a number of articles about drugs and policing.

Tim Newburn is Joseph Rowntree Foundation Professor of Urban Social Policy at Goldsmiths College, University of London. He is the author or editor of fourteen books, covering such issues as policing, private security, youth crime and criminal justice policy. He is currently carrying out research on police drugs strategies, on peer education and drugs prevention, and on drugs and youth justice.

Vincenzo Ruggiero is Professor of Sociology at Middlesex University in London. He is the editor of the book series 'Transnational Crime' for Routledge. His latest books are *Organised and Corporate Crime in Europe* (1996), *Economie Sporche* (1996), and *The New European Criminology* (edited with N. South and I. Taylor, 1998). He is currently working on a new book on the city and social movements in Europe.

Harry Shapiro has been employed as an information officer, author, journalist, editor and researcher at the Institute for the Study of Drug Dependence, London, since 1979. He is also a regular broadcaster and author of many articles and books on both drugs and popular music, including *Waiting for the Man: the Story of Drugs and Popular Music* and biographies of Jimi Hendrix and Eric Clapton.

Michael Shiner is a Research Officer at Goldsmiths College, University of London. Prior to this he was employed by the Policy Studies Institute.

His research has focused on peer approaches to drug education and he is joint author of *Young People, Drugs and Peer Education: An Evaluation of the Youth Awareness Programme* (Drug Prevention Initiative, Home Office Paper 13, 1996) and 'Definitely, maybe not? The normalisation of recreational drug use amongst young people', *Sociology*, 31 (3), 1997.

Nigel South is Professor of Sociology and Director of the Health and Social Services Institute at the University of Essex (email: soutn@essex.ac.uk). He teaches in the areas of criminological theory, health and social policy, and drugs issues. Recent books include V. Ruggiero and N. South *Eurodrugs* (1995) and N. South (ed.) *Drugs, Crime and Criminal Justice*, 2 vols (1995). He has also co-edited (with V. Ruggiero and I. Taylor) *The New European Criminology*, (with R. Weiss) *Comparing Prison Systems*, and (with P. Beirne) *For a Green Criminology*, (a special issue of *Theoretical Criminology* (2, 2)) all published in 1998.

INTRODUCTION

1

DEBATING DRUGS AND EVERYDAY LIFE: NORMALISATION, PROHIBITION AND 'OTHERNESS'

Nigel South

We are all natives now, and everybody else not immediately one of us is an exotic.

(Geertz, 1983: 151)

Sobriety is supposed to be the primary or 'natural' condition, the thesis, and intoxication is assumed to be secondary, unnatural, and anti-thetical.

(Lenson, 1995: 3)

This collection is concerned with 'drugs and everyday life'.[1] It therefore raises many questions about the past, present and future place of drugs in our society and culture.[2] Such questions seem to me to be well worth asking. Not least because if ever there was a time when the answers were straightforward, it is surely not today. Indeed, even my starting points – the topic of 'drugs' and the idea of 'everyday life' – require a certain amount of unpacking or deconstruction.

Let me first consider our 'context' in this collection – the idea of everyday life. Late modernity has brought rapid and astonishing changes in the social, cultural and economic spheres of everyday life and our everyday world reflects a new relationship between the 'local' and the 'global' (Giddens, 1990; Robertson, 1995). A variety of signs and experiences of diversity have accompanied such changes. For some writers, living with, accommodating and sampling this diversity epitomises the 'postmodern turn' (Kellner, 1990). Given the critique of the superficiality of everyday life inherent here, the idea of a shift to hyperreality, and the emphasis on consumption as a newly dominant form of social expression (Feather-stone, 1987; de Certeau, 1988), it is unsurprising that drugs and drug use have been seen as elements of this 'rave new world' (Redhead, 1991; Parker et al., 1995). In such a context, it is argued that the routines and orders of 'everyday life' have been subject to considerable rupture and challenge. Yet, somehow, 'everyday life' remains 'liveable' and we carry on living 'it' however 'it' may be changing or defined.

Such adaptability is vital, for the pace of change would otherwise confound and overwhelm us all. As Pickering and Green (1987: 13) note, the disintegration of the traditional social bases of community life is incontestable. In the past, these bases saw everyday experience and everyday life as rooted in:

> identification with one's own home, family, friends, fellow workers, locality, customs and institutions. These subjective alliances and loyalties are of course readily courted into extended, abstract constructs such as country, nation and race precisely because the more immediate and concrete identifications of everyday life have been subject to a long process of ideological infiltration (e.g. self-interest equated with national interest) and social change (e.g. the loosen-ing of community ties and indigenous patterns of mutual aid), and because such broader constructs are metaphorically experienced in terms of local and particular identifications.

Today, the 'local' and the 'particular' no longer *mean* what they *meant* (Robertson, 1995). Van Hoorebeeck (1997: 509) has recently commented on 'the sociology of everyday life' in a way that is very useful here.

> Everyday life could be described as those aspects of life that are related to reproduction, maintenance, common routines, receptivity and sociability (Featherstone, 1992) . . . Everything which is common though hard to explain ('irrational') gets thrown in with it, so, although mundane, the notion has something very heterogeneous as well. Moreover, behind its apparent self-reproducing static surface, there is a great deal of resistance (Maffesoli, 1989), in the sense that it is often referred to as containing elements opposing rationalization and regulation by authorities. It also has a tendency to promote *sociality*, to be understood as the desire to be immersed in collective and frivolous Dionysiac activities. As an example of tendencies to transcend official morality that are built into what we would think to be the stable, self-reproducing patterns, the carnivalesque is often mentioned (Featherstone, 1990).

The use of drugs and spread of drug cultures are reflective of these everyday tendencies toward opposition to 'rationalization' and 'regula-tion', and the embrace of indulgence in Dionysiac activities and the 'carnivalesque'. Indeed, since antiquity, people have sought means to facilitate momentary or illusory transcendence of the routine demands of everyday life (Rudgley, 1993; Goodman et al., 1995): points of departure from one timetable of the diurnal round to a different story with a different script. As van Ree (1997: 93) argues, while drugs are 'taboo' in societies which fear the artificial inducement of irrationality,[3] it is for this very reason that, ironically, they are an increasingly popular part of everyday life: 'as a "chemical carnival", providing a temporary and reversible slackening of the bonds of reason, they in fact indirectly serve to strengthen the societal framework'. Here we see the suggestiveness of neo-functionalist notions about the relationship between drugs, cultures and controls, in the everyday life of society (cf. Douglas, 1966).

Having considered the everyday *context*, let me turn now to consideration of the main issue for this book – drugs. The discussion is divided into two sections, reflecting the two key themes of this volume, 'cultures' and 'controls' of drug use. The subsequent chapters are divided along the same lines, further developing these themes The concluding chapter offers a contrasting argument about 'normalisation' to that put forward here.

DRUGS AND THE CULTURE(S) OF EVERYDAY LIFE

What I might be referring to when using this word 'drugs' could actually be a wide variety of substances with a place in everyday life. For example, medicines, poisons, foods and drinks. As Lenson (1995: 4) observes:

> the ordinary usage of the term 'drug' is utterly ambiguous. While the War on Drugs rages on, you can still drive past a mall and see a seven-foot neon sign reading DRUGS on the façade of a chain pharmacy. We assume that this is possible because there is a clear distinction between drugs taken for medical purposes and those taken for recreation, but this boundary too is far from rigid. In my lifetime amphetamines have crossed over from prescription to street drugs, and marijuana may soon cross back into prescribability as a treatment for glaucoma, the side effects of chemotherapy, and some AIDS-related illnesses.[4] And with the advent of molecular engineering the distinction has blurred even more. The difference between Prozac and Ecstasy is mostly a matter of marketing.

This point, regarding the blurring of the legal and illegal status of drugs, is one among several thought-provoking features of the emergence of a late modern 'pick 'n' mix' (Parker and Measham, 1994) poly-drug culture. Here a variety of legal substances (alcohol, tobacco, prescription and 'over-the-counter' drugs) are found alongside the range of illegal drugs available and used, providing a smorgasbord of items for selection and consumption. Let me therefore, albeit briefly, consider the recent shift over the past twenty or so years, which has taken drugs and drug use from marginal subcultures to the situation where they are widely sampled and used in late modern consumer culture.

From 'escape attempts' to everyday life

In 1976, Cohen and Taylor published the first edition of their book *Escape Attempts: the Theory and Practice of Resistance to Everyday Life*. Unsurprisingly, the use of drugs featured among the 'escapes' reviewed. It is illuminating to reflect here upon how much both 'everyday life', as well as the meaning and use of 'drugs', have changed since this book was first published. The book as a whole was a serious engagement with themes and preoccupations of the late 1960s and the 1970s and naturally the authors' descriptions of drug use reflected the times. For these authors, use of drugs could be a way of escaping the boundaries of 'paramount reality'. Drugs offered '*extra*-ordinary' (my emphasis) ways of defying the tedium of the 'ordinary'; drug use could be seen as a way of 'slipping away from reality' to explore the 'mindscape', and as a means to experience profound though (with a touch of realism) 'momentary' 'slips through the fabric' (1992: 145–7, 170–85). Although the examples given to illustrate such activities reflect meanings and styles of use that are mirrors of their time and culture, there is no denying that the motives and experiential goals concerning drug use have remained, in some ways, remarkably constant.

Cohen and Taylor were clearly aware of emergent features of contemporary consumption and leisure patterns which came to be identified with late or postmodernity (see the introductory chapter in the second edition of the book, 1992). Furthermore, their interest in the sociology of deviance meant that they were intrigued by the *diversity* of available subversions of reality and the question of 'why more people did not resort to them.' What would surely have intrigued them even more then, is the profound change (which would have been hard to predict), whereby in just over twenty years, experimentation with or use of drugs has become so closely woven into the experiential and cultural fabric of 'ordinary' everyday life in Western society. Drug use may still represent a route to 'unreality' and a means to slip away from the constraints of routine, but today, in many more different ways for many more different people, drug use is *actually a part* of the 'paramount reality' of everyday life. Furthermore, for non-users, *awareness* of drugs as a significant consumable in today's youth, leisure and street culture markets, and *acquaintance* with peers who are or have been drug experimenters or users, have shifted from the realm of the esoteric to being ordinary 'facts of everyday life'.

Here, let me add a note of caution. I am aware that this is a portrait of contemporary drug use in which amazement at the significance of change veers dangerously close to celebration. It is important to emphasise that drugs and drug use may be attended by many problems, not all of which, by any means, are simply the result of their illegal status. Human beings and intoxicants of whatever legal status have a propensity to mix dangerously at times. Let me therefore set out the points made above in a different way.

In recent years there have been changes in the spread and use of drugs in society. However, it is not this point alone that is significant: it is also important that *awareness* and *ideas* about drugs have been changing. Today, personal and popular awareness of drugs as a social, lifestyle and/or crime-related issue is now pretty universal in Western culture. Familiarity with images of drugs and drug users, and of related hedonism, crime, and drug-related illness and deaths (e.g. withdrawal from or overdose on 'hard drugs'; the impact of AIDS/HIV), has become widespread as a result of media fascination and representation (see Shapiro and Murji, Chapters 2 and 4). A wide variety of illegal and legal drugs are available and extremely easy to buy or sample. Finally, for young people, the 'lifetime' possibility of personal acquaintance with drug users and/or drug use now approaches 'lifetime' probability.[5] These propositions are fairly straightforward and, apart from the last one, difficult to argue with seriously. But the conclusions that can be drawn from them are rather less straightforward. Common agreement on 'the place of drugs in everyday life' still eludes politicians and pundits, researchers and commentators, 'ordinary' voters as well as professionals involved in drugs services, clinical treatment and law enforcement.[6]

The difficulty in arriving at any consensus about how society should respond to drug use is unsurprising. Politicians and 'experts' should be more ready to acknowledge this point. Such difficulty is more understandable if we consider just a few of the 'big' questions and proposals raised and contested around the issue of the illegality of drugs and their consumption. Many of these matters lie at the heart of the drugs debate and are examined in the chapters below. For example: why do different cultures (national, gendered, ethnic, subcultural, etc.) have such varied drug consumption profiles and preferences (see Chapters 2–4)? What should be the nature of criminal justice responses to illegal drug use? Can such responses ever be effective (see Chapters 6 and 7)? Why should some drugs be illegal and others not? Would legalisation or decriminalisation of all (or even just some) drugs be a great step forward or a disastrous step backward (see Chapter 8)? Do prevention approaches work? Does treatment work? Does anything work (see Chapters 5 and 9)? What is the kernel of the problem – is it supply? demand? social environment? deficiency in the individual? simply a primal urge to 'get wrecked'? Is there a 'kernel' to the problem? Is there 'a problem' at all?

One way of thinking about these issues and the place of drugs in late modern society is to consider the proposition that drug use has now become a 'normal' part of everyday life. In other words, it is non-acquaintance with drugs or drug users that has become the 'deviation from the norm'. Consideration of this thesis, particularly associated with the work of Howard Parker and colleagues (Parker et al., 1995), links this introductory essay with the concluding chapter by Michael Shiner and Tim Newburn. This link follows my *partial* agreement here with the argument of Parker et al., that the dominant theme in the late modern, end-of-20th Century story about drugs is a move *towards* 'normalisation'. To qualify this position, evidently drug *use* has not become a normal activity for all or even the majority of young people and the prohibition of drugs is still powerfully in place. A future scenario of full 'normalisation' of drug use may be glimpsed in some surveys, as well as in many instances and expressions of the lifestyle of contemporary youth (Parker et al., 1995: 24–5) (and older consumers), but it does not at present correspond to the lifestyle activity of the majority of people. As Shiner and Newburn (1997; and Chapter 9) convincingly argue, peer group resistance and preference for other socially expressive or pre-occupying alternatives to the use of illegal drugs, remain significant in the lives of most young people. Nonetheless, something profound has happened in relation to the place of drugs in everyday life since the mid-1980s and the diffusion of heroin use (Dorn and South, 1987), followed by the emergence of Ecstasy and rave culture (see Chapters 2 and 3).

At one level, this contention returns us to the question of the definition of 'drugs'. We must clearly distinguish between different kinds of drugs and their relative popularity. Predictably, on the traditional spectrum of 'soft' to 'hard' drugs, it is the main drug at the soft end – cannabis – that will have greatest use, and 'hard end' drugs such as heroin and cocaine that remain exceptions in use. 'Dance drugs' such as Ecstasy and LSD occupy an anomalous position, generally viewed by users as at the 'soft end' yet officially classified as at the 'hard end'. Regardless of such classification, they are undeniably popular (BMA, 1997: 13–14). However, Shiner and Newburn (1997 and Chapter 9) are rightly concerned about the evidence for *the numbers of young people* experimentally or regularly using drugs. They engage critically with the data employed by Parker et al. (1995; Parker and Measham, 1994) and other interpreters of data (e.g. Coffield and Goften, 1994) who suggest that a process of normalisation of drug use is under way. This critique is, it must be said, a convincing one.

However, to my mind, equally persuasive (and of some importance as the background to the Chapters in this collection), are the intellectual and cultural dimensions of the argument about normalisation (Parker et al., 1995: 23–6). The very generation of this debate about normalisation, its serious implications, and the public and policy contexts in which it is taking place, are all indicative of the need for a new perspective on drugs and everyday life. The essentials of such a perspective might be that:

- it cannot be denied that drug use is of enormous contemporary importance – whether as symbol, social problem or fashion accessory;

- data, however challenged, indicate socially significant changes in patterns and degree of use over the past twenty years;
- the balance of probability is that prevention efforts, peer influence and other factors will exert some downward pressure, restraining, *perhaps* even stabilising, rates of increase in the use of drugs but that these will not reverse recent increases;
- the availability of drugs, a key factor in introduction to and maintenance of drug use, will not be significantly diminished;
- hence, the whole issue and persistence of drugs *as a feature of everyday life* has become and will remain 'normalised'. While drug use has not itself become the *true* norm, it has moved some way from the status captured by the term 'exception to the norm': from 'exceptionality' to being part of everyday life.

It is the view of Parker et al. (1995: 25) that:

> Adolescents of the 1990s are growing up in and with this new level of drug availability. Whether or not they become drug users is a decision based on personal and peer group choice since the availability of drugs is a *normal* part of the leisure-pleasure landscape. Their current illicit drugs of 'choice' are marketed in such ways as to make them appear safe, attractive and good value for money; the sorts of qualities we are all encouraged to embrace as we push our trolleys around the supermarket.

Furthermore, as Blackman (1996: 139) observes, while it is not entirely clear quite 'how normalisation operates', marketing and consumption-culture are central:

> One of the visible links between youth culture and drug culture is the visual display of youth styles. It is possible to argue that there exists a repository of ideas and images within popular youth culture which are drug influenced through processes of the mass consumption of products such as songs, music, videos, T-shirts, clothes logos, jackets, badges and posters . . . Consumer capitalism plays a central role in the marketing of drug referenced products as part of young people's leisure and lifestyle.

Whether or not as individuals we actually use drugs, we now all live in a cultural, media and consumption environment saturated by references to and images of drugs, as well as explicit and implicit connections between drugs and various other consumption items. What is most significant about late modernity and the quest to control and reduce the use and misuse of drugs is not simply the question of 'how many people actually use them?' Rather, it is *the sheer volume of social activity* concerned with, or referring to, 'drugs'. Daily examples include, expressions of cultural, media, political, medical, and enforcement engagement, attention and reaction. Drugs are simultaneously officially damned yet dragged ever more firmly into the everyday discourse of social life. Shiner and Newburn (1997) conclude an earlier paper with a quote from

Plant (1985) which they employ to illustrate how the media recurrently 'talk up' drug problems in society, generally engaging in the scare-mongering particularly beloved of the popular press. My point however is that what Plant notes should be read in another way: that 'drugs' have become just another part of normal everyday discourse albeit one that, like crime as an everyday topic, can be classified as 'bad' behaviour as opposed to 'good' (see Chapters 2 and 4). Writing in the mid-1980s, Plant (1985: 350) observed that:

> Hardly a day passes without either a radio or television documentary or the front page of a tabloid newspaper being devoted to the subject of drugs. This attention is reinforced by a veritable barrage of gloomy forecasts and sharply rising levels of recorded drug-related crimes. Some of this interest has been factual and considered. But sadly much of it has been couched in highly emotive terms.[7]

DRUGS AND THE DISCOURSES OF CONTROL IN EVERYDAY LIFE: 'EXCEPTIONALITY' AND 'OTHERNESS'

This book draws on perspectives on illegal drugs and questions of cultures and controls, from within sociology, cultural studies and criminology. In the social sciences, work in these traditions has typically approached drugs issues in a liberal, tolerant and enlightening fashion. Commitment has been to description of hidden and frequently misunderstood worlds, and/or to suggestions about appropriate approaches to understanding and helping drug users, and/or controlling drugs and the use of drugs in society (South, 1995, 1997). These descriptions and prescriptions have provided ideas, critiques and debates that have been influential – but only up to a point. Since the nineteenth century (Berridge and Edwards, 1981), it has been medical, criminal justice, political and policy responses that have largely both shaped and reflected the status of illegal drugs as what Cohen has termed 'The Great Prohibition of the Twentieth Century'.[8]

The significance of the 'policy, public health and prohibition' matrix

The dominant policy and control discourses surrounding drugs and drug use are largely the products of the powerful frameworks of the psychiatry and psychology of dependence (Smart 1984; Strang and Gossop, 1994; Booth Davies, 1997); of public health concerns with epidemiology, 'infection' and 'contagion' (Berridge and Edwards, 1981; Lupton, 1995; Harding, 1998); and of international and domestic law-enforcement priorities and obligations (by virtue of international agreements) concerning control (Bruun et al., 1975; South, 1998). All of these discourses emphasise the theme of *exceptionality*: in other words, the proposition that illegal drugs are exceptions to the norm of acceptable intoxicants.[9] As consumers of such, 'drug users' are seen to have placed themselves 'outside' normal cultures and controls. It is right then that they should attract appropriate responses – whether medical or enforcement – to bring them back 'within' the disciplinary social order of acceptability (Smart, 1984: 34), and/or to punish their deviation. The 'labelling' tradition within the sociology of deviance has been the most profoundly influential perspective on this social construction of the 'Otherness' of drug users, as reflected in the title of Becker's (1963) classic work, *Outsiders*.

As already noted, it has been a common starting point within the sociology of deviance, as well as in cultural anthropology (Douglas, 1966), to pursue the neo-functionalist observation that in certain respects a society 'needs its deviants' (Rock, 1997: 253–4). Along these lines, Nils Christie (1986) has neatly outlined the ways in which drugs and their consumers make perfect 'suitable enemies' for society to declare war upon. If society constructs drugs and drug users as 'suitable enemies' to be feared and hence fought (cf. van Ree, 1997), this provides one powerfully suggestive (if somewhat *overly* functionalist) way of looking at the place of drugs in the control discourses of everyday life. For Christie (1986: 42–3):

> Social problems are what people see as social problems. But there are so many unwanted conditions in society. It is impossible to wage war against all of them. A choice has to be made . . . Five characteristics are peculiar to suitable enemies:
>
> 1) . . . It is obvious that major problems – and particularly the conditions that are supposed to create the problem – will not be defined in ways that threaten centrally-positioned and powerful groups in society. The enemy must not be defined in such a way that strong groupings line up behind him and object to the definition of the problem as a problem . . .
>
> 2) A good enemy ought to be seen as dangerous, often inhuman . . .
>
> 3) . . . The enemy is so strong that extraordinary powers are granted.
>
> 4) Good enemies are those that never die . . . 'The enemy is almost exterminated' the war-bulletins claim, 'just give us some more time and resources, and the job will be done'. Wars fought by professional experts against unclear and vaguely defined targets are particularly suitable. In such cases the enemy can be defined so that suitable targets can be included or excluded according to needs . . .
>
> 5) . . . The greater an evil, the more such an enemy can unite and dissolve other conflicts within any society.

As Christie then goes on to show, 'Three features' make narcotics [i.e. drugs] 'perfect as an enemy' (1986: 46–7):

First: It is unclear what should be defined as narcotics. The enemy can be changed according to needs . . .

Secondly: As with drugs, so with users. Actions are directed towards those most suitable . . . As described by Virginia Berridge and Griffith Edwards in their excellent book on *Opium and the People* (1981): ' "Stimulant" opium use in the cities [of the nineteenth century] was part of the threat posed by the industrial working class . . . Middle class, and respectable, opium use was, of course, rarely a matter of concern, even in the case of stimulants used by the Romantic writers.' (p.48).

Thirdly: As with the users, so too with the producers [and distributors]. Attention is directed toward the most suitable. Guinness, Heineken and Tuborg, and the tobacco industry are not. The pharmaceutical industry has also been surprisingly – or perhaps not so surprisingly – good at fending off attacks.

Producers, distributors and users of 'exceptional', illegal drugs are very valuable 'suitable enemies' for societies uncertain about their moral and constitutional strengths in other areas of life.

Pursuing a similar argument, Marek Kohn (1997: 142) neatly summarises the sequence of images of 'drugs and related enemies' that have been conjured up by the twentieth-century imagination of Western reaction to drugs:

As always, drugs are feared because of their otherness. In the 1920s, the menace they were believed to pose found its most acute expression in fears of miscegenation. Similar alarms were sounded in a reprise that developed after the Second World War, this time revolving round marijuana and black men instead of cocaine, opium and Chinese men. In the 1980s, the symbolism took more elliptical forms, but drugs reappeared as a means of expressing fears of a foreign threat to a nation unsure about its fortunes and direction . . .

At present . . . the otherness of drugs that the dominant culture seems to fear above all is not that of race, or crime, but the other world of hallucinatory states.

Collison (1996: 439) also notes how:

Drugs and drug economies are repetitively thought about as other. Local communities in the industrial world are corrupted by outsiders – Mafiosi, Yardies, Colombians, Triads, or, less poetically, existing criminal organizations. Thus, drug economies are represented in public discourse as 'alien' conditions precipitating the repeat victimization of naive and impressionable young drug users and the wider community of the respectable poor (HM Government, 1994).[10]

The consigning of drugs and drug users to the realm of the 'Other' and to the symbolic 'zones of danger and exclusion' in society, is a largely twentieth-century phenomenon in the UK, USA and other Western societies.[11] In various other societies, within the developing world for example, the classification of drugs as illicit by Western governments may be at odds with local culture and convention. In some parts of the world, drugs still have important and traditional, economic or cultural uses in everyday labour or relaxation, or are vital in the context of ritual. The place of drugs in global everyday life deserves more sensitive appreciation than the politics of international 'drug wars' allow.

The combined efforts of contributors to the 'policy, public health and prohibition matrix', devoted to the aims of regulating or controlling drugs, have, so far, failed to produce any demonstrable success, even in their own terms. This is surely a twentieth-century 'record of achievement' which must tell us something! As Coomber (1998: xii) observes:

> That existing drug control policies may have developed from a drug-centric foundation of exaggeration and falsity, interrelated with notions of 'otherness' (xenophobia/racism) and misplaced (and essentially contradictory) moralities as well as international and national politics, among other biases, suggests that until these influences have been acknowledged and neutralised, rational debate on drugs and drug use controls will remain difficult.

DEBATING DRUGS AND EVERYDAY LIFE

It is not, I should emphasise, my argument that *all* regulatory and control efforts or prevention and education initiatives are misplaced (though some are certainly misconceived). Or, alternatively, that the 'drug problem' would simply cease to be 'problematic' if society immediately embraced decriminalisation or legalisation. My dissatisfaction is with the way in which drugs discourses so unhelpfully polarise. The bequest of debates about drug cultures and controls to date has been a set of entrenched positions, vested interests, intellectual timidity and general myopia. A situation which has produced a *fin de siècle* exchange about 'what's wrong' which resembles a Möbius strip – prohibition proponents engage in a debate with legalisation proponents, endlessly repeated on an unreal and unrealistic terrain.

The twentieth-century 'Great Prohibition' on drugs has also been a 'Great Prism' through which the dominant ways of looking at drugs are focused in particular ways and yet distorted. The drugs debate still has a considerable way to go and the chapters in this book make valuable contributions to it.

NOTES

1. By 'drugs' I generally mean those deemed illegal, although in this and in other chapters in the present book, there will also be reference to use of legal drugs. For further discussion, see South, 1997: 925–7; and, generally, Gossop, 1993.

2. As well as in non-Western societies and cultures. However, this book is primarily concerned with the UK, Europe and North America. It is arguable that one should not really examine 'drugs' in Western or non-Western societies without including substantial reference to alcohol as a legal (or, in some societies, illegal) intoxicant. Some might argue that tobacco should be similarly treated. However, to incorporate these properly would produce a rather different (and certainly lengthier) book.

3. This taboo and fear reflects points made by Smart (1984: 34) in asserting that the 'disciplining of everyday life is seen to arise from the emergence of rational scientific knowledge as applied to human behaviour', and that 'Policy on drug addiction, and indeed alcohol addiction, is part of this general movement precisely because hedonistic addiction runs counter to the ethos of a disciplinary society.'

4. Lenson's speculation was valid. In November 1996 voters in California and Arizona approved balloted initiatives which permit the cultivation and use of marijuana for medical purposes. In Arizona, following the ballot, doctors may also prescribe other previously forbidden drugs for legitimate medical purposes.

5. 'Lifetime' measures are a frequently used element of surveys which ask whether a person has ever used drugs 'during their lifetime', or had close acquaintance with a drug user 'during their lifetime'. There are acknowledged problems with this measure and a critical discussion is provided by Shiner and Newburn in Chapter 9 of this volume.

6. Media, commercial and academic surveys relating to the legal status of drugs have been carried out many times in recent years in the UK and North America. Predictably, these produce a diversity of conclusions and breadth of disagreement between polls which is of very little value in any attempt to clarify 'general public' opinion.

7. Emotive messages about 'the dangers of drugs' were recurrent in late nineteenth- and early twentieth-century drugs discourses (Kohn, 1992). In the 1980s, opportunities for both 'factual and considered' as well as highly emotive reporting were amply provided by the dramatic increase in experimental and dependent use of heroin (perceived as the most powerful and sinister, yet also the most fascinating drug of all), coinciding with the impact of HIV and AIDS. These phenomena provided extremely clear markers about the dangerous waters into which drug users swam at their peril (Strang and Stimson, 1991). The majority of 1990s drugs have not offered the same clear contours of risk. Poly-drug users of the decade have predominantly favoured non-addictive drugs (apart perhaps from tobacco) and drugs have increasingly become identified as an item within an open leisure and lifestyle 'consumption culture', rather than a subterranean 'drug culture' *per se*. Harm minimisation advice about drinking water at raves in order to avoid dehydration is sound and important but lacks the almost apocalyptic sense of urgency and warnings of dire consequences for the whole of society that accompanied campaigns to prevent HIV transmission by reducing the sharing of intravenous injection equipment. Nonetheless, see Kohn, 1997.

8. Stanley Cohen, personal communication.

9. 'Why?' is a matter of great debate. While the difference between acceptable (tobacco, alcohol) and unacceptable (illegal) drugs has something to do with

perceptions of dangerousness, it also has much to do with the state of scientific knowledge (the classic question is, 'Were tobacco to be discovered today, would it be made legal or illegal?'), historical contingency, and the political, moral and professional interests involved. Such matters are frequently addressed in pro- and anti-prohibition debates (see Ruggiero, Chapter 8; South, 1995: vol. 1).

10. Relations between drugs, social reaction, ethnicity and 'Otherness' are explored further by Karim Murji in Chapter 4 of this volume; and see also Ruggiero and South, 1997.

11. See Sibley, 1995: 60–4, for discussion of representations of the defiled urban 'Other'.

REFERENCES

Becker, H. (1963) *Outsiders: Studies in the Sociology of Deviance*. Glencoe, NY: Free Press.

Berridge, V. and Edwards, G. (1981) *Opium and the People: Opiate Use in Nineteenth Century England*, 2nd edn. New Haven, CT: Yale University Press.

Blackman, S. (1996) 'Has drug culture become an inevitable part of youth culture? A critical assessment of drug education', *Educational Review*, 48 (2): 131–42.

Booth Davies, J. (1997) *The Myth of Addiction*, 2nd edn. Amsterdam: Harwood.

British Medical Association (1997) *The Misuse of Drugs*. Amsterdam: Harwood.

Bruun, K., Pan, L. and Rexed, I. (1975) *The Gentlemen's Club: International Control of Drugs and Alcohol*. Chicago: University of Chicago Press.

Christie, N. (1986) 'Suitable enemies', in H. Bianchi and R. van Swaaningen (eds), *Abolitionism: Towards a Non-repressive Approach to Crime*. Amsterdam: Free University Press. pp. 42–54.

Coffield, F. and Goften, L. (1994) *Drugs and Young People*. London: Institute for Public Policy Research.

Cohen, S. and Taylor, L. (1992) *Escape Attempts: The Theory and Practice of Resistance to Everyday Life*, 2nd edn. London: Routledge. First published 1976.

Collison, M. (1996) 'In search of the high life: drugs, crime, masculinity and consumption', *British Journal of Criminology*, 36 (3): 428–44.

Coomber, R. (1998) 'Preface', in R. Coomber (ed.), *The Control of Drugs and Drug Users: Reason or Reaction?* Amsterdam: Harwood.

de Certeau, M. (1988) *The Practice of Everyday Life*. Berkely, CA: University of California Press.

Dorn, N. and South, N. (eds) (1987) *A Land Fit for Heroin? Drug Policies, Prevention and Practice*. London: Macmillan.

Douglas, M. (1966) *Purity and Danger*. London: Pelican.

Featherstone, M. (1987) 'Lifestyle and consumer culture', *Theory, Culture and Society*, 4: 55–70.

Featherstone, M. (1990) 'Postmodernism and the aestheticization of everyday life', in S. Lash and J. Friedman (eds), *Modernity and Identity*. Oxford: Blackwell. pp. 265–90.

Featherstone, M. (1992) 'The heroic life and everyday life', *Theory, Culture and Society*, 9 (2): 159–82.

Geertz, C. (1983) *Local Knowledge: Further Essays in Interpretive Anthropology*. New York: Basic Books.

Giddens, A. (1990) *The Consequences of Modernity*. Cambridge: Polity Press.

Goodman, J. Lovejoy, P. and Sherratt, A. (1995) *Consuming Habits: Drugs in History and Anthropology*. London: Routledge.

Gossop, M. (1993) *Living with Drugs*, 3rd edn. Aldershot: Ashgate.

Harding, G. (1998) 'Pathologising the soul: the construction of a 19th century analysis of opiate addiction', in R. Coomber (ed.), *The Control of Drugs and Drugs Users: Reason or Reaction?* Amsterdam: Harwood.

HM Government (1994) *Tackling Drugs Together*. London: HMSO.

Kellner, D. (1990) 'The postmodern turn: positions, problems and prospects', in G. Ritzer (ed.), *Frontiers of Social Theory: The New Synthesis*. New York: Columbia University Press.

Kohn, M. (1992) *Dope Girls: The Birth of the British Drug Underground*. London: Lawrence & Wishart.

Kohn, M. (1997) 'The chemical generation and its ancestors: dance crazes and drug panics across eight decades', *International Journal of Drug Policy*, 8 (3): 137–42.

Lenson, D. (1995) *On Drugs*. Minneapolis: University of Minnesota Press.

Lupton, D. (1995) *The Imperative of Health: Public Health and the Regulated Body*. London: Sage.

Maffesoli, M. (1989) 'The sociology of everyday life (epistemological elements)', *Current Sociology*, 37 (1): 1–17.

Parker, H. and Measham, F. (1994) 'Pick 'n' mix: changing patterns of illicit drug use among 1990s adolescents', *Drugs: Education, Prevention and Policy*, 1 (1): 5–13.

Parker, H., Measham, F. and Aldridge, J. (1995) *Drugs Futures: Changing Patterns of Drug Use amongst English Youth*. London: Institute for the Study of Drug Dependence.

Pickering, M. and Green, T. (1987) 'Towards a cartography of the vernacular milieu', in M. Pickering and T. Green (eds), *Everyday Culture: Popular Song and the Vernacular Milieu*. Milton Keynes: Open University Press.

Plant, M. (1985) 'The real problem with drugs', *New Society*, 7 June: 350.

Redhead, S. (1991) 'Rave off: youth, subculture and the law', *Social Studies Review*, 6 (3): 92–4.

Robertson, R. (1995) 'Glocalisation: time–space and homogeneity–heterogeneity', in M. Featherstone, S. Lash and R. Robertson (eds), *Global Modernities*. London: Sage.

Rock, P. (1997) 'Sociological theories of crime', in M. Maguire, R. Morgan and R. Reiner (eds), *The Oxford Handbook of Criminology*. Oxford: Oxford University Press.

Rudgley, R. (1993) *The Alchemy of Culture: Intoxicants in Society*. London: British Museum Press.

Ruggiero, V. and South, N. (1997) 'The late modern city as a bazaar: drug markets, illegal enterprise and the "barricades" ', *British Journal of Sociology*, 48 (1): 55–71.

Shiner, M. and Newburn, T. (1997) 'Definitely, maybe not? The normalisation of recreational drug use amongst young people', *Sociology*, 31 (3): 511–29.

Sibley, D. (1995) *Geographies of Exclusion: Society and Difference in the West*. London: Routledge.

Smart, C. (1984) 'Social policy and drug addiction: a critical study of policy development', *British Journal of Addiction*, 79: 31–9.

South, N. (ed.) (1995) *Drugs, Crime and Criminal Justice*, Vols 1 and 2. Aldershot: Dartmouth.

South, N. (1997) 'Drugs: use, crime and control', in M. Maguire, R. Morgan and R. Reiner (eds), *The Oxford Handbook of Criminology*, 2nd edn. Oxford: Oxford University Press.

South, N. (1998) 'Tackling drug control in Britain: from Sir Malcolm Delevingne to the new drugs strategy', in R. Coomber (ed.), *The Control of Drugs and Drug Users: Reason or Reaction?* Amsterdam: Harwood.

Strang, J. and Gossop, M. (eds) (1994) *Heroin Addiction and Drug Policy: The British System*. Oxford: Oxford University Medical Press.

Strang, J. and Stimson, G. (eds) (1991) *AIDS and Drug Misuse*. London: Routledge.

Van Hoorebeeck, B. (1997) 'Prospects for reconstructing aetiology', *Theoretical Criminology*, 1 (4): 501–18.

Van Ree, E. (1997) 'Fear of drugs', *International Journal of Drug Policy*, 8 (2): 93–100.

CULTURES: FORMS AND REPRESENTATIONS

2

DANCES WITH DRUGS: POP MUSIC, DRUGS AND YOUTH CULTURE

Harry Shapiro

Opium? No! Cocaine? No! The Great . . . Brain Killer is Dance Music.

> (*Portland Oregonian*, 1932, quoted in Silver, 1979: 167)

there has always been a relationship between club culture and drugs. In the Seventies when I was immersed in the Northern Soul club underground, you would see clubbers who were patently addicted to the whole experience . . . Rave culture's hardcore is similarly addicted . . . Only there are a hell of a lot more of them and they take a hell of a lot more drugs.

> (Stuart Cosgrove interviewed by Sean O'Hagan, *The Times*, 22 February 1992)

The 1990s have seen a dramatic rise in the incidence of recreational drug use among young people in the UK (Health Education Authority, 1996; Miller and Plant, 1996; UK Parliamentary Office of Science and Technology, 1996; ISDD, 1997). The prevalence of adolescent drug use had been on an upward curve since the late 1970s (Wright and Pearl, 1995), and then through the 1980s focused largely on the use of solvents and heroin. Use of such drugs was generally regarded as a marginal activity linked closely to urban deprivation and social dislocation, and undertaken by those stereotypically labelled by the media at least as 'mad, bad or sad' (ISDD, 1976). What has happened since the late 1980s is a significant broadening of the drug-using constituency encompassing a much wider range of substances taken by ever-larger groups of young people. For a significant minority who would consider themselves otherwise 'ordinary' members of the community, drug taking has become an unremarkable part of the lifestyle kit (Hirst and McCamley-Finney, 1994; Parker et al., 1995). Key developments within popular music and the catalytic appearance of Ecstasy on the British drug scene have combined in a unique symbiosis to herald the 'normalisation' of illicit drug use on a hitherto unknown scale. However, although the current drug/music scene in the UK has been brought about by the special circumstances described below, the relationship between drug use and popular music has a long and diverse history, strands of which have played a significant part in creating the contemporary drugs/music nexus (Shapiro, 1990).

By itself, rave culture has revitalised the sociological literature on youth culture, and in particular has provoked a revisionist view of its history challenging the hegemony of the key writers of previous decades (cf. Redhead, 1990, 1993; Merchant and MacDonald, 1994; Thornton, 1995). However, few of the debating points are germane to this present chapter, which is more by way of highly condensed socio-cultural narrative than sociological analysis. Whatever the difference of viewpoint as to the nature and history of youth subcultures in Britain, there seems to be consensus concerning at least one point: that drug use has been one of the defining features of many of these groups and has been linked to particular phases in the history of popular music (Rietveld, 1993).

As well as sketching in the history of the subcultural palette into which the artists of rave culture have dipped, this chapter will also suggest (as others have done) that initial reactions by the body politic at national level to rave culture carried all the hallmarks of one of the most deeply enshrined constructs of subcultural sociology, the 'moral panic' (Young, 1971; Cohen, 1972). However, other developments at a local level have suggested a more tempered approach.

There has yet to be a detailed analysis of the cultural threads attached to the apparently ill-matched partners who came together to form the loose and disparate confederacy of music, fashion and drug styles which became known as rave culture.[1] Tentatively there appear to be at least two distinct and broad-based strands – one whose cultural heritage was interior, the world of the club; the other being exterior, from the 'be-ins' and 'happenings' of 1960s west coast America to the open air free parties of early 1990s Britain.

BRITISH CLUB CULTURE 1920–70

Sarah Thornton (1995) has argued that (with the exception of America's gay community) the club scene in the UK has played a more central role in the history of British youth culture than its American counterpart. Firstly, so much of American culture is based on the car: when the bulk of middle-class American teenagers go out, they go out driving, a leisure option denied to many British teenagers. Secondly, British houses are smaller and so a young person has far less space of their own. Young people in Britain also have less control over their 'virtual' space – unlike many young middle-class Americans, few in this country have their own phone lines (and not just for phone calls, but latterly for use of the Internet). This means that much of British youth is forced outside to the street or clubs (where paradoxically they enjoy hardly any personal space at all), reflecting a general assumption that many cannot get into pubs and even if they could, often they do not want to go there. So the club scene has played a pivotal role in the history of British youth culture, and repeatedly over the years the clubs have hosted a variety of fashions in all-night dancing, none of which (club-goers would claim) could have been sustained without the use of stimulant drugs. Arguably it was the deep roots put down by British club culture which allowed the dance scene to flourish so dramatically and so much in advance of other countries in Europe and the USA.

During the inter-war years, and with the first drug laws in place,[2] the illicit drug scene in Britain was limited to a few dance and drinking clubs in London's West End. The most popular illicit 'fun' drug of the time among the 'sporting' crowd of prostitutes, gamblers, theatre people and the more louche elements of the British aristocracy, was probably cocaine. The *Evening News* (14 March 1922) published an account of clubland, claiming that women in particular were driven to prolonged wild dancing by the cocaine rush: 'One [of the "girl-addicts"] was a frail-looking creature of about twenty in a flimsy frock that left three-quarters of her back bare. During the interval of her vivacious dancing in an underground room, she gave herself over to almost hysterical attacks of inane purposeless laughter' (Kohn, 1992: 131). The cocaine overdose death of dancer Freda Kempton in 1922 made the national press and prompted the *Daily Express* to run a campaign against drugs and 'dance dens' illustrated by a cartoon of a skeleton doorman standing outside 'The Dope Dance Club' beckoning in would-be revellers under the caption 'The Shadow of Death.' Apart from basement dives (and in images which resonate down the years) the *Express* also described dances held in 'unlit buildings in foreboding neighbourhoods' where the participants were 'perpetually seized with hysterical laughter and ogling foolishly' (Kohn, 1992: 131). However, after this period of sensationalist attention, apart from a few sensational tabloid stories about 'Indian hemp' in the early 1950s and a drugs raid on a West End jazz club, the non-medical use of drugs was simply not an issue until the early 1960s.[3] Concern at this point was prompted by the use of another stimulant drug by young people – amphetamine.

First developed as a pharmaceutical product in 1927, amphetamines had been supplied to soldiers in wartime to fight battle fatigue (Grinspoon and Hedblom, 1975). During the 1950s, they were marketed in a number of formulations mainly as a slimming aid and to ward off sleep – and so were used regularly for example by students studying for exams and by long distance lorry drivers. By the late 1950s, around 2.5 per cent of all NHS prescriptions were for amphetamine drugs (Connell, 1968). Many British pop stars, like the Beatles who cut their performing teeth playing gruelling sessions in German clubs in the early 1960s, survived on a steady diet of Preludin and Drinamyl (so-called Purple Hearts) amphetamine tablets (Norman, 1982: 98). The habit spread from bands to fans. The bands gathered more fans and new music venues sprang up, often on the same sites that had hosted the jazz bands of the previous decade – a spatial and geographical continuity which has been repeated in London's West End up to the present day.

It was around 1964 that a new club culture emerged dubbed 'Mod'. Framed by a sartorial elegance based on Italian fashion bought from the newly emerging clothes shops or boutiques catering for young people with growing amounts of disposable income, mods sped along on Italian scooters and amphetamine tablets, a drug supplying both an arrogance and tension to the culture and the fuel for all-night dancing. Although the name 'mod' derived from lovers of 'modern' jazz, the mods of the 1960s had their own heroes, bands like the Who (who immortalised their fan base in the concept album *Quadrophenia*) and the Small Faces whose anthems expressed the amphetamine experience in both style and lyrics. Roger Daltrey of the Who punctuated 'My Generation' with the amphetamine stutter typical of the user who cannot get the words out fast enough, while the Small Faces 'got away' with singing 'Here Comes the Nice' on *Top of the Pops* with an explicit mention of 'speed' and 'Itchycoo Park', rumoured to be a reference to amphetamine formication.[4]

Once the mod era gave way to psychedelia in 1966, there was little in the way of a distinctive club culture in London to take its place. Rock music quickly outgrew clubs and became first campus and then arena-based. What remained were the mainstream discotheques, such as the Speakeasy and Blaises, venues for the rock aristocracy and regular clubs such as the Marquee, the 100 Club, Klooks Kleek and others which provided the launch pad for up and coming blues/rock bands.

BRITISH CLUB CULTURE 1970–90

For the next development in stimulant-based dance culture, we must look to the north of England, to venues in Wigan, Blackpool and elsewhere and the phenomenon of the early 1970s known as 'Northern Soul'. The devotees of Northern Soul were carrying on a long-established tradition whereby British music fans have embraced American black music often far more enthusiastically than the home base. During the 1950s, for example, American blues artists were fêted in Britain by white audiences at a time when young black American music fans regarded the blues as best-forgotten sounds of slavery. The blues buffs of the 1950s were primarily older and middle-class whereas the fans of 1960s soul music and West-Indian-derived bluebeat and ska were often from working-class backgrounds. Paradoxically, the most enthusiastic admirers included the 'skinheads' who were otherwise intractably racist. The driving force of similarly working-class-based Northern Soul were so-called 'rare grooves'. These were obscure American soul records which became the focus for a nocturnal dance culture which again employed amphetamine. However by this point, prescribing of pharmaceutical amphetamines had been much reduced; instead the illicit market was developing. Now, use of illegally manufactured amphetamine sulphate powder added to the sense of exclusivity among aficionados.

The other amphetamine-based dance culture of the 1970s was punk. This had a rather more profound impact on the recent history of popular music in the UK. Many books and articles have been written on the punk phenomenon. For the purposes of this chapter, it is sufficient to say that, at least in its musical heritage, punk recalled the days of the mods. The punk style grew and set up home in some of the old London venues – even taking over, on one infamous occasion early in its history, the 100 Club in Oxford Street, one of the bastions of British jazz. Again, punk generated a furious chemically sustained all-night dance culture. Leader of the seminal punk band the Sex Pistols, Johnny Rotten, took his name from the state of his bad teeth, a common problem among amphetamine users, who suffer from calcium deficiency as a side effect of regular use. So important was the drug image to punk style that many young people cultivated the cadaverous amphetamine look without actually taking the drug (Burchill and Parsons, 1978). Club culture came much more to the fore during this period and set the scene for the arrival of a 'new age' in the mid-1980s. Aside from Northern Soul and punk, there was a strong club network among the gay community. A post-punk club scene centred around the 'New Romantics' and briefly around neo-psychedelia, an abortive attempt to recreate the 1960s without the use of drugs. There were also the beginnings of illegal warehouse parties which owed something to the blues or rent parties and shebeens of the Afro-Caribbean community where alcohol would be served. However, by the late 1980s the club scene in the UK had run out of steam and was in need of fresh inspiration.

The source for its revitalisation derived from a combination of two distinct but related developments – both from outside the UK. The first was house or garage music from the USA. Named after the Warehouse in Chicago and the Paradise Garage in New York, this was the first black electronic music, inspired initially by the experimental futuristic sounds of the German band Kraftwerk. In contrast to 1970s disco and funk, this harsher, industrial sound (additionally sampling from the whole tradition of black music, especially the soul sounds of James Brown) appealed to young black city dwellers, reflecting as it did the grim realities of urban life. The street DJs who invented the style often overlaid the soundtracks with their own lyrics or 'rap', a tradition borrowed from their Jamaican reggae counterparts. House music began to filter across the Atlantic to venues in the north-west of England where underground black music like Northern Soul had always found a ready audience.

The second and far more unlikely source came from the Mediterranean island of Ibiza. A long-standing 'hippy hideaway' (Neville, 1996), Ibiza developed its own dance club culture based on the house/garage sounds of black urban America recast as the 'Balearic sound'. The core of this largely instrumental music was a relentless and regular percussive beat which has defined all subsequent developments of dance music – from the almost beatless, melodic wash of 'ambient' music up to the 150 beats per minute of jungle and its various offshoots and beyond to gabba at a maniacal 200 b.p.m.

British DJs coming back from their 'Club Ibiza' experience decided to try and stimulate the flagging London club scene by recreating the island sounds of summer, and in 1987 a whole new generation of clubs sprang up including the pioneering Shoom and Future. As in previous times, a new stimulant drug went hand in hand with a new dance culture: this time a near relative of amphetamine, 3,4, methylenedioxymethamphetamine, MDMA or as it became widely known, Ecstasy.

MDMA was first synthesised in 1914 by the German pharmaceutical company E. Merck, as an appetite suppressant, but never marketed. It was rediscovered in the USA during the 1960s by a Dow Chemical research chemist, Alexander Shulgin. MDMA was used by some therapists, particularly those dealing with marital problems, as the drug that uniquely encouraged empathy between users and helped dissipate anger and hostility. Alongside its stimulant properties, this 'empathogenic' quality of MDMA is arguably one of the keys to its popularity as a street drug in the 1990s.

Inevitably the drug leaked onto the streets, and during the late 1970s and early 1980s Ecstasy (as it became known) was legally available in the USA. Millions of tablets were sold, especially to the young middle classes seeking new spiritual experiences as an antidote to the harsh economic environment of the period, until in 1985 it was dubbed by one American writer as a 'Yuppie way of knowledge' (Nasmyth, 1985). However, in the same year, fears over reported Ecstasy-related brain damage to rats led to its banning in the United States.

By that time the drug had found its way to Britain with returning travellers from the US and also from the orange-robed disciples of Bhagwan Rajeesh (Saunders, 1995). But rather than providing 'time-out' transcendence for the professional classes, Ecstasy was quickly assimilated to head the pantheon of dance drugs in the new club scene across the country and from there rapidly took its place as the cultural signifier of a generation.

THE GREAT OUTDOORS

The second major plank on which rave culture was founded was the tradition of outdoor music events inaugurated on the west coast of America in the early 1960s as a prelude to psychedelia. The catalytic chemical was LSD. Once the drug had escaped the academic testing ground, crusaders for the experience such as writer Ken Kesey held 'Acid Tests' where young people gathered to dance to embryonic psychedelic music (provided by who else but the Grateful Dead) and drink LSD dissolved in orange juice (Stevens, 1987). The notion of young people gathering together in large numbers to dance and listen to music, take drugs and make love gained momentum through the decade among mainly white middle-class students in revolt against the monolithic straitjacket of American society in general and the Vietnam War in particular. From 'be-ins' and 'happenings' in Golden Gate Park in San Francisco in the early 1960s to Woodstock in 1969, spiritual and political aspirations were rapidly (and perhaps inevitably) overtaken by commercial venality. Nevertheless, the tradition of transcendent hedonism combined with a hefty dose of spiritual, pagan and even paranormal desires and a polymorphous sense of communion was established and exported to Britain – not so much in the explicitly commercial environment of, for example, the Isle of Wight Festival of 1970, but beginning perhaps with the first free Stonehenge Festival of 1974 (Clarke, 1982).

Although much has been made of drug use in Britain in the 'swinging sixties', the actual extent of use has probably been overplayed. From about 1966 onwards (when the 'sixties' as a socio-cultural phenomenon actually started), use of cannabis and LSD 'exploded'. However, this was from a virtually non-existent base and was largely confined (socio-demographically) to elements of the student population and (geographically) to London and the Home Counties, where, by and large, the new high-profile artistic elite lived (musicians, writers, painters, photographers, etc.) alongside the media who eagerly reported their drug use.

Among students there is some evidence to suggest that, as artefacts of a past decade, drugs fell out of fashion in the early 1970s (Auld, 1981) but even so drug use began to permeate the UK as a whole. However, the messianic/tribal aspects of the communal drug experience which surrounded the use of hallucinogenic drugs did decline except in pockets of the underground which kept the spirit of 'the sixties' alive at Stonehenge and Glastonbury right through to the 'new wave' open air rave parties. By the mid-1970s, as Chris Stone describes it,

Anger had replaced the placid self-indulgence of the hippie era, but the institution of Stonehenge fitted in well with the DIY punk ethos. It was anarchy incarnate, a riot of self-expression and celebratory culture. A new breed of punk was born from contact with the festival scene; the so-called rainbow punk. Hippies in all but name. They bought trucks and took to the road. They became the core of what we now call New Age Travellers. The fusion of hippie idealism with punk politics is at the root of the counter-cultural scene and the social cement of the underground was 'we all take drugs. (Stone, 1996: 111)

By the summer of 1991, the rave scene met the festival-goers and travellers 'and a new philosophy was born'. This was based on the ethos of Spiral Tribe, one of a number of sound systems touring Europe as part of the free party circuit. They had a corporate identity, logos and uniform, but 'it was as if they'd learnt all the lessons of corporate capitalism, but to a different end. They aped capitalism in order to subvert it' (Stone, 1996: 177). Here perhaps is one of the paradoxes of the rave scene in 1990s Britain. Arguably, use of Ecstasy and other drugs by young people was a natural reaction to the hard-nosed materialism and insecurities of the 1980s – but it was also a strange endorsement of its hedonistic and entrepreneurial values. An explanation for these apparently contradictory viewpoints is required but in the absence of hard evidence must remain tentative.

RAVE CULTURE

The 1980s were a period of great insecurity for all sectors of British society. For the first time middle-class professionals were experiencing the same kind of employment uncertainties as those experienced by the working classes. There was a sense of alienation, lack of community, looking after 'number one' – a sea of individuals each fighting for their own survival and fearful of what the future might hold. Young people entering their mid-teens at the turn of the decade were deeply cynical about the political process and found little solace in their own communities, nor did the Church have much to offer in the way of spiritual comfort. Thus we find a generation, not only looking for alternatives to reality, for altered states of consciousness (like its predecessor in the 1960s), but also in search of 'community', for almost tribal identification and a sense of belonging. Many young people seem to have found it on the rave scene through the use of Ecstasy with its capacity to promote empathy and fellowship among users. For supporters of the drug, it would seem to be very much the right drug in the right place at the right time. To this search beyond the everyday and ordinary, of course, we might add the current intense interest in aliens from outer space (*The X-Files*, *Independence Day*, etc.) and 'virtual reality' on the Internet.

But as Stone indicates, there has also been an apparent endorsement of the values of the 1980s; much of what goes on every weekend in clubs and other venues up and down the UK is all about having a good time – and for many, a good time cannot be had unless drugs are involved. To an extent this mirrors the picture of conspicuous consumption enjoyed by a lucky few that was so characteristic of the previous decade. The abiding stereotypical image of 1980s Britain was the 25-year-old financial broker with mobile phone, Porsche and unlimited supplies of cocaine. One might argue that many more are now joining the party – going to the 'in' clubs, helping to define the infinite varieties of dance music (an exercise in niche marketing which mainstream business would be proud of), wearing fashionable designer labels and taking the fashionable drugs. This has increasingly meant alcohol becoming a part of the menu of fashionable intoxicants, as the breweries have fought back with drinks aimed at young people in a bid to retrieve customers from the other purveyors of drugs. Alcohol is now routinely available at most dance venues. And as for the early entrepreneurs of rave who made large amounts of money from staging events, far from being dubbed 'bread heads' (the ultimate hippie insult) they became cult heroes. Only now is the corporate (for which read bland) face of rave coming in for criticism in the letters pages of the dance magazines like *MixMag* and *Musik*.

At the beginning of this decade, there was a substantial new youth culture in Britain which dominated both the internal and external landscapes of the drugs/music nexus, drawing it closer to the main-stream of British youth culture than at any time this century. Dance music and Ecstasy stood astride this new culture even to the point of a palpable synergy between the rhythm of the music and the effect of Ecstasy on the brain whereby the drug stimulates certain receptors which encourages the user to engage in repetitive acts without necessarily being aware of them. A combination of the repetitive 4/4 house music beat and Ecstasy consumption produced dancers who entirely synchronised their bodies to the music.

But looking past the pharmacology of Ecstasy, the relatively benign image of the drug has arguably made most other forms of drug use more acceptable. During the 1980s, the government ran Britain's first mass media anti-drugs campaign targeting heroin in the 'Heroin Screws You Up' series of billboard, television and magazine advertisements. How-ever, the subsequent evaluation of the campaign showed that most of those interviewed had been firmly antipathetic to heroin (and cocaine) in the first place. The campaign's main achievement was to reinforce existing viewpoints. Ecstasy was very different. The early 'Smiley' logo defined the nature of the drug – a happy, fun party drug – an image which subsequent high-profile Ecstasy-related deaths have done little to dent. Among users, most of the bad publicity has centred on the content of Ecstasy on the street, ranging from pure drug to complete fake (Forsyth, 1995).

Ecstasy and the dance culture it supported has opened the gateway to experimentation with a whole range of substances: established drugs on the UK scene such as LSD and amphetamine and new drugs (as yet uncontrolled by the Misuse of Drugs Act) such as ketamine, amyl nitrite (poppers) and gammahydroxybuterate (GHB).

The resurgence of interest in cannabis has been particularly striking. Over the decades, cannabis has informed the light, bouncy sound of 1920s New Orleans jazz, the introspection of bebop jazz, the mystic meanderings of cosmic 1960s hippies and the almost stationary beat of Jamaican Trench Town roots rockers. Then in the 1980s, the celebration of cannabis became a central theme of new developments on the black American music scene tagged hip hop, rap, dance hall and gangsta. The breakthrough song for 'dance hall' was 'Under Me Sleng Teng', a paean to cannabis smoking, as were multimillion-selling crossover albums by artists like Dr Dre and Cypress Hill. Disparate and independent developments in the UK have coalesced to produce a widespread 'cannabis culture' including the influence of rap music, the hemp fashion industry based on licensed growing of hemp in East Anglia and the revitalisation of the pro-cannabis lobby backed by supportive editorials in the broadsheets and medical press and among some of the judiciary.

Apart from overt references to the drug in such songs as 'Ebeenezer Goode' by the Shamen, Ecstasy has informed just about every aspect of what has latterly been dubbed Ecstasy culture. This takes many forms, including the use of relaxing ambient music, a gentle backdrop of easy-listening sound, almost aural wallpaper in chill-out areas where people might be recovering from a long night of Ecstasy-driven dancing. To take account of the fact that it can be dangerous to become overheated through taking Ecstasy (with its effect of raising body temperature) in combination with extended bouts of non-stop dancing, club fashions in clothes changed to much looser, more baggy styles. Before the drug element of rave became so public, high street chains like Miss Selfridge and Top Shop were keen to exploit the 'Smiley' logo on ranges of fashion clothing. This enthusiasm among retailers waned briefly, but the relentless pulse of rave culture and the sales revenue it promised proved irresistible, and now, for example, television and cinema screens throb to the beat of 'hyperreal' advertisements for soft drinks – another indication of how well-publicised health and safety aspects of drug use in clubs have permeated the commercial consciousness.

The 'new' drug users still believe that by using heroin (smoking or injecting) and/or cocaine (in its new formulation crack), a line has been crossed. Hence, use of these drugs remains a minority activity among the rave generation. Nevertheless, Ecstasy-inspired 1990s rave music provided the soundtrack of *Trainspotting*, a film about the Edinburgh heroin scene of the mid-1980s. The upbeat soundtrack supplied ammunition for those critical of the alleged glamorisation of heroin use in the film, a criticism also directed at fashion photographers for cultivating the much-emulated 'wasted junkie' look of young models like Kate Moss. And on the back of grunge rock music we also have the return of the wasted rock star, most notably the late Kurt Cobain of Nirvana, an image that is replicated throughout the industry.[5] It is perhaps a sad irony that Jerry Garcia, leading light of the most famous psychedelic band, the Grateful Dead, should have succumbed in 1995 to the effects of long-term heroin use. Overall, drug use among musicians has never been so prominently exposed. Although undoubtedly children of the rave generation, the musical sensibilities of bands such as the Happy Mondays, Stone Roses, Blur, Pulp and Oasis were wedded to more conventional rock forms far removed from techno dance music, and in that guise these bands became rock stars in the traditional sense with all the attendant trappings of the lifestyle, including drugs. What is different is the degree to which they have been prepared to talk openly and with some fondness about their chemical indulgence in the full knowledge that drug use among the fan base is commonplace. In the 1960s, revelations about a musician's use of drugs were considered extremely bad for business.[6] Nowadays it seems almost part of the armoury of marketing. A major record retail chain who recently ran a window display in support of Britpop under the legend 'Homegrown', would have known only too well that many customers would see beyond the reference to 'local boys made good'. Not that the rave scene entirely escaped the banalities of the conspicuous consumption mostly associated with the drug-strafed lifestyle of rock. Thornton describes the Millennium Club which imagines itself as entirely VIP chiefly because its members are 'heavily into cocaine', while the owner of Cloud Nine 'snorts coke off a friend's Visa card' (Thornton, 1995).

Of course, even in the 1990s, pop stars can go one step over the line. Brian Harvey of East 17 had opprobrium heaped upon his head for the 'revelation' that he had taken twelve Ecstasy tablets and then driven home. The comment in support of Harvey by Noel Gallagher of Oasis, that 'drugs are just like tea' (see Shiner and Newburn, Chapter 9), caused equal outrage. Coming on the back of criticism of the police for simply cautioning brother Liam for possession of cocaine, there were calls from politicians to have Noel Gallagher prosecuted for incitement. Pro-drug views from Oasis should have caused no surprise, but there are two interesting aspects to the Harvey incident.

Firstly, it was subsequently revealed in the press that Harvey's relationship with the rest of the band and the manager had been strained for some while and that his sacking from East 17 was almost waiting to happen. If Harvey was looking for a swan song to damage the reputation of the band, then he rightly concluded that an outrageous statement about drugs was still the way to grab the attention of the media. Secondly, the Daily Mirror (which first published his comments) then organised a poll among its readership which came out in support of Harvey's 'honesty'. This suggests that what politicians and the media conclude is the 'public consensus' on drugs may be far from monolithic.[7] (See Chapter 1, p. 5 and Note 6, p. 12).

RAVE AND THE MEDIA

The media backlash against dance music was inevitable and swift, although perhaps not swift enough for some of the leading lights of the new scene who appeared anxious to receive the press opprobrium necessary to validate their underground status. The music press and the rave spokespeople danced a strange two-step with the mainstream media. On the one hand, between February and August 1988, through the summer which became rave's 'Summer of Love' equivalent to the Sergeant Pepper/LSD season of 1967, *Record Mirror*, *New Musical Express* and *Melody Maker* (all owned, incidentally, by mainstream publishing corporations) were predicting that rave would be linked to drug use by the tabloid press. *Time Out* (17–24 August 1988) even went so far as to helpfully write the headlines (LONDON GRIPPED BY ECSTASY and DRUG CRAZED NEW HIPPIES IN STREET RIOT). For a time, the tabloids failed to rise to the bait. On 1 October the *Sun* ran a feature which set out a glossary of Acid House terminology and invited readers to purchase a Smiley logo T-shirt. However, only a week later the paper's resident doctor Vernon Coleman was warning about the dangers of Ecstasy, followed by a plethora of the predicted headlines, of which DICING WITH A COCKTAIL OF DEATH (*Daily Star*, 2 November 1988) and MR BIG BEHIND THE LATEST FRENZIED POP PARTY CULT (*Daily Mirror*, 2 November 1988) are but two examples. This latter was a reference to Tony Colston-Hayter, one of the earliest entrepreneurs of rave who organised large unlicensed warehouse parties. Immediately, party organisers and major drug dealers were cast as one and the same people. Although in practice the police dealt with rave events as a public order issue, because they knew they couldn't possibly arrest every drug user (Collin and Godfrey, 1997), it was clear from the outset that the running battle between rave culture and their opponents among the mainstream press, police, local authorities and politicians would focus on the use of drugs.

Having achieved the notoriety they had arguably sought, supporters of rave culture began backpedalling to play down the drug connection. The immediate assumption about Acid House was that it concerned LSD. In fact, this turned out to be correct, as LSD figured quite prominently in the early period just ahead of or alongside Ecstasy as a drug of choice. But at the time, the term was linked to the Chicago music scene: Paul Staines of the Freedom to Party Campaign later claimed he made up this connection to put journalists off the scent by linking the word 'acid' to the technique of sampling. The contention was that 'acid' was black American slang for stealing (Saunders, 1995: 18). Radio 1 DJ Simon

Bates for one was taken in: 'Acid is all about the bass-line in music and nothing to do with drugs' (*Daily Mirror*, 12 November 1988).

CONTROL RESPONSES

Increasing or introducing penalties for drug use has been a key weapon of the state in dealing with youth movements viewed as a threat to society. In 1964, in response to mod culture, hastily conceived legislation resulted in the banning of amphetamine without a prescription.[8] In the same year, it became an offence to allow premises to be used for the smoking of cannabis, and in 1966 LSD was outlawed almost before it became established on the drug scene. It is particularly interesting to note that in a decade of unprecedented liberalising legislation which saw controls relaxed on gambling, censorship, abortion, homosexuality, the beginning of anti-discrimination laws in favour of women and ethnic minorities and even the abolition of hanging – the laws against drug use were tightened.[9] This says much about the mythological and symbolic nature of drug use in society which goes far beyond the scope of this chapter. However, when it came to Ecstasy, the laws were already in place. Most of the amphetamine analogues were already categorised by the Misuse of Drugs Act 1971 as Class B drugs. The discovery of MDMA and related compounds during a police raid on a laboratory in the mid-1970s caused them to be added to the control list, although not as Class B (like amphetamine), but as Class A for which the penalties for possession and supply are much harsher.[10]

It became obvious that as soon as the media began highlighting the spectacle of large numbers of young people gathered together, dancing all night to loud music under the influence of illegal drugs, the police would be forced to act. The early years of rave organisation and control can best be described as anarchic. Unlicensed events were taking place in any available location: fields, aircraft hangars, derelict buildings and motorway underpasses. Initially, the police and local authorities relied on legislation such as the 1967 Private Places of Entertaining (Licensing) Act which requires private (as well as public) events to be licensed by the local authorities and the Licensing Act of 1988 which gave the police greater discretionary powers in the granting of licences. There was also recourse to various public order legislation, health and safety laws as well as the Misuse of Drugs Act. The police and party organisers played cat and mouse with each other as a whole network of subterfuge was established. Convoys of young people would meet in cars at, for example, motorway service stations awaiting instructions as to how to locate that evening's event. Where attempts were made to hold large open air festivals, police would cordon off roads and shepherd would-be attendees into neighbouring areas away from the site. The police set up a

Pay Party intelligence unit based at Gravesend police station to monitor the activities of party organisers and over a two-year period from 1988 to 1990 there were some serious public order disturbances around the country as police either clashed with those trying to reach sites or arrived to break up an event already under way. Although much was made by the media of the risks posed to public order by these large outdoor events, most if not all of the violence occurred as a direct result of police intervention.

However, it was not strong-arm tactics that ended the illegal raves (if anything police action made activists even more determined) but new and much tougher licensing legislation. Under the Entertainments (Increased Penalties) Act of 1990 first tabled by Graham Bright, MP, organisers of unlicensed parties could face fines of up to £20,000 and six months in prison. This put most organisers out of business and some went abroad to the more liberal climate of mainland European countries such as Germany. However, the free party movement was by no means dead in the UK and outdoor events continued around the country in Liverpool, Cheshire, Warrington, the Lake District, Wales, Gloucester-shire and Southport, often accompanied by violent clashes between police and ravers (Newcombe, 1992), and culminating in the rave Woodstock held at Castlemorton in May 1992 attended by up to 40,000 people. The organisers, the Spiral Tribe sound system, were charged with public order offences and there were a number of other arrests over the ten-day period of the event. In a trial costing an estimated £4 million (Saunders, 1995), all those whose cases came to court were acquitted. The adverse publicity attending the event laid the groundwork for the Criminal Justice Act 1994 (CJA) which put the final nail in the coffin of the unlicensed event.

As with most legislation assembled in the white heat of media glare, the sections of the CJA which specifically refer to raves have been described as 'piecemeal' (Card and Ward, 1994). For the purposes of the Act, a rave is defined as 'a gathering on land in the open air of 100 persons or more . . . at which amplified music is played during the night . . . and is such as, by reason of its loudness and duration and the time at which it is played, likely to cause serious distress to the inhabitants of the locality'. This does not apply to events where public or private licences have been granted. Under the Act, the police can intervene to stop an event from happening, even if only three people have gathered, if the superintendent has reason to believe that eventually more than 100 people *will* gather illegally. Police can also seize equipment, and have the power to redirect people who may be on their way to a site. As it stands, the Act is open to interpretation. For example, there is no definition of 'night': what about an outdoor event that started in daylight, which would be quite common in the summer months? Would it be legal up to the time when it got dark? Nor is it clear whether a fully enclosed venue such as an aircraft hangar with doors would be exempt, because the Act only mentions venues which are in the open air or 'partly open to the air'. How do you define 'serious distress'? The wording of the Act is vague enough to suggest that the complaint of one individual in an otherwise isolated rural location would be enough.

There is less controversy over the attempts of local authorities to regulate the activities of indoor venue owners. In these cases, real risks to the customers exist in clubs where, in pursuit of profit, health and safety regulations have been ignored or violence allowed to continue unchecked. Certainly the lack of alcohol in rave clubs meant an absence of the usual type of customer-on-customer violence that is a regular feature of mainstream discos and pubs. However, any club or pub in an inner city area is a likely target for criminal gangs eager to provide protection, supply drugs or simply take over the business as 'sleeping partners'. For example in Liverpool a number of clubs hosting house music were closed down because of violence on the premises. The issue of drugs, of course, has caused widespread controversy.

Police and local authorities have objected to the licence renewal of clubs where drug dealing is alleged – Club UK in south London lost its entertainment licence in January 1997 and closed down. Owners often counter criticism with assertions that they do all they can to stop drugs coming into clubs and employ security guards to search all customers, although they are not empowered to conduct intimate searches and the determined user or dealer can secrete drugs to avoid detection. Clearly the situation will vary from club to club. The larger urban venues have been tightening up on their 'no drugs' policies, and many venues now actively cooperate with the police. But there will always be circumstances where venue owners will be colluding in (willingly or not) or actually organising drug dealing on their premises. In addition, research indicates that it is something of a myth to indict rave venues as being 'drug supermarkets' because most drug users take their drugs before they arrive (Forsyth, 1996).

In March 1997 a government-backed private member's bill received the Royal Assent: this enables local councils to shut down clubs immediately if there is evidence of drug use and drug dealing. It is too early to establish exactly how this will work in practice. There are some councils who are used to dealing with club owners in urban settings and are aware of the virtual impossibility of guaranteeing a drug-free venue. Other councils, perhaps those outside the major conurbations who have less contact with dance venues, may take the opportunity of more stringent legislation simply to attack rave culture by closing down clubs.

Local authorities have been keen to act against those venues where health and safety regulations have been routinely flouted in respect of fire hazard, maximum numbers on the premises and so on. But the health and safety issue that has received most attention has been that related to minimising the dangers of drug use. As we have seen, dancing for long hours in packed venues sustained on stimulant drugs is nothing new on the British club scene. For all the untold amount of amphetamines consumed during the 1960s, there is not one case report of an amphetamine-related club death recorded in the literature. However, if Ecstasy has a uniquely benign pharmacological action which has secured its popularity, then it also has a more malign property which has helped claim the lives of around seventy young people since 1989. To a much greater extent than amphetamine, Ecstasy interferes with the thermoregulatory mechanism of the body, by raising body temperature, even when the user is at rest. The combination of drug plus its use in hot ambient temperatures has made the equivalent of heat stroke type deaths the major cause of fatality in those seventy or so cases. However, thanks to the efforts of drug agencies such as the Merseyside Regional Drug Information Service (now called HIT)[11] and the Manchester agency Lifeline, club-goers were warned about the dangers of overheating, and advised to wear baggy clothes and drink non-alcoholic fluids if they were going to take Ecstasy and then dance for long hours in hot, humid and tightly packed venues. Club owners responded cynically by turning off the cold water supply in the toilets and then charging anything up to £2 a bottle for water.

It would have been expected that local authorities would not want to take up the issue of safeguarding the health of drug users for fear of being accused of condoning drug use. And for some time, this was exactly the situation; the drug agencies were left to help users as best they could. But in the face of unrelenting Ecstasy use, some local authorities with the assistance of drug agencies have taken on board the harm minimisation issue. Manchester City Council, for example, launched the Safer Dancing Campaign, and in December 1996 the London Drug Policy Forum issued guidelines for London rave venues in advance of a major safer dancing campaign for the capital. Harm minimisation proposals have also been adopted at a national level by the Home Office and the Scottish Office in association with the Scottish Drugs Forum.[12] In any event, both for humanitarian and commercial reasons, many club owners are confronting the health and safety issues around drugs, following the guidelines and allowing drug agency workers in to offer advice and act as drug paramedics for those in difficulty.[13]

After a decade of development, rave culture, in all its manifestations, is now a legitimate and lucrative arm of the leisure industry with highly commercialised venue organisations such as Ministry of Sound and Cream, glossy magazines, record labels, merchandising and the DJ (rather than the musician) as star. Inevitably, the rave scene has balkanised into many different genres and sub-genres. The drug scene will almost certainly go down the same route. Certain drugs such as cannabis and LSD will undoubtedly remain central. But the demands of fashion, the search for some new experience and, more prosaically, the controls on precursor chemicals which are used in drug manufacture, will encourage the underground chemists to become more ingenious in 'designing' new drugs. As drug use becomes increasingly a fashion accessory, it may be even more at the whim of fashion than in previous times – which means that mass consumption of dance drugs as a normal activity of growing up might go out of fashion or that at least the experimenters and occasional users will become bored (or decide the legal risks are not worth the trouble), leaving regular users to carry on.

There are some indicators that recreational drug use associated with dance culture may have reached a plateau in some parts of the UK. However, on the basis of our knowledge of the drug scene, prevalence of use and drug seizures, all the indicators of the extent of drug use and the range of substances available show increases dating back to the early 1960s. Ecstasy in particular has created a 'platform of acceptability' among substantial numbers of young people who are now willing to experiment with all manner of psychedelic drugs which will no doubt dance hand in hand with whatever the music industry has to offer, be it top-down corporate product or innovations from the back bedrooms.

NOTES

1. Although much of the ground relating to developments in the club scene that brought about rave has now been covered by Matthew Colin and John Godfrey's *Altered State: the Story of Ecstasy Culture and Acid House* (1997).
2. The Dangerous Drugs Act, passed in 1920, outlawed the possession without a prescription of opiate drugs like opium, morphine and heroin, and also cocaine.
3. In discussing the 'Hemp Problem' in Britain, the main concern of *The Times* of 27 July 1957 was not the effects of the drug, but the sexual danger posed to white women by black men who might seduce them using drugs.
4. Chronic amphetamine users often report a feeling that insects are crawling all over their skin and they scratch to get rid of them. This sensation is called 'formication'.
5. Recent overdose deaths include those of members of the bands Blind Melon and Smashing Pumpkins. For the first time, the US music business has set up a service to help musicians with drug problems.
6. When Paul McCartney admitted to trying LSD in 1967, Beatles manager Brian Epstein felt compelled to say he had tried it too, even though he hadn't, just to try and defuse what could have been a very damaging situation
7. This notion is supported by two further examples. During 1996, viewers of the BBC *vox pop* programme *You Decide* voted in favour of law reform both before the debate was screened (which included comments from bereaved parents) and after. Lewisham Council in south London convened a 'Citizens' Jury' which considered evidence on the drugs issue and concluded that law reform, especially in relation to cannabis, should be actively considered.

8. Personal communication. Bing Spear, former head of the Home Office Drugs Branch who sadly died in 1995.
9. South (1997: 940) makes a similar point.
10. Heroin and cocaine are also Class A drugs, but because they are deemed to have some medical uses, e.g. morphine for intractable cancer pain, they are in Schedule 2 of the Misuse of Drugs Act which allows them to be used for such purposes. Ecstasy and LSD are in Schedule 1 (drugs which have no recognised medical uses).
11. The agency was the first to publish health and safety information about using drugs at raves. The leaflet was called *Chill Out* (1992) and readers of the *Daily Star* were invited by the paper to visit the agency in order to throw the author in the River Mersey. It wasn't long before similar advice about harm reduction was appearing in the medical press and it is now standard issue government drug campaign information.
12. As far as can be established, no Ecstasy-related deaths have taken place at the outdoor events which were the focus of so much control activity. Free party campaigners have made the point that the deaths only arose when raves were forced indoors by legislation. (cf. Saunders, 1995).
13. However, with the Barry Legg bill now law – The Public Entertainments Licences (Drug Misuse) Act 1997, some drug workers are concerned that they will be barred by club owners now fearful that the presence of drug workers on the premises will signal a drug problem to the police.

REFERENCES

Auld, J. (1981) *Marijuana Use and Social Control*. London: Academic Press.
Burchill, J. and Parsons, T. (1978) *The Boy Looked at Johnny*. London: Pluto Press.
Card, R. and Ward, R. (1994) *The Criminal Justice and Public Order Act 1994*. Bristol: Jordans.
Clarke, M. (1982) *The Politics of Pop Festivals*. London: Junction.
Cohen, S. (1972) *Folk Devils and Moral Panics*. London: MacGibbon & Kee.
Collin, M. and Godfrey, J. (1997) *Altered State: the Story of Ecstasy Culture and Acid House*. London: Serpent's Tail.
Connell, P. (1968) 'Clinical aspects of amphetamine dependence', in C. Wilson (ed.), *The Pharmalogical and Epidemological Aspects of Adolescent Drug Dependence*. Oxford: Pergamon.
Forsyth, A. (1995) 'Ecstasy and illegal drug design: a new concept in drug use', *International Journal of Drug Policy*, 6 (3): 193–209.
Forsyth, A. (1996) 'Are raves drug supermarkets?' *International Journal of Drug Policy*, 7 (2): 105–10.
Grinspoon, L. and Hedblom, P. (1975) *The Speed Culture: Amphetamine Use and Abuse in America*. Cambridge, MA: Harvard University Press.
Health Education Authority (1996) *Drug Realities: National Drugs Campaign*. London: HEA.
Hirst, J. and McCamley-Finney, A. (1994) *Place and Meaning of Drugs in the Lives of Young People*. Sheffield: Health Research Institute, University of Sheffield.
ISDD (1976) 'Seeing glue through heroin spectacles', *Druglink*, 2 (3): 4.

ISDD (1997) *Drug Misuse in Britain 1996*. London: Institute for the Study of Drug Dependence.

Kohn, M. (1992) *Dope Girls*. London: Lawrence & Wishart.

McDermott, P. (1993) 'MDMA use in the north west of England', *International Journal of Drug Policy*, 4 (4): 210–22.

Merchant, J. and MacDonald, R. (1994) 'Youth and rave culture, Ecstasy and health', *Youth and Policy*, 45: 16–38.

Miller, P.M. and Plant, M. (1996) 'Drinking, smoking, and illicit drug use among 15 and 16 year olds in the United Kingdom', *British Medical Journal*, 313 (7054): 394–7.

Nasmyth, P. (1985) 'The agony and the Ecstasy', *The Face*, 78: 53–5.

Neville, R. (1996) *Hippie, Hippie Shake*. London: Bloomsbury.

Newcombe, R. (1992) *The Use of Ecstasy and Dance Drugs at Rave Parties and Nightclubs: Some Problems and Solutions*. Liverpool: 3D Research Bureau.

Parker, H., Measham, F. and Aldridge, J. (1995) *Drug Futures: Changing Patterns of Drug Use amongst English Youth*. London: ISDD.

Redhead, S. (1990) *The End-of-the-Century Party: Youth and Pop towards 2000*. Manchester: Manchester University Press.

Redhead, S. (ed.) (1993) *Rave Off: Politics and Deviancy in Contemporary Youth Culture*. Aldershot: Avebury.

Rietveld H. (1993) 'Living the dream', in S. Redhead (ed.) *Rave Off: Politics and Deviancy in Contemporary Youth Culture*. Aldershot: Avebury.

Saunders, N. (1995) *Ecstasy and the Dance Culture*. London.

Shapiro, H. (1990) *Waiting for the Man: the Story of Drugs and Popular Music*. London: Mandarin.

Silver, G. (ed.) (1979) *The Dope Chronicles 1850–1950*. New York: Harper & Row.

South, N. (1997) 'Drugs: use, crime and control', in M. Maguire, R. Morgan and R. Reiner (eds), *The Oxford Handbook of Criminology*. Oxford: Oxford University Press.

Stevens, J. (1987) *LSD: the Storming of the Heavens*. New York: Atlantic Monthly Press.

Stone, C. (1996) *Fierce Dancing*. London: Faber & Faber.

Thornton, S. (1995) *Club Culture: Music, Media and Subcultural Capital*. Cambridge: Polity Press.

UK Parliamentary Office of Science and Technology (1996) *Common Illegal Drugs and their Effects: Cannabis, Ecstasy, Amphetamines and LSD*. London: POST.

Wright, J.D. and Pearl, L. (1995) 'Knowledge and experience of young people regarding drug misuse 1969–94', *British Medical Journal*, 310: 20–4.

Young, J. (1971) *The Drugtakers*. London: MacGibbon & Kee.

3

DRUGS AND CULTURE:
THE QUESTION OF GENDER

Sheila Henderson

> They're smart and hold down careers, but they spend coffee breaks
> chasing their dealers and lunch breaks chasing the dragon . . .
> Professional addicts. Women who take drugs to stay on top.
>
> (Jaynes, 1997)

As recently as the early 1990s, trying to get women's magazines to cover
illegal drug use was mission impossible. In my experience, journalists
responded to approaches by asserting that drugs were an inappropriate
topic for their readers. Now the social climate surrounding drug use has
changed so much that sniffing, swallowing and smoking powders,
potions and pills at work, rest and at play has become part of 'having it
all' for 'Cosmo girl' and many another 'modern girl' culture (or so we
may well believe from media tales of fashion models, movie and pop
stars and other representatives of 'girl power'). Women, it would seem,
have achieved the (dubious) equality of consuming as many illegal
mind-changing substances as the next man. In fact, some recent surveys
suggest they surpass their male equivalents when it comes to sniffing
solvents (Parker et al., 1995) and when it comes to drug-offer situations
(HEA, 1997). Something has happened to the gender dimensions of drug
use but do we know what it is? And should we care?

In this chapter, it is my task to explore and offer comment on the
gender question as we approach the twenty-first century. To do this
(awesome) task justice would take far more than a few thousand words
on the current state of play in gender and drugs research. So I will limit
my remarks to what my research on drug use over the last eight years
has equipped me to do: to argue that we do not know what is happening; that it is important that we should; and that, to achieve this
understanding, a dramatic change in the paradigm for understanding
gender and drug use is needed. In order to reach this point, I ask three

pertinent questions: What is the general state of the art of 'thinking' gender and drug use? Why does the general state need to change? How does it need to change? I shall attempt to provide some answers by referring to my early work on women and dance or rave culture.

GENDER AND DRUG USE: NOW YOU SEE IT . . .

First question: what is the general state of the art of 'thinking' gender and drug use?

If, like any inquirer into the question of gender and drug use, you began by consulting the drugs research literature (key search word 'gender'), one of the early articles you would discover asserts the following:

> Drug dependent females are seen as characteristically pathetic, passive, psycho-logically and socially inadequate, isolated and incapable of shouldering responsibilities . . . These images are drawn from a view of woman's major role as centrally responsible for the 'private' side of life – housework, child-care, emotional support and family servicing . . . the illegal addict is seen as first rejecting and then being rendered incapable of performing these functions effectively by a lifestyle which is initially wilfully perverse and then inescap-ably pathetic . . . Female dependence is a reality – female drug dependence is an inappropriate and undesirable side-effect to be redirected to more conveni-ent and controllable forms of dependence. (Perry, 1979: 1)

This quote offers a powerful clue to the ways in which the question of gender has historically been addressed within drugs research. The pamphlet's assertion of the need to focus on women's drug use and to look beyond socially stereotypical representations and responses, reflects both the gender state of play within the drugs research literature at that time and feminist responses to it. This, predominantly medical and psychological, literature presented a picture of drug use in which drug users just happened to be male (if you bothered to notice) and women hardly figured. When they did, they appeared as sicker, more deviant, more psychologically disturbed than their male peers: as weak and pathetic creatures. Women's drug use figured as a 'deviation' from 'normal' femininity due to mental or physical deficiencies, or disease (Rosenbaum, 1981; Cuskey, 1982). It was worthy of attention only when it affected others: through childbirth and child rearing.

Understandably, the rising influence of the women's movement within the drugs policy, treatment and research field meant this traditional wisdom was questioned. In 1979, addressing the question of gender and drug use meant attempting to enforce a new focus on women's drug use as a matter of equal concern – one worthy of specialist drug service provision and research. This feminist project attempted to shatter a heavily medicalised and psychologised picture of drug use that had ignored its social, economic and cultural aspects. Feminists pursued a perspective which viewed the very fabric of everyday life as a political landscape in which gendered social relations – within the private spheres of the home and the family as well as the public world of work and media representations – were arenas of power: arenas within which women were oppressed by the economic, social and cultural power afforded to men as a matter of course. Examining the specific arenas of drug use and drug treatment only served to prove the point – both were ultimately geared to the needs of men. Men were agents of women's oppression through drug use – as doctors, pimps and dealers.

Although this feminist perspective contributed a great deal to our understanding of the social meaning of drug use it stopped short at differentiating between cultures of drug use. True, the range of drug use that received attention broadened. Women's use of tranquillisers now figured alongside the legitimate (male) use of prescribed drugs or alcohol, and the illegal use of heroin and other opiates. But these early days of the project on gender and drug use reproduced the research norm of the time – a focus on problem drug use gleaned from users of drug services.

But that was 1979, two decades ago. Why revisit the past? For one simple reason: the state of the art of understanding gender and drug use I have described has changed surprisingly little. A 1993 review of the literature found a similar picture: one based largely on the problematic end of the spectrum of women's drug use drawn from women contacted through drugs services (Taylor, 1993). A picture which emphasised the exclusive role of men in introducing women to drug use; women's dependence on men to inject them to maintain their habit; women's desire to have babies to affirm their role as women and their irresponsibility as mothers; and their inevitable involvement in prostitution. No dramatic change since that time is to be found in published research: a database search of English-language publications on gender and drug use between 1993 and 1996 yielded 200 references, the vast majority of which focused on women in services of various kinds and the criminal justice system. Just under a third of the references were concerned with pregnancy and motherhood. A concern with women's drug use as it affects others still appears to dominate the gender and drug use literature.

There is one very good explanation for this, and it is directly related to a key change in the drugs research literature as a whole: the growth of policy-led research in the wake of HIV/AIDS. In the context of concerns about HIV and AIDS, drug use was deemed a potential threat to the health of the nation. The focus of research was now policy-led and included the goal of minimising the threat of AIDS to society and, to a lesser degree, minimising the harms involved in drug use for drug users. The research spotlight was therefore trained predominantly on those whose health behaviours were considered to be most risky to others and themselves: hence, the many studies of the injecting and sexual behaviour of drug users conducted since the mid- to late 1980s and a particular focus on prostitution and pregnancy. To some extent, these studies do represent a significant change in gender-related research in the field. Although they have been geared to informing public health policy rather than a more abstract gender research agenda, they have nonetheless tended to incorporate the gender question as a matter of fact – because the task in hand required it. What is more, this focus on gender did lead to examination of the gender *dynamics* of, and relations *between*, the sexes within specific drug cultures – even if the narrowly defined cultural dimensions of drug use were limited to sexual and injecting behaviour.

No doubt there are further explanations as to why the explicit project of research on gender and drug use still seems to equate with a narrow concern with 'women's drug use' *per se*. This situation sometimes seems reminiscent of a strangely Victorian 'separate spheres' arrangement (for 'a question of gender', read 'women's issues'), and to have increasingly offered a one-size-fits-all approach to understanding gender and drug use. However, rather than pursue these, I want to move on to briefly discuss my own answer to my question 'What is the general state of the art of "thinking" gender and drug use?' In response, I argue that such 'thinking' is out of step with broader social developments and associated trends in drug use.

GENDER AND DRUG USE: NOW YOU DON'T . . .

Second question: why does the general state of the gender and drug use art need to change?

I have previously argued (Henderson, 1993a, 1993b), that the current state of the art suits those concerned to maintain the status quo. For those who have no interest in exploring the impact of gender on drug use, a 'women's issues' ghetto is ideal: it can be easily avoided. For those content to focus only on negativity, the puritanical (female) victim mentality (PVM) which the business of inquiring into gender and drug use seems to fall into so readily, is a veritable comfort blanket. And there are certainly more than enough examples of women out there for whom this perspective seems to 'fit' – for example young women with few social options selling their bodies for crack. Hence, the status quo. But this gender and drug use paradigm really does not 'fit' all cultures of drug use. I discovered this well and truly in the early 1990s, in the context of a study of young women and dance/rave/Ecstasy culture carried out in the north-west of England between October 1991 and 1993 (Henderson, 1993c).

This study was a continuation of the established approach to gender and drug use in that it focused on women. But it focused on women within youth culture, not problem users and/or service clients, and a brief review of some of its findings should demonstrate just how inadequate the PVM was as a means of making sense of them. The young women (aged between 15 and 25) that I interviewed varied in how 'often, many, much and long' they used Ecstasy, amphetamine and LSD (from three months to three years, mostly on a weekly basis). But, they shared a view of their drug taking as an integral part of a culture. In Britain, this culture first emerged as the minority Acid House scene in the 1980s and grew and diversified beyond all expectation (Collin and Godfrey, 1997; Redhead, 1997). To fully grasp the drug use, one has to understand the culture. This revolved around large social events in which euphoria was the name of a new game and its many, exciting components included group feeling, dance movements, facial and hand expressions, massage, and roaring when the empathy between the crowd, the DJ and high points in the music peaked. A whole host of visual, aural and oral stimuli brought crowds of diverse young people together in a sensual social space on a grand scale.

The young women I spoke to came from a range of class, race and ethnic backgrounds; the majority smoked tobacco and cannabis on a regular basis but had little taste for alcohol. They generally found it hard to identify which features they liked most about the scene – the music, drugs, dancing, social interaction, a feeling of belonging, style and fashion, auto-eroticism, flirtation – but their appetite for the pleasures of this nocturnal culture was outstanding (Henderson, 1993d, 1996, 1997):

With really good 'E's, I mean at a really good club, you're just dancing on totally sort of a sexual high. It's just something totally incredible. The dancing and being in the club, that high is what it's all about – and you just don't get it anywhere else, in any shape or form.

When I took E in the beginning, it was a new thing . . . travelling in convoys on motorways trying to find the parties dressed in mad, casual clothes . . . People travelled from all over the country to be there. Everybody wanted to know one another, it was so exciting . . . I used to get up on the speakers and get the crowd going . . . I got these euphoric rushes through my body . . . I just wanted to love everybody . . . I lived for the weekend just to experience that feeling again, the whole atmosphere. (Henderson, 1997: 69)

What was very clear at the time was that all this sensuality and hedonism lacked an important ingredient – it was not tied into a straightforward sexual narrative: 'doing' sex had lost its pride of place in the new chemical Britain after dark. The old nightclub codes involving measured display and a commonly understood purpose of finding a sexual partner were seemingly swept away. Cigarettes, water, massages were part of social exchange between strangers of either sex (with no strings attached). In a context of recession and diminishing opportunities in the education and job markets, these young women had self-confidence, drive and keenness to get on (either outside or inside the official world), common sense *and* an extraordinary capacity for pleasure in their own physicality. In the age of AIDS, this was safer sex writ large:

> The thing I remember is the second time I took 'E' at a club . . . I was in a near orgasmic state. I remember, like, looking round as if I was like saying with my eyes, 'Ah this is what it's like!' but it felt like everyone was going, 'Eiow this is what it's like!' – they all knew . . . I can't remember if I came or not but for a long time I was like really just about to and it was just brilliant really. (Henderson, 1997: 70)

> We do fancy blokes at raves and enjoy flirting with them . . . but it's like going back to when you were younger, you don't want to get them into bed, you're just friendly. (Henderson, 1997: 71)

> It's always been affectionate, hugging and kissing girls you never met before like they're your lifelong friend but recently you can see girls grinding together. A year ago they would have been called lezzies or something but nobody bats an eyelid. (Henderson, 1993d: 128)

MAKE-OVER TIME

Question three: how does the general state of the art need to change?

Answer 1: Thinking on gender and drug use needs to change from a one-size-fits-all approach and adopt some flexibility and responsiveness to changing trends and patterns of drug use, drawing on the most useful tools for the job.

Let me illustrate by recapping. To witness young women's involvement in this culture and to listen to their stories in the early 1990s (arguably the peak of the popular rave scene in Britain), was, then, to be faced with a somewhat empty tool-kit when it came to 'thinking' gender and drug use in this context. Not least because, as has been argued more recently:

> The rave dance-floor . . . is one of the few spaces which afford – and indeed, encourage – open displays of physical pleasure and affection. Explicit displays of 'ecstatic' happiness, and the relentless drive to achieve this, have never been so central to a youth culture's meaning. (Pini, 1997: 167)

These young women were evidently not being frog-marched into drug use by men and were not leading deeply unhappy lives as a result of their drug use. Their drug use was (only one) part of buying into a lifestyle to which pleasure was central. Granted, their participation within the culture was different from that of their male counterparts on the dance floor:

A lot of girls who go to 'raves' are looking for something different . . . they take it more easy with the drugs but they do seem to get a better buzz you know . . . I can walk past a lot of people when I'm 'E'ing, a lot of lads, and they won't give me a buzz you know. A lot of them have, like, shady faces and stuff but more girls are dead friendly . . . Lads seem to be more tied up in their own field . . . They don't seem to sort of give out as much, I've noticed . . . I think girls go out there to give everybody a buzz. They look round for people more when they're dancing, you know, smile more. They seem like they want to put their love across more over than what the lads do. (18-year-old female) (Henderson, 1993c: 40)

And they were predominantly consumers of the culture, not its producers – the DJs, the promoters, the entrepreneurs of all kinds were predominantly male. But they were like chalk to the cheese of the prevailing images of femininity within other studies of drug use.

This new trend in gender and drug use needed new analytical tools. Here was a phenomenon which involved mass pleasure-seeking on a grand scale and yet the state of the literature on gender and drug use seemed to remain largely as described by Elizabeth Ettorre in 1989. Ettorre observed that 'pleasure for most women appears as a subverted or hidden reality' and highlighted the 'need to look perhaps more closely at the pleasurable effects of substances and in particular to ask ourselves why and how women experience their substance use as pleasurable' (Ettorre, 1989). The obvious 'kit' to examine was that of studies of youth culture. Perhaps unsurprisingly, a similar debate around gender had already taken place in this area of social inquiry – with feminists, and some male writers, questioning perspectives which portrayed young women as perpetually draped on the passenger seat of youth culture without questioning why (McRobbie, 1980; Dorn and South, 1983). Where female drug use was touched upon at all in this context, the old familiar gender story was retold:

So intransigently male are the mythologies and rituals attached to regular drug-taking that few women feel the slightest interest in their literary, cinematic or cultural expressions . . . It would be foolish to imagine that women do not take drugs – isolated young housewives are amongst the heaviest drug users and girls in their late teens are one of the largest groups among attempted suicides by drug overdose. Instead I am suggesting that for a complex of reasons the imaginary solutions which drugs may offer boys do not have the same attraction for girls. (McRobbie, 1980: 29)

The most useful tools came from the (albeit, often contorted, abstract and overly complex) discipline of Cultural Studies. In a nutshell, these were perspectives developed in response to the growing significance of the world of consumption in defining our identities: perspectives which embraced the possibility of women being social actors, rather than merely passive subjects of power; and which explored the many dimensions of female (and later, male) pleasure, desire, identity and power in relation to consumer culture (Coward, 1984; Nava, 1991); perspectives which were developed in the context of analyses of popular consumer culture – from the female bedroom culture of 'teenyboppers' (McRobbie, 1991), to the teen magazine (Winship, 1987), the sexuality of Madonna (Frank and Smith, 1993), advertising, fashion, the shopping mall, TV and so on – but which had fought shy of female drug culture on the whole. For the young women in my study, drugs were one of a wide range of (in this case, illicit) cultural products with which they composed a lifestyle and through which they made sense of themselves within the broader context of the social world.

However, to take this argument further, my early 1990s study does illustrate my general point – but also has its limitations. Clearly, adopting new perspectives to allow me to make sense of my findings at the time was a necessary development in my thinking on gender and drug use (and, to be honest, made it possible for me to pick up on the trends I identified when I did) but these perspectives were not sufficient for understanding the gender dimensions of *all* cultures of drug use. They simply represent a much-needed addition to the tool-kit. For example, a recent analysis of the gender dimensions of the new and growing phenomenon of heroin use in the 1990s suggests that, unlike the gender-neutral epidemic of the early 1980s, this is a predominantly male culture of use (Strang and Taylor, 1997). Very different analytical tools may be needed to investigate heroin culture at the end of the century. Nonetheless, if Taylor's (1993) rare ethnography of a group of female injecting drug users in Glasgow is anything to go by, a straightforward return to the PVM as the most appropriate means of understanding women's position within modern heroin culture is by no means inevitable. Taylor's study illustrated how the adoption of a perspective which identified women as social actors could uncover important aspects of a drug culture in which women have traditionally been seen either as moral reprobates or as passive victims of their social circumstances or of male power over them. She found that the women took what forms of independence and purpose they could: they were more likely to be autonomous agents in their move to 'hard' drugs; have a sense of pride in injecting themselves; be every bit as involved in 'taking care of business' as men; not inevitably support their habit through prostitution; have complex responses to pregnancy – among them a deep desire to come off drugs; and make strenuous efforts to keep their drug-using lifestyle from affecting their children (Taylor, 1993; see also Maher, 1997).

Answer 2: Thinking on gender and drug use needs to be informed by broader social changes

Even more importantly, a truly flexible and responsive approach necessarily involves continual reassessment in the face of broader social change. What was broadly true of the gender dimensions of dance culture in the early 1990s is by no means so applicable across the board of a vastly diversified and transformed phenomenon. The advent of what has been described as post-Ecstasy club culture, with its plethora of cultural forms, identities, associated forms of drug use (which incorporate an increasingly wide range of drug use) and (much more traditionally sexualised) gender relations, requires further investigation, not least from a gender perspective: investigation which goes further than the surveys which repeatedly suggest the normalisation of drug use (Parker et al., 1995) without fleshing out the detail of the social meaning of drug use among young people (Shiner and Newburn, 1997 and Chapter 9 in this volume)

A flexible and responsive approach would necessarily reassess the broader changes within the social definition of gender and gender roles. It would be important to recognise, for example, that the original manifestation of the young postmodern woman my research identified, who knew what she wanted and went out and got it – on and off the dance floor – was not a short-lived fluke, a brief encounter before the harsh realities of female adulthood took over (Henderson, 1997). Recent research among 3,000 young women aged 13–19 suggests that not all modern-day claims of 'girl power' are a media invention and that the 'can-do' girl is alive and kicking (Katz, 1997). Such a broader social framework within which the expectations of femininity are so much higher – even if the options open to individuals do not match them – has powerful implications for the *experience* of femininity and, hence, social inquiry.

Answer 3: Thinking on gender and drug use needs to take account of both sides of the gender equation

This is best illustrated by returning to the example of the early 1990s. The changing shape of gender relations on the Ecstasy-fuelled dance floor affected young men as well as young women. Masculinity was remixed within the dance culture too, at least on the dance floor – as the young women in my study described:

> You see lots of lads hugging each other, a lot . . . Sometimes they hug for so long you think 'When's the big snog coming?'

> You can always spot them, men who think 'let's go to one of these here raves' and 'these girls are probably goers'. They stand there with pints of beer and ask you if you come here often. (Henderson, 1997: 94)

As a (male) student described:

> When you are on Ecstasy you can quite happily spend the whole night hugging, stroking, smiling together, acknowledging the people around you, and saying very little . . . ideas of actually having sex do not arise until after

the rave (where the need for sleep usually quenches the desire for sex). (Creed, 1993)

Irvine Welsh, acclaimed Scottish writer on the new chemical culture, graphically presents the case of an E-induced 'transformation' of masculine response to rave culture. Here, in his book *Ecstasy* (1995), the same character moves from disdain to appreciating that 'something special' is happening:

A lot of the boys in the cashies took Es, a lot of them didnae. I never saw the point. I'd always liked the Becks, and couldna get intae that fucking music. It was shite, that techno, nae lyrics tae it, that same fuckin drum machine, throbbin away aw the time. I hated dancing . . .
   I was lost in the music and the movement. It was an incredible experience, beyond anything I'd ever known. I could never dance but all self-consciousness left me as the drug and the music put me in touch with an undiscovered part of myself . . . My body's internal rhythms were pounding, I could hear them for the first time. They were singing: You're alright, Roy Strang . . . People, strangers, were coming up to me and hugging me. Birds, nice-looking lassies n that. Guys n aw; some ay them cunts that looked wide and whom I would have just panelled before . . . Something special was happening and we were all in this together. (Welsh, 1995: 237)

With the benefit of hindsight, it would be all too simple to put the female identities and pleasures the study described exclusively down to Ecstasy's reported effects, especially on men:

It is curious that a drug which can increase emotional closeness, enhance receptivity to being sexual and would be chosen as a sexual enhancer, does not increase the desire to initiate sex. (Buffum and Moser, 1986)

But masculinity was on the change within the broader Ecstasy culture – beyond the dance floor, house music democratised the music creation business to such a degree that the new-style DJ took over from the live music venue as a central feature of pop culture (see also Shapiro, Chapter 2 in this volume). Across the country, young men went to the bedroom or garage with a pile of vinyl (fetishised in the age of CDs, audio tapes and digital technology), a bag of cannabis, two turntables, a mixer, a sampler and some good friends – and produced dance floor and chart hits. Suddenly many a boy's fantasy was, not to be a rock star complete with wailing guitar and mirror-formed pose, but the man who (facelessly and silently) orchestrated the moods and emotions of the dance crowds. Now, in a reversal of early feminist studies of teenybopper bedroom culture, young men were occupying this domestic space, staying home and 'cooking tunes'. Granted, technological know-how was a key component of this new form of masculinity, but the creative form also became an emotional language for young men. Planning and composing remixes of non-stop tunes, raided from almost every type of music you can think of, became a kind of emotional currency. A form of cultural exchange. Something to give to those you were close to, those on the same 'vibe', and a form of social identity.

Finally, of course, these changes in masculinity within dance cultures were by no means unrelated to broader social changes. On the one hand, we are told, as a result of the massive economic and social shifts in the late modern world, masculinity is in crisis: sperm counts are taking a nose dive, the Equal Opportunities Commission is getting more complaints from men than women about job discrimination and recruitment, fathers are harassed by the Child Support Agency and boys are turning to anorexia. 'A Bad Time to Be a Man', 'The Men's Ward', 'The Male Survival Guide', 'Men Aren't Working' and 'Women on Men' have become part of an evening in front of the television. Men are (successfully) committing suicide more (young ones especially), complaining about too much use of the male body as a sexual object in advertising, while, at the same time, they are entering a male version of the Miss World beauty competition called Mr UK, cashing in on popular 'boy' bands and 'Full Monty' hen nights, and buying into 'new laddism' – the latter appearing in the shape of football fandom, beer consumption, an obsession with 'babes', more or less criminal forms of 'ducking and diving' and generally 'behaving badly'.

My central point here is that the changes in masculinity and femininity I have described are by no means unrelated. It is difficult to make sense of one form of gender culture without reference to the other.

CONCLUSION – AND

Answer 4: Thinking on drug use would benefit enormously from more research on gender and drug use

I began this chapter by asking if we knew what was happening to the gender dimensions of drug use and whether we should care. I conclude that it is obvious that we know very little. Qualitatively, for example, we have insufficient information about patterns of illicit drug use as we approach the turn of the century. Granted, a (happily) increasing number of surveys have provided more quantitative data. However, while some surveys tell us first that drug use is now 'normalised' among young British people, more recently, others have told us that levels of drug use have peaked and we now appear to be witnessing a 'levelling out' (Ramsay and Spiller, 1997). Regardless of the problems of interpreting such ups and downs in empirically measured trends, we still know too little about the broad cultural flesh which needs to be put on these numerical bones. Never mind the cultural specifics underpinning trends in modern drug use. This is a state of affairs that should be remedied and we should certainly care enough to pursue the research needed. Planning for the future is always a fundamentally flawed occupation. Nonetheless, if drug treatment and prevention policy (beyond the criminal justice system) are to respond with any degree of effectiveness in the twenty-first century, then they must tune into the many different cultures of drug use modern British society currently supports, and identify key areas of concern. These are essential steps for the agenda if we are to gain a better sense of the place of drugs in everyday life. This is an agenda to which research has much to contribute and on which the gender question should be prioritised.

REFERENCES

Buffum, J. and Moser, C. (1986) 'MDMA and sexual function', *Journal of Psychoactive Drugs*, 18 (4), October–December: 353–9.

Collin, M. and Godfrey, J. (1997) *Altered State. The Story of Ecstasy Culture and Acid House*. London: Serpents' Tail.

Coward, R. (1984) *Female Desire. Women's Sexuality Today*. London: Paladin.

Creed, T. (1993) 'Social interactions at raves: a raver's/sociologist's study'. Dissertation, University of Manchester.

Cuskey, W. (1982) 'Female addiction: a review of the literature', *Journal of Addictions and Health*, 3 (1): 3–33.

Dorn, N. and South, N. (1983) 'Of males and markets: a critical review of youth culture theory'. *Occasional Paper 1*. London: School of Social Science, Centre for Occupational and Community Research, Middlesex Polytechnic.

Ettorre, B. (1989) 'Women and substance use/abuse: towards a feminist perspective or how to make dust fly', *Women's Studies International Forum*, 12 (6): 593–602.

Frank, L. and Smith, P. (eds) (1993) *Madonnarama. Essays on Sex and Popular Culture*. Pittsburgh, PA and San Francisco: Cleis Press.

HEA (1997) *Young People and Health: The Health Behaviour of School Aged Children*. London: Health Education Authority.

Henderson, S. (1993a) 'Time for a make-over', *Druglink*, September–October: 14–16.

Henderson, S. (1993b) 'Keep your bra and burn your brain?' *Druglink*, November–December: 10–12.

Henderson, S. (1993c) *Young Women, Sexuality and Recreational Drug Use. Final Report*. Manchester: The Lifeline Project.

Henderson, S. (1993d) 'Luvdup and deeelited: responses to drug use in the second decade', in P. Aggleton, P. Davies and G. Hart (eds), *AIDS: Facing the Second Decade*. London: Falmer Press.

Henderson, S. (1996) ' "E"' types and dance divas: some implications for research and prevention', in T. Rhodes and R. Hartnoll (eds), *HIV Prevention in the Community: Perspectives on Individual, Community and Political Action*. London: Routledge.

Henderson, S. (1997) *Ecstasy: Case Unsolved*. London: Pandora.

Jaynes, L. (1997) 'Professional addicts: women who take drugs to stay on top', *Cosmopolitan*, October: 33–8.

Katz, A. (1997) 'All about Eve', *Guardian*, 8 October: 2–3.

McRobbie, A. (1980) 'Settling accounts with subcultures: a feminist critique', *Screen Education*, 39: 29.

McRobbie, A. (1991) *Feminism and Youth Culture. From 'Jackie' to 'Just Seventeen'*. Basingstoke: Macmillan Press.

Maher, L. (1997) *Sexed Work: Gender, Race and Resistance in a Brooklyn Drug Market*. Oxford: Clarendon Press.

Nava, M. (1991) 'Consumerism reconsidered: buying and power', *Cultural Studies*, 5 (2).

Parker, H., Measham, F. and Aldridge, J. (1995) *Drug Futures*. London: ISDD.

Perry, L. (1979) *Women and Drug Use: an Unfeminine Dependency*. London: ISDD.

Pini, M. (1997) 'Women and the early British rave scene', in A. McRobbie (ed.), *Back to Reality? Social Experience and Cultural Studies*. Manchester: Manchester University Press.

Ramsay, M. and Spiller, J. (1997) *Drug Misuse Declared in 1996: Latest Results from the British Crime Survey*. London: Home Office, Research and Statistics Directorate.

Redhead, S. (1997) *The Club Cultures Reader: Readings in Popular Cultural Studies*. Oxford: Blackwell.

Rosenbaum, M. (1981) *Women on Heroin*. New Brunswick, NJ: Rutgers University Press.

Shiner, M. and Newburn, T. (1997) 'Definitely, maybe not? The normalisation of recreational drug use amongst young people', *Sociology*, 31 (3): 511–29.

Strang, J. and Taylor, C. (1997) 'Different gender and age characteristics of the UK heroin epidemic of the 1990s compared with the 1980s', *European Addiction Research*, 3: 43–8.

Taylor, A. (1993) *Women Drug Users*. Oxford: Clarendon Press.

Welsh, I. (1995) *Marabou Stork Nightmares*. London: Jonathan Cape.

Winship, J. (1987) *Inside Women's Magazines*. London: Pandora.

4

WHITE LINES:
CULTURE, 'RACE' AND DRUGS

Karim Murji

A few years ago, during fieldwork for the book *Traffickers* (Dorn et al., 1992), a couple of colleagues and I went to visit a police station in London. After a meeting with the chief officer we were taken on a guided 'walkabout' by a detective from the local drugs squad. While we were not aware of what instructions he had been given, it seems that he saw his duty as being to demonstrate his knowledge of the territory and its people. At the end of the walkabout we arrived near to a street well known for its many 'Asian' shops and restaurants. One of my colleagues asked the officer if he thought that the local Asian community was involved in drug trafficking. He replied: 'Oh yes, they import it in foodstuffs, wrapped inside fish and things like that.' At the point at which he said 'they', he looked and nodded directly at me. (To stress that I did not just imagine this, I can add that my colleagues also noticed the gesture.) Was this an involuntary action? A sign of his discomfort at my presence? Or perhaps he thought that I might have some information to offer on this observation? The issue was not pursued and nothing more was said of it. The reader's attitude to or interpretation of this anecdote may well indicate much about how this chapter will be read. There could be many ways of reading the gesture in my direction and there may, at face value, be little basis on which to choose one explanation rather than another. But its undertone seemed clear to me and, perhaps, will also be so to those who believe that racial or racist meanings do not have to be spelt out for their meaning to be apparent. Racism may not always, or even often, be made explicit but it is there to be read into situations from which it cannot be explained away.

This chapter examines a number of aspects of the racialisation of drugs, including culture and culturalism and the depiction of dangerous places defined by the linking of drugs, crime, race and violence. Analyses of the coupling of race and drugs have been well developed in a number

of accounts of the history of drug control, principally those looking at the
USA. Various authors have examined periods when the dangers of,
and need for controls on, drugs have been based upon fears about their
effects on racial minorities, often mixed into a dizzying pot-pourri of
tales or fantasies of sexual mixing, vice and violence (for example see
Musto, 1973; Helmer, 1975). Such themes are of course not unique to the
US and several narratives in Britain have been explored by Kohn (1987,
1992).

RACE, CULTURE AND DRUGS

There are a number of difficulties in writing about race and culture in
relation to drugs. The status and utility of the term 'race' has been
questioned. Since it has no biological basis, its unqualified use can serve
to perpetuate, rather than question, commonsense ideas about race
differences. Such ideas include the problem of essentialism, the belief
that different groups, racially defined, have fixed inner characteristics
that distinguish them from other 'races'. But, when it comes to explaining or understanding drug use and supply, what can meaningfully be
attributed to racial difference? Race itself does not exist independently of
other social factors such as class, gender and age. These may be every bit
as important as race, or perhaps even more so. Hence it is difficult to
impute any essential traits to racial groups and most attempts to do so
have been discredited. Questioning how worthwhile it is to use race does
not however mean that we cannot refer to something that can be called
racism, or examine the ways in which racist discourse produces and
seeks to cement ideas about race as the principal source of difference and
identity.

Culture is every bit as problematic as race. It is frequently used as a
synonym for race, most commonly when the term multi-culturalism is
used as a code to connote and subsume it. Britain, it is often said, is now
a multi-cultural (and some add, multi-ethnic, multi-faith) society. The
insinuation is that it is immigration – racially defined – that brought
about this change. One of the most questionable aspects of this linking of
race and culture is the implication that Britain was once a racially pure,
culturally homogeneous flat land before the 'outsiders' came in. Race
and culture are linked in an unproblematic way that reinforces rather
than refutes 'cultural difference' as a code for those forms of racist
discourse which deny racism by redefining it as merely a cultural
preference for 'our own kind of people'. In the process, racism is
ethnicised or culturalised and cultural difference is treated as the signifier of a hard and fast boundary that separates 'us' from 'them'. The
depiction of the 'culture' of ethnic or racial minorities is used as a means
for simultaneously denying, while implicitly reasserting, hierarchies

through which racial categories are 'smuggled' back in. A linked problem is the way in which 'black culture' has been represented in fields such as anthropology and sociology, as well as in education. These accounts have been criticised for producing stereotyped and pathological views of black culture and families, in which the dividing line between liberal and reactionary views has sometimes been a very thin one.[1] The most recent expression of this has been the widely shared, and often racialised, meanings associated with the idea of an underclass. In bringing together 'culture of poverty' and 'cycle of dependency' perspectives, the use of the underclass as an analytical term has perpetuated a form of culturalism where culture itself is seen as a governing force while wider structural elements, as well as a sense of agency, tend to be lost.

A more complex and dynamic depiction of culture, stressing multiplicity and hybridity in the making of personal and collective identities, has been advanced in recent years. The presence of such perspectives within studies of drug cultures seems weak, though some research examining drug use by women and young people, mostly Ecstasy use within rave culture, has served to widen the field of vision (cf. Henderson, Chapter 3 in this volume). Such opportunities remain most underdeveloped in relation to race, perhaps because of a feeling that it has become a taboo subject (see Ruggiero and South, 1997). This seems to have led to a view that it is better not to write about race at all, rather than risk the dangers of stereotyping. However, a number of ethnographic accounts of the lives of black and Latino groups have emerged in the US (for example, see Bourgois, 1995). Selling and using drugs feature as principal elements within the culture, though not without an attempt being made to place this into an overall picture of group and individual lifestyles. While ethnography as a methodology is sometimes criticised for paying insufficient attention to social and economic forces, in Britain approaches to race, drugs and crime have usually fallen into the opposite camp. In emphasising structural determinants, they tend to miss out on differentiation and detail within categories such as race and gender. There have been attempts to bring the two sides of the picture together, though one assay in this direction – the work of British left realists – provoked controversy precisely because it was seen as promulgating a crude and dangerous view of 'black youth culture' to explain black involvement in street crime (Lea and Young, 1984). There are other approaches. From a political economy perspective, Ruggiero (1995) has argued that to the extent that the illicit economy broadly mirrors the structure of the licit economy, we would expect blacks in the main to be at the lower end of criminal hierarchies rather than the kingpins, just as they mostly are in the economic structures of the legitimate world. While this approach does seek to make the visibility of black drug sellers in some streets and areas understandable, unlike left realism it does not do so by using a culturalist explanation.

Race has figured in other recent research on drug markets, law enforcement and prevention, though not as the central concern. A study of drug treatment and advice services sought to explore some of the reasons why relatively few black and Asian people are seen at such services (Awiah et al., 1992; see also Pearson et al., 1993). In terms of drug use itself, a source of evidence about patterns of usage has emerged in the form of a number of self-report surveys, in which people have been asked to declare their own use of some or all drugs. Some surveys report that some ethnic or racial minority groups declare higher drug use. But other surveys have found the opposite. A more detailed consideration of methodology, sample size and the age groups surveyed might shed a little more light on the findings. Even so, whether drug use is found to be higher or lower amongst particular groups still requires some explanation that is not detectable from the data itself, leaving questions about influences on drug use unanswered. Again the issue is, what is the significance of race or ethnicity in variations uncovered by such surveys? Perhaps, as Awiah et al. conclude, there is a need to move beyond the 'quite useless (and sometimes implicitly racist) debates over whether or not drug use *per se* is more or less common in black and other ethnic minority communities compared with the white population' (Awiah et al., 1992: 9).

The heroin 'epidemic' in Britain in the early and mid-1980s appeared to include very few black people. Their absence has been acknowledged though not really explained – for instance, it has been suggested that one reason may have been that heroin was seen a 'dirty, white man's drug' and thus shunned by black drug users and perhaps sellers too (Pearson, 1995a). Although Asians have been associated with heroin (chiefly its supply, because of its production in parts of Asia), African-Caribbean communities in Britain seem to have been connected with two main drugs: cannabis initially and latterly crack-cocaine. Cannabis has been associated with Rastafarianism where the use of ganja is seen as an aid to spirituality. More secular uses were seen as common place on the front lines and in the shebeens of areas with sizeable black communities. The widespread use of cannabis, or perhaps the idea that use was common, meant that drugs often became a source of conflict between the police and black people, especially when the police were seen as exceeding their powers of 'stop and search' and using drugs as an excuse to harass many young black men for no obvious reason other than their blackness. It is an indication of the extent to which the link is taken for granted that an analysis by a police officer of cannabis arrest statistics in London should be regarded as newsworthy because it revealed that the majority of people arrested were not black (*Guardian*, 9 July 1994). The all too common linkage between African-Caribbean people and cannabis was also part of a period of controversy when blacks seemed to be 'unusually eligible' (Miller, 1996) for the diagnosis of cannabis psychosis.

Like heroin, Ecstasy, *the* drug of the 1990s, has also not been seen as attracting a sizeable number of black users. For the Labour MP Bernie Grant, young blacks are 'too smart' to take Ecstasy. Grant said: 'I'm sure that black kids have more sense . . . Fortunately it doesn't appear to be a drug that is popular with the Black community' (*The Voice*, 20 January 1997: 1). A number of deaths linked to Ecstasy, certainly all the most publicised ones, have been of young white people (see Murji, 1998a). None of this means that black and Asian people do not take or sell heroin, Ecstasy or any other drugs, though, in terms of *representation* the reasons why some drugs do, and others do not, seem to become associated with black people remain open to further investigation. There seems to be no particular reason to believe that belonging to a racial or ethnic minority group provides some sort of inoculation or barrier that protects people from these, or any other, drugs, or makes their usage totally unacceptable. Nonetheless, as Awiah et al. (1992) point out, the Advisory Council on the Misuse of Drugs (ACMD) has alluded to some sort of cultural blanket acting to prevent or contain drug problems, particularly for Asian communities. This is one aspect of an invidious culturalism. Asian culture is seen as strong and offering protection, while the culture of African-Caribbean groups is seen as somehow lacking and deficient. The idealisation of the former finds its corollary in the denigration of the latter, to reverse Pitts' (1993) formulation (see also Webster, 1997). Cultural deficiency is commonly used to explain initiation into drug use (see Dorn and Murji, 1992). Sometimes, as with left realism, such approaches are combined with a vaguely sociological analysis about a lack of social/economic integration that is presumably supposed to add to their plausibility. Clutterbuck, for instance, claims that ethnic minorities are most subjected to the attentions of drug sellers because a new 'underclass contains a disproportionate number of immigrants, whose unrewarding lives makes them prey to the drug pushers' (Clutterbuck, 1990: 184). A closely related view can be found within what is probably intended to be a liberal explanation:

Among cultural minorities within the United States, historically there have been higher rates of unemployment and poverty level existence. Payton (1981) acknowledges and discusses the characteristics and stresses of poverty, such as feelings of hopelessness, alienation, and powerlesness, as high correlates of chemical abuse within African-American communities. Youth raised in these communities are often subjected to a culture of origin that appears to tolerate and support the trafficking and use of chemicals for non-medical purposes . . . This does not imply that all members of low income communities succumb to or tolerate the abuse of chemicals. In fact, the majority of people in these communities do not. Yet, in terms of prevention or intervention program development, the visibility and accessibility of trafficking and use does impact the culture and lifestyle evolution in many of these communities. It is evident historically that the trafficking of illegal chemicals within minority communities has served to fulfil some of the economic needs of a population that was systematically and legally ostracized from the job market. Over time, the culture has adapted to a situation thrust upon them but not accepted by the majority. (Griswold-Ezekoye, 1986: 209–10)

This sort of culturalism is precisely what has made the idea of 'black culture' so questionable as either an explanation for drug use or a medium that makes it understandable. The idea of a black drugs culture that is permissive, casual and tolerates 'the trafficking and use of chemicals' employs a malignant and dangerous culturalism, no matter how much it is dressed up as an effect or an outcome of social and economic pressures.

'Good people gone bad'

An objectionable differential culturalism is applied to each of the two main minority groups in Britain, an example of which has already been seen from the ACMD (cf. Awiah et al., 1992). Most discussions of race and drugs have centred on the representation of African-Caribbean people and, for at least two decades, they have most often been portrayed as the dangerous 'Other', 'lesser breeds without the law' (Gilroy, 1987a). Asians have generally taken a back seat in this field, though it would be wrong to imagine that they have been totally absented from the arena in which drugs, crime and race come to be linked. Some of the contributors to Daniels and Gerson's book (1989) examine media images of Asian involvement in drugs and crime in television programmes since the 1970s. More recently, the widely acclaimed Hanif Kureishi scripted film *My Beautiful Laundrette* (sic) was criticised by some Asian groups because Omar, one of the protagonists, finances the renovation of his laundry from the proceeds of heroin imported from Pakistan by his cousin.

Since the mid-1980s there have been attempts to uncover Asian gangs in places such as Southall. The two main groups named, the Tooti Nungs and the Holy Smokes, were said to define themselves territorially, from which it is but a short step to see them as engaging in turf wars, which spill over into the community generally. But crime, culture and religion were tied together in confusing ways; thus, the gangs were seen as engaging in crime and drug dealing, but also fighting for 'honour' and to protect their sisters. This culturalisation of Asian gangs resembles the 'traditional crime family', most notably the Mafia, as depicted in various books and films. Such characterisations have been criticised for their sweeping generalisations about Italian culture and family life. It is, once again, notable that the 'strong family' theme is rarely applied to African-Caribbean people. Susan Benson has nicely summed this up in the title of her paper, 'Asians have culture, West Indians have problems' (Benson, 1996). The media and others find it difficult to move beyond the assumption that while West Indians are the troublesome minority or 'enemy within', Asians are basically lawful and that culture is the main source of self-restraint and control. Stories about the latter are cast as a 'sad departure' from the norm, as a *Sunday Times* (21 August 1994: 6) headline (and the report that went with it) demonstrates: ASIAN YOUTHS REBEL AGAINST GOOD IMAGE. Some changes in representation have been evident in more recent coverage. In the 1990s media attention has focused from time to time on young Asian people and their involvement in drugs and crime, most notably in Bradford (see Webster, 1997), Tower Hamlets (see Keith, 1995; Thompson, 1995) and King's Cross (for example, see 'Asian teenage gangs terrorising London', *Evening Standard* 13 November 1996: 12–13). In all these areas, evidence that young people whose parents and grandparents came from Pakistan and Bangladesh have the highest failure rates at schools and are increasingly among the most likely to be unemployed adults, has led to warnings about the dangers of a new underclass being created in which crime and virtual ghettos are inevitable. The availability of drugs features as one element within this cocktail, though not (yet?) the main one.

DANGEROUS PLACES

Since the late 1980s crack-cocaine has been the drug most linked with race in Britain. The onset of the 'crack panic' has been discussed elsewhere (Bean, 1993). The association of crack with black people and Yardies in particular has been made explicit in journalism (Silverman, 1994; Small, 1995; Thompson, 1995), fiction (Headley, 1992) and police discourse and official reports (see Murji, 1998b). Crack tales have combined a heady brew of black men with a fondness for guns and extreme violence, 'loose living' and a fragile valuing of their own and other people's lives. Their 'live fast, die young, devil may care' attitude has been presented as wreaking havoc on black communities, furthering a 'spiral of decline' in particular places as they acquire a reputation for being ruled by drug warlords. The links between specific places, drugs, crime and most recently, crack-cocaine and Yardies, are too intertwined to disentangle. They form part of a discursive chain of social problems that could be lengthened almost indefinitely to include high crime, inner city neighbourhoods, 'white flight', social pathology/disorganisation, low school attainment, poor parenting, problem housing estates, single motherhood, poverty, welfare dependency, etc. That some of these terms may also be connected to developments outside this chain – for example, 'inner city' could also be linked to gentrification and consumption – does not undermine the main point about the familiarity of the chain. Attempts to deconstruct and destabilise the 'obviousness' of such chains with regard to specific places often rely upon a contrast between the media representation of those places with their more mundane everyday reality. The distinction between representation and reality may not be so straightforward in what some see as an era of the death of the real. Nevertheless, in the conclusion I will suggest that there is still scope for more work that stresses the ordinariness of areas and places that have been pathologised.

Various writers have argued that it is race that primarily shapes the imaginary geography of places depicted as the dreaded Other:

> Race is a privileged metaphor through which the confused text of the city is rendered comprehensible . . . blackness now commonly serves as the cautionary urban other . . . Blackness, or at the very least a racialised vocabulary set which does not need to be spelled out explicitly within the acceptable rules of public discourse has come to play a cautionary role similar to, indeed sometimes becomes a racialised variation of, that once occupied by nineteenth century fears of the crowd. (Keith and Cross, 1993: 9–10)

For instance, in the early 1980s, the then Commissioner of the Metropolitan Police identified several 'symbolic locations' mostly specific roads and streets in London. These were defined as areas with high crime rates and where challenges to the police were said to be commonplace (see Keith, 1993). It did not need to be spelt out that all of these were 'black areas', or, more properly, they had come to be seen as areas with a significant number of black residents. It probably also did not need to be stated explicitly that all of them had regularly been linked with drug availability and, sometimes, with open street-level drug dealing.

If race or blackness acts as the Other which gives shape to anxieties about particular places, it has also been seen as the medium through which fears about crime – and drugs, as Kohn (1987) has proposed – are focused and given a recognisable shape (Hall et al., 1978; Gilroy, 1987a; Keith, 1993). Hence it is possible to delineate the continuity in racialised images of black crime from the mugger to the rioter and now the drug trafficker. Tales of the city and of particular places, fears about racial ghettos and drugs and crime are mixed in with concerns about vice and moral decline through discourses of contagion and pollution (Goldberg, 1993). Drugs, race, culture and particular regions of the city all have distinct histories and geographies of contagion and danger, that have been weaved together at various times. Goldberg (1993: 45) argues that these impose 'a set of interiorities and exteriorities' (Goldberg, 1993: 45), or a relational symbolism between inside and outside, that define the basis for geographies of exclusion and danger, of which the most prominent marker is the visibility of the ethnicised or racialised Other.

Moss Side in Manchester is notable as a location that has come to bear the burden of representation as a dangerous place where drugs, race, guns and violence are said to coexist in an unstable mix. It has been described as England's 'Bronx' by Silverman (cf. *Guardian*, 13 January 1996) who, in furthering the theme of a place and a race apart, adds that it 'stands on its own [as] the only place where drug dealing has followed the American model' (Silverman, 1994: 232). Paddy Ashdown, the leader of the Liberal Democratic Party has related that: 'I used to find the arguments about the legalisation of cannabis quite powerful until I went to see Moss Side. Now, I'd been a soldier on the streets of Belfast, but I'd never been so frightened in all my life' (interviewed in *The Big Issue*, 3–9 February 1997: 13). Before looking further at such images of Moss Side it should be noted that, as I have already suggested, the everyday life of all such places may be very different from the received images. Detailed studies of and in symbolic locations have brought out the local histories that are usually ignored or underplayed in discussions of crime and social problems (Keith, 1993; McLaughlin, 1994). A fuller analysis would also have to address the social and economic context which produces 'black ghettos'. As Taylor et al. point out, places like Moss Side have often 'been relinquished and residualised by the dominant society and then defined as criminal areas' (Taylor et al., 1996: 203; see also Fraser, 1996).

The professionalisation of drug markets has been traced by Dorn et al. (1992). Looking at Manchester generally, an informant given the name 'Eileen' pointed to the increased participation of established criminals in the drug scene. Accompanying this growth was a rise in the number of violent incidents, particularly those involving firearms. In the late 1980s and the early 1990s, six killings were linked to gang rivalries over drugs. Eileen refers to a period 'when there was nearly a shooting every night of the week for something like a month' (Dorn et al., 1992: 40) and, around this time, firearms were said to have become akin to fashion accessories and Manchester acquired the nickname 'Gunchester'. The Greater Manchester Police (GMP) force issued patrol officers with body armour in 1991. In 1993 there were 1,048 firearms offences in the GMP area, more than double the figure only two years earlier. The nadir of this period was the shooting of a 14-year-old boy Benji Stanley, apparently caught up in a case of mistaken identity in January 1992. The incident focused widespread media and public attention on Moss Side as the arena where violent turf wars between gangs were being played out. Enhancing the image of territorial conflict – and, in consequence, an explicit comparison with the street gangs of south-central Los Angeles – the 'Goochies' and the 'Doddies' were said to take their name from streets on a local housing estate (*Guardian*, 24 December 1993 and 14 January 1994; Taylor et al., 1996). Because of this, by the early 1990s Moss Side had become powerfully established as a criminal area, a place where 'drug gangs fight for power' (*Independent*, 18 April 1991: 5) or 'gun gangs rule the rat-runs' (*The Times*, 29 June 1993: 7). Taylor et al. (1996) found this view reflected by some of their respondents who felt that it was a 'bad area' and one that was not safe for whites to be seen in. The apparently unique dangerousness of Moss Side, and the fear that its problems or 'disease' might infect the rest of the city, is summed up in the view that it was:

inescapably exerting its irresistible criminal influence on what local common sense wants to see as a relatively non-criminal city. The presence of Moss Side was symbolic in a very contemporary sense; that is, in symbolising the presence not just of a racial Other . . . but also of a specific kind of violent criminality, signified in particular by discussion of the 'Yardie', implicitly linked into the 'international drugs and firearms trade'. (Taylor et al., 1996: 206)

Thus Thompson can glibly state that 'In some areas, notably Manchester's Moss Side, the Yardie-led gun culture has spread through an entire generation' (Thompson, 1995: 59). Moss Side therefore seems to typify Lash and Urry's (1994) idea of the 'wild zone' as an arena defined by disorder and danger (see also Stanley, 1996). Race and place become intertwined as features that demarcate the boundaries of civility, distinguishing the respectable from the disreputable. The stain of infamy became even more apparent when it was reported that the author Joanna Trollope retracted a 'slur' on the Gloucestershire village of Aston Magna after complaints about her comparison of it to Moss Side. Unsurprisingly, race can be read as a key signifier because she saw the village as having 'a population . . . significantly immigrant. It's a place where all the goings-on you are accustomed to associate with a place like Moss Side are commonplace' (*Guardian*, 20 January 1996: 2). It hardly needs to be added that there was no apology to the residents of Moss Side.

'Alien culture'

The Yardies have come to symbolise social disorganisation in black communities. Their presence in places such as Moss Side signals the depths to which we, or rather 'they', have plunged. This narrative establishes a contrast within cultures of crime. While the East End of London was acknowledged to have a criminal culture, it was basically a stable one, with a sense of order given by the established hierarchies. But drugs and disorganised crime, accompanied by guns and random violence (epitomised in the storyline of the innocent victim caught up in the crossfire of a turf war, or the drive-by shooting in the US) which the Yardie has brought about, depicts a culture of instability, in which even suburban Croydon runs the risk of 'turning into Chicago' (*Croydon Advertiser*, 18 June 1993: 2). The effects of crack are mimicked in portrayals of the excitability and instability of Yardies as dealers and users. As Stanley has written, 'The "controlled" gang violence of the 1960s and the 1970s has declined in favour of new and more arbitrary forces of violence. Where gang rule provided a veneer of respectability in the distribution of the criminal activities of protection, gambling and vice . . . the dominant commodities are now drugs and guns implicating embryonic Jamaican Yardie and Asian Rajamuffin influence' (Stanley, 1996: 103). Drugs and race are connected and twinned as threatening foreign/alien imports, a state of mind that underlies liberal perspectives too.

Hence, several television and radio documentaries on crack and the Yardies have chosen to go to Jamaica to investigate a 'drugs and guns' culture in that country. However this attempt at 'contextualisation' simply ends up reaffirming a discourse of foreign importation in the sense that the Yardies are then seen as having brought this (alien) culture with them into Britain. It therefore buttresses an idea that guns and violence are virtually a cultural proclivity. In a context where Yardies have been described by the National Criminal Intelligence Service as a threat to the very 'security and stability of the nation' (quoted in the *Guardian*, 3 February 1997: 1), the representation of groups in this way serves to reinforce notions of the dangerous Other, those 'without law' who threaten 'us'.

There is a parallel discourse in which an invasion/flooding metaphor is used so that drugs are described as 'pouring' into Britain which is then at risk of being 'awash' with, or 'swamped' by, them. Kohn (1987) has noted the use of this discourse with regard to heroin, though Pearson (1995b) has argued that drugs in general always seem to be represented as coming from 'outside' or 'somewhere else' (see also Gould, 1994). The 'Otherness' of drugs has consequently been linked in with both terrorism and illegal immigration into a discursive chain that enables politicians and others to call for enhanced border controls to contain and counter all these threats. National and transnational security discussions tie together various demands for controls to monitor and prevent the movement of all 'undesirables'. Critics have described this as the establishment of a 'Fortress Europe' policy in which all such groups are categorised together in order to keep everyone, from refugees to terrorists, out of the 'safe European home'. Sivanandan has described this policy as a form of racism, 'which cannot tell one black from another, a citizen from an immigrant, an immigrant from a refugee – and classes all Third World peoples as immigrants and refugees, and all immigrants and refugees as terrorists and drug dealers' (quoted in Read and Simpson, 1991: 2).

Returning to crack-cocaine again, the image of the flood/invasion was apparent in the original speech by Robert Stutman, a DEA (Drug Enforcement Administration) special agent who in a speech to the Association of Chief Police Officers set much of the subsequent reaction in motion. Stutman (1989: 7) stated that, 'We are so saturated with cocaine in the United States, there ain't enough noses left to use the cocaine that's coming in and where it's coming is right here.' The idea that the US drug market was 'saturated' was questioned at the time (*Druglink*, 1989) and Kohn (1987) points out that a saturation thesis had been applied to heroin since at least 1984. But in the years since Stutman's speech there have followed innumerable stories from official sources as well as others (Hargreaves, 1992) suggesting that the cocaine cartels of South America are turning to Britain and/or Europe as an easy or soft target (for example, 'Breaking the white wave of evil', *Independent on Sunday*, 5 April

1992: 6; 'Crack trade turning to "safe" Britain', *Guardian*, 2 July 1994: 8). These stories provided another racial theme. The idea that there are easy points of entry for Latin American drug traffickers, especially through Greece, Turkey, Spain, Portugal and Italy, presents these countries as the 'weak links' or the 'soft underbelly' in the European security cordon. Pictorially, this conception was neatly summed up by an illustration headed 'Protecting the Nation' that accompanied a Customs and Excise press release. In a scene reminiscent of the opening titles of the TV comedy series *Dad's Army*, it depicted a map of Europe on which an arrow indicates a consignment of drugs coming from the south/east and progressing unimpeded through half a dozen European countries until it is finally halted at the British border.

'Flooding' as a way of emotively describing the spread of drugs may find a mirror image in other, more radical and critical analyses. For example, Rumsey (1990) discussing the increase in the use of drugs in black communities in parts of the USA argues that: 'In the late 1960s, the black movement was raising all kinds of hell, and then the black community was *flooded* with heroin, to break the back of the black movement. You *flood* them with heroin, you set them up with needles, and then you make a law that says they have to share them. And on top of it, you have a virus that's transmitted sexually and by blood' (emphasis added). The view that increased drug availability and usage in black and white communities has functioned as a control mechanism has been commonplace, anecdotally at least. Heroin use in Britain escalated in the 1980s: the drug was felt by some to be, literally, an 'opiate of the people' at a time when the government had to find ways of coping with mass youth unemployment. Similarly, drug use in general has been characterised as functioning to quell or pacify potentially riotous inner city populations and prisoners. Drugs, HIV and AIDS have also been described in terms of an invasion from 'outside' (Rumsey, 1990) and both crack-cocaine and HIV have been seen by some commentators as being visited upon particular communities as a form of official control or agent of death reaping the disorderly and the disreputable, the latter image also associated with the idea of divine intervention and retribution against sin and depravity. Lacking evidence of intention, such tales are usually treated as the stuff of conspiracy theories (which does not necessarily mean that they are untrue). In this context it may be significant that investigations by a local newspaper in California revealed that the spread of crack-cocaine in black communities in the USA may have involved a CIA operative as part of the Agency's involvement in the drugs and guns trading that underlay the Iran-Contra scandal. The newspaper reports that the agent admitted that he specifically sought out black dealers in south-central Los Angeles to whom he sold thousands of kilograms of cocaine, at just the time when crack use in black communities was taking off ('America's "crack" plague has roots in Nicaragua war', *San Jose Mercury News*, 18 August 1996; 'War on drugs has unequal impact on black Americans', ibid., 20 August 1996).

Gilroy has argued that the problem with the depiction of black people in crime (or, for current purposes, drugs) is that 'images and representations of black criminality . . . achieve a mythic status' (Gilroy, 1987b: 118). This problem amounts to more than that a casual emphasis on ethnicity and race assists the establishment of racialised boundaries that distinguish civility from dangerousness. It is also that, spoken of in terms of nationality, race or ethnicity, these groups seem all too easily to coalesce into an all-encompassing Other: a 'them' who threaten 'us'. For example, an article in a British newspaper concerning the decline of the Mafia concluded with this warning about new threats emerging to fill the void: 'As well as the growing influence of the ruthless Russian gangs, Chinese Triads and Japanese yakusa compete for spoils. On the west coast of the United States, Korean gangs are active alongside Mexican organised crime collectives which recruit from the smaller street gangs of young disaffected Latinos' (*Guardian*, 4 January 1997: 2). When the Other is characterised so all-inclusively, it seems rather ineffectual to draw upon the 'tiny minority' argument. Thompson (1995) for instance, prefaces his account of 'gangland Britain' with the words, 'in every case, organised criminals make up only a fraction of a percentage of the population – [I] do not seek to tar every Jamaican, Colombian, Sicilian or Asian with the same brush, it [this book] merely focuses on the tiny underworld element within each group' (Thompson, 1995: 5). However since the rest of his book concentrates on 'ethnic' criminal enterprises, employing descriptions such as 'Jamaicans', 'Asians' and so on, it is difficult to see who is being excluded from his broad brush.

'WE GOTTA GET OUT OF THIS PLACE'?

Does writing about, or more particularly naming, specific places run the risk of reaffirming the image of them as problem areas? To some extent this is an academic issue; after all, the representations of the places mentioned here are sufficiently well embedded in popular and local discourses to make liberal hand-wringing fairly pointless. It could be argued that some places are so 'well known' that naming them again does little more damage. But, like the subject of whether and how we use the term 'race', an unquestioning approach can re-entrench that which ought to be made problematic. Racial thinking combines with other factors to 'define out' some people as not 'one of us' and some areas as 'not like ours'. Some of the consequences of this have been discussed above. Similarities and differences with the representations of other places that have also been associated with drugs – parts of Glasgow,

Paisley and Oxford for example – but which lack the identification of a racialised Other, ought to be subjected to closer scrutiny.

I also want to raise the question of whether 'drugs tourism' to inner city areas that have become known as sites of drug availability should be regarded as a problem or not. In *The Fall* (1956), Camus intimates that while 'The poor don't go into the luxury districts . . . eventually the gentlefolk always wind up at least once . . . in the disreputable places'. My own inquiries in Brixton during the mid-1980s suggested that a number of visitors from other parts of London and elsewhere had heard of and visited the 'front line' as a place where drugs were perceived to be quickly and easily available (indeed the police, local residents and others have made the same point about people congregating in the King's Cross area). Such visitors established a reflexive relationship with would-be suppliers, although, significantly, the latter are likely to be the most amateur and disorganised dealers, since intensive surveillance and enforcement efforts are unlikely to be absent. Various questions arise here. Do these other 'outsiders' vicariously benefit from, while serving to reaffirm, an image that the residents of some areas have to live with on a daily basis? Alternatively, does the 'reputation' of some places actually make them more attractive and appealing to some people, who in turn help to drive a localised alternative economy? The double-edged nature of these questions suggests that the wild zone can be both a place of excitement and of squalor and, for some, these may amount to the same thing. The reputations that areas acquire may become sedimented and difficult to shake off, though the question of how the representation of some places has changed over time merits further investigation.

Finally, I wish to revisit the idea of dangerous places. To some extent, any person in Britain attentive to the media will 'know about' Brixton or Moss Side, not least because these areas have been subject to so much coverage. Indeed this 'knowledge' has, at least to some extent, been internationalised. I once noticed in the early 1980s that the then President of South Africa was moved to warn against developments that could lead to that country becoming 'like Brixton'. However, this knowledge claim ignores a somewhat tricky question concerning the boundaries of disreputable and dangerous places: of where they begin and end and, in consequence, what is 'in' and 'out'. Close inspection suggests that the phenomenological boundaries of places, even, or perhaps especially, those with a reputation, are far from clear. The 'East End' for example, is a famously loose term that can cover anything from quite a small geographical area to a state of mind of residents of parts of Essex. 'King's Cross' refers loosely to an area around the station, but its boundaries are also unclear. Events such as gang fights in Somers Town, around Drummond Street and the Regent's Park Estate, as well as parts of Islington, have all been classified under the umbrella heading of being 'in' King's Cross. (Though, perhaps, the boundaries of King's Cross can be more certain, in some respects, since it is difficult to imagine events in Bloomsbury being mistakenly included). A similar point may be made about the front line. The front line in Brixton runs between Brixton and Herne Hill, though clearly the latter has escaped the typifications that have so often been made about the former. Even then, the front line may not be fixed and could shift as a result of influences that have not received much attention. Also, one might ask, where is the elusive Crack City, so frequently referred to in journalism? In his book on crack, the BBC journalist Jon Silverman attaches the title to an estate in Kilburn – although actually some might argue that the estate he refers to is on the borders of Paddington or Ladbroke Grove. But, in any case, the term Crack City has much more commonly been associated with an estate in Deptford, south London (Pearson et al., 1993). Crack City seems to have become a free-floating signifier that is or can be anywhere. This is not just a matter of naming or geographical (in)accuracy. The real point of Silverman's use of the term is that the predictable front lines have changed to anywhere where crack is traded. This picture of a dis-organised and increasingly fragmented drug market corresponds with research findings (Dorn et al., 1992) but, as with the identification of the ragged nature of the boundaries of dangerous places and their changing character over time, it is not a view that appears to have made much impact on popular or racialised 'ways of thinking' about either drug markets or particular places. Going to and writing about symbolic locations, as hordes of students, journalists and academics (including me) have, conveys the message that these are the places where the action is. The emphasis on and the search for the spectacular means that what is commonly ignored are the mundane features of everyday life in all of these places that are not characterisable in terms of drugs, social prob-lems, gangs, turf wars, etc. The humdrum repetition of daily routines may come closer to relating the 'structure of feeling' even of Moss Side (cf. Taylor et al., 1996). This does not mean that we have to try to paint a rosy or romantic picture of social life in dangerous places. But, rather than 'naming and shaming', it is an outlook that does at least open a route to a different meaning of normalisation, one that seeks to em-phasise the unexceptionality of such places rather than their status as 'wild zones' of danger.

NOTE

1. In this chapter, I use the term 'black' to refer to people of African-Caribbean origins and 'Asian' to refer to people of mostly South Asian origins. Both these expressions, as well as the term 'white', gloss over considerable differ-ences within each of these categories.

REFERENCES

Awiah, J., Butt, S. and Dorn, N. (1992) *Race, Gender and Drug Services*. London: ISDD.

Bean, P. (1993) 'Cocaine and crack: the promotion of an epidemic', in P. Bean (ed.), *Cocaine and Crack: Supply and Use*. Basingstoke: Macmillan.

Benson, S. (1996) 'Asians have culture, West Indians have problems', in T. Ranger et al. (eds), *Culture, Identity and Politics*. Aldershot: Avebury.

Bourgois, P. (1995) *In Search of Respect*. Cambridge: Cambridge University Press.

Clutterbuck, R. (1990) *Terrorism, Drugs and Crime in Europe after 1992*. London: Routledge.

Daniels, T. and Gerson, J. (eds) (1989) *The Colour Black*. London: BFI.

Dorn, N. and Murji, K. (1992) *Drug Prevention*. London: ISDD.

Dorn, N, Murji, K. and South, N. (1992) *Traffickers: Drug Markets and Law Enforcement*. London: Routledge.

Druglink (1989) Special issue on crack, September/October.

Fraser, P. (1996) 'Social and spatial relationships and the "problem" inner city', *Critical Social Policy*, 49: 43–65.

Gilroy, P. (1987a) *There Ain't No Black in the Union Jack*. London: Hutchinson.

Gilroy, P. (1987b) 'The myth of black criminality', in P. Scraton (ed.), *Law, Order and the Authoritarian State*. Milton Keynes: Open University Press.

Goldberg, D. (1993) 'Polluting the body politic', in M. Cross and M. Keith (eds), *Racism, the City and the State*. London: Routledge.

Gould, A. (1994) 'Sweden's syringe exchange debate', *Journal of Social Policy*, 23: 195–217.

Griswold-Ezekoye, S. (1986) 'The multicultural model in chemical abuse prevention and intervention', in S. Griswold-Ezekoye et al. (eds), *Childhood and Chemical Abuse*. New York: Haworth Press.

Hall, S. Critcher, C., Jefferson, T., Clarke, J. and Roberts, B. (1978) *Policing the Crisis*. London: Macmillan.

Hargreaves, C. (1992) *Snowfields*. London: Zed.

Headley, V. (1992) *Yardie*. London: X Press.

Helmer, J. (1975) *Drugs and Minority Oppression*. New York: Seabury Press.

Keith, M. (1993) *Race, Riots and Policing*. London: UCL Press.

Keith, M. (1995) 'Making the street visible', *New Community*, 21: 551–65.

Keith, M. and Cross, M. (1993) 'Racism and the postmodern city', in M. Cross and M. Keith (eds), *Racism, the City and the State*. London: Routledge.

Kohn, M. (1987) *Narcomania*. London: Faber & Faber.

Kohn, M. (1992) *Dope Girls*. London: Lawrence & Wishart.

Lash, S. and Urry, J. (1994) *Economies of Signs and Space*. London: Sage.

Lea, J. and Young, J. (1984) *What Is To Be Done about Law and Order?* Harmondsworth: Penguin.

McLaughlin, E. (1994) *Community, Policing and Accountability*. Aldershot: Avebury.

Miller, J. (1996) *Search and Destroy*. Cambridge: Cambridge University Press.

Murji, K. (1998a) 'The agony and the Ecstasy', in R. Coomber (ed.), *The Control of Drugs and Drug Users*. Amsterdam: Harwood.

Murji, K. (1988b) *Policing Drugs*. Aldershot: Ashgate.

Musto, D. (1973) *The American Disease*. Oxford: Oxford University Press.

Payton, C. (1981) 'Substance abuse and mental health', *Public Health Reports*, 96: 20–5.

Pearson, G. (1995a) 'City of darkness, city of light', in S. MacGregor and A. Lipow (eds), *The Other City*. New Jersey: Humanities Press.

Pearson, G. (1995b) 'Drugs, crime and aliens'. Paper presented to the American Society of Criminology, Boston.

Pearson, G., Mirza, H. and Phillips, S. (1993) 'Cocaine in context', in P. Bean (ed.) *Cocaine and Crack: Supply and Use*. Basingstoke: Macmillan

Pitts, J. (1993) 'Thereotyping', in D. Cook and B. Hudson (eds), *Racism and Criminology*. London: Sage.

Read, M. and Simpson, A. (1991) *Against a Rising Tide*. Nottingham: Spokesman.

Ruggiero, V. (1995) 'Drug economics', *Capital and Class*, 55: 131–50.

Ruggiero, V. and South, N. (1997) 'The late modern city as a bazaar', *British Journal of Sociology*, 48: 54–70.

Rumsey, S. (1990) Interview (1988) reprinted in *HIV/AIDS and the Asian Communities*, report of a seminar at London Lighthouse, 29 August, London: SHARE.

Silverman, J. (1994) *Crack of Doom*, new ed.. London: Headline.

Small, G. (1995) *Ruthless*. London: Warner.

Stanley, C. (1996) *Urban Excess and the Law*. London: Cavendish.

Stutman, R. (1989) 'Crack stories from the States', *Druglink*, September–October: 7–9.

Taylor, I., Evans, K. and Fraser, P. (1996) *A Tale of Two Cities*. London: Routledge.

Thompson, T. (1995) *Gangland Britain*. London: Hodder & Stoughton.

Webster, C. (1997) 'The construction of British "Asian" criminality', *International Journal of the Sociology of Law*, 25: 65–86.

CONTROLS: POLICY, POLICING AND PROHIBITION

5

MEDICINE, CUSTOM OR MORAL FIBRE: POLICY RESPONSES TO DRUG MISUSE

Susanne MacGregor

THE PROBLEM OF DRUGS

Social policy responses reflect the way a social problem is defined, which is in its turn affected by the character of social policy in that society.

In an account of historical concepts and constructs of drug dependence, Virginia Berridge has described how one commentator 'writing about the "discovery" of morphine addiction in the 1870s, awarded praise to those whose views accorded with "modern" and "scientific" views:'

> While tools were not yet at hand to dissect the inner character of the addiction problem, there were clinicians who now saw a responsibility for the health professions in prevention, and that the addiction problem involved a medical dimension as well as social custom and moral fibre. (Sonnedecker, 1962). (Berridge, 1990: 1)

The three categories of explanation identified can be used to illustrate differing perceptions of the drugs problem and they can be shown to have dominated twentieth-century perceptions of the problem and policy responses to it.

MEDICAL EXPLANATIONS

Criticisms of the medicalisation of social problems were part of the rather crude 1970s debates between 'medical' and 'social' models of deviance. Medical definitions stress the interplay of psychological, bio-chemical and biological factors. More socio-medical approaches see these factors as mediated through a social environment. Recently, with the rise of genetics, pre-determined individual characteristics as explanations for behaviour have become more prominent. In the field of drug dependence, some medical explanations give central prominence to the toxicology of drug use, stressing the effects of various drugs on brain functioning, personality change and other physical effects such as liver damage. Important work has been done on the interactions of drugs taken together but this is still an under-researched area. Attention focuses on treatments for drug use utilising alternative drugs, methadone rather than heroin for example, and various treatment regimes to cope with withdrawal. These approaches dominate discussion in some European countries, such as Italy, where pharmacological explanations and inter-ventions play a key role in responses to drug dependence. In Britain and the United States, medical practitioners are more likely to work in partnership with behavioural scientists like psychologists and adopt approaches to treatment which combine drug therapies with inter-ventions based on theories of behaviour as conditioned or learned. So for these theorists, dependence on drugs is partly physical, involving a chemical dependency but is also partly learned. Interventions, which reprogram individuals to recognise signals triggering a desire to take drugs and encouraging them to respond differently to these, are part of treatment programmes focusing on each individual's reactions to stimuli. Much work in traditional psychiatric departments is patient-centred in this way. These regimes are open to evaluations which follow cohorts of patients over time through a structured programme: outcomes can then be measured and treatment regimes evaluated for their effectiveness (Effectiveness Review, 1996).

Criticisms of these approaches are that they bracket out a range of influential factors, such as the characteristics of those recruited to treat-ment programmes, the situational and contextual features of the clinical regime, and the strong influence of other variables (including the activities of other health and social agencies) separate from the intervention programme itself. The key difference is between the individualism of the psychological perspective and greater awareness of the influence of social factors. This latter awareness is found among other medical practitioners (like GPs, public health physicians or social psychiatrists) who differ from those working closely with psychologists and pharma-cologists in clinical settings. An alternative individualistic approach, often found in psychiatry and in social work, is that based on various forms of psychoanalytic theory. In a strong form, these explain drug dependence in terms of early childhood experiences and, in a weaker form, are the basis of much of the counselling which still characterises the activities of most treatment and care agencies.

The socio-medical type of explanation is found in the field of social psychiatry (a field more concerned with epidemiological research and with debates about the shape of policy and practice than that of the clinical psychiatrists with a special interest in drug dependence). This approach will be illustrated by reference to a collection edited by Michael Rutter and David J. Smith (1995), which focuses on young people, especially teenagers. It asks the *fin de siècle* question 'Are things getting worse?' The writers review the best scientific evidence available and focus on disorders where there is 'serious malfunctioning of individuals in their social setting' (Smith and Rutter, 1995: 1).

These analysts look at the interconnection of 'individual factors (including the process of individual development) and social structures and conditions' (1995: 1). They rely on a notion of dysfunctionality, arguing that disorder is most often (with rare exceptions) a sign of individual and social failure. Social context plays a part in the explanation. Contemporary contextual features which, it is hypothesised, have influenced the rise in rates of disorder among young people in late twentieth-century Western societies, include: changing patterns of adolescence; increase in life expectancy; a reduction in the proportion of young people in the population; improvements in general health and living conditions; increase in leisure; and the growing instability of family units. Concepts utilised in the most recent of this literature and coming increasingly to influence the design of intervention strategies are 'risk' and 'opportunity'.

Currently social conditions exhibit rapid transformation in 'populations, migration and social institutions . . . [change in] family's shape and structure [and] . . . rapid technological advances [which] have transformed the meaning of work and the roles associated with it' (Hess, 1995: 104). The family is seen as crucial in affecting human psychosocial development. Changes include more divorce, remarriage, cohabitation, lone living and lone parenting. These trends are most evident in northern Europe (Hess, 1995: 172–3) and are sources of stress to which individuals have to adapt. Different individuals respond differently to these stresses – some are more resilient, others more vulnerable.

This approach has informed recent social policy responses to a wide range of problems. Such accounts typically conclude that 'young people embedded in families characterised by high levels of conflict or by parents who are not able to provide adequate supervision, effective discipline and emotional support, have an increased risk of experiencing a range of psychosocial disorders'. (Hess, 1995:173). At the same time, it is acknowledged that there is evidence that some young people seem to have a resilience that protects them from adverse effects, in spite of being subject to these influences. Protective factors include:

1 the use of external sources of support: Peer groups can be very influential: the culture of the peer group is an important influence.

Schools and relationships with teachers can be crucial. '[I]ncreased involvement in social institutions outside the family – whether structured through youth organisations, schools, sports clubs, churches, local businesses, or community agencies – may increase adolescents' interactions with supportive peers and adult role models and can decrease feelings of isolation and marginality' (Hess, 1995: 174–5);

2   close affectional ties to family members: 'Regardless of family constellation, low family conflict and high family cohesion is most conducive to healthy adolescent adjustment, including positive self-esteem and motivation to achieve academically, high goal-directedness, and low severity of psychopathology' (Hess, 1995: 175, quoting from Kurdek and Sinclair, 1988);

3   other protective factors: These are personality-based, like temperament (activity level and reactivity) intelligence and cognitive abilities, and social and communicative skills. 'These intra-individual characteristics modify the effects of contextual conditions' (Hess, 1995: 175).

One chapter in the Rutter and Smith collection focuses specifically on alcohol and drug abuse (Silbereisen et al., 1995). The authors review changes in the availability of illicit drugs through the twentieth century, noting rises in the range, amount and accessibility of illicit drugs since the 1960s. As many commentators have suggested, this development was interwoven with the cultural revolutions of that decade (youth culture, hedonism, challenges to and declining respect for authority, etc.). Silbereisen et al. also point out that Europe is the continent with the highest alcohol consumption, with consumption in central and eastern Europe growing rapidly in recent years. These authors note that American data has monitored a massive increase in illicit use of drugs there between the 1950s and 1970s. There was something of a decline in the 1980s (apart from cocaine use). The data still show a high level of use (Silbereisen et al., 1995: 501–3): 'data from drug shipment seizures, mortality statistics, and clinic attendance all confirm that the rise in occasional or regular recreational drug use was closely paralleled by a similar marked increase in substance abuse and dependency (1995: 503). European countries experienced a comparable although slightly later upsurge in both drug use and abuse and the phenonemon of 'recreational' drug use is now a recognised aspect of the lifestyle of a large minority of young people in Britain.

A key principle of this type of explanatory framework, which rests on carefully collected social data, is that 'the medical and social ill-effects of alcohol [and use of other substances] tend to increase and decrease in line with changes in overall levels of consumption' (Silbereisen et al., 1995: 518). This fundamental public health/epidemiological finding informs policy responses: policies which can effectively reduce overall levels of consumption in a society will reduce the rate of 'problems' or 'disorders' encountered. This view has recently been challenged by researchers like Eric Single, who has argued that the overall level of consumption is too crude a factor on which to base public policy (Single, 1996). Measures of the overall level of consumption disguise important factors, such as whether consumption follows regular but moderate patterns or whether the pattern varies substantially and frequently, i.e. where 'binges' are present. Binge use is most likely to cause harm to the individual's health and to the safety of others. Policy responses, Single argues, should therefore be more subtle and focused, aiming to control and regulate *patterns* of substance use and, especially, to modify/regulate the environment in which substance use takes place (by reducing potentially harmful features like access to vehicles and the presence of dangerous objects, like glasses which smash or furniture with sharp edges, and increasing protective factors, such as availability of trained service personnel, in clubs and pubs for example, or providing plenty of free, clean water and cooling-off areas). These ideas are already being developed in practice, particularly in the alcohol field, and are often being applied to environments in which illicit drug use takes place.

Explanatory factors for rises in illicit drug consumption found in this type of socio-medical account include: economic factors (such as increased personal disposable incomes, increased availability/supply of drugs, changes in the ecology of work); beliefs, attitudes and values (the growing influence of peer groups, lessening of disapproval in the general culture); demographic and economic conditions (age cohort size – baby boom and baby bust – combined with the expansion or contraction of the demand for labour); family structure; status transition to adulthood (changes in the meaning and experience of adolescence); and conduct disorder.

This socio-medical approach is probably still the most influential one in social policy in the English-speaking world and possibly elsewhere. It is informed by social epidemiological data and utilises the concept of 'risk' as a key explanatory variable. Related concepts are those of 'lifestyle' and 'problem'. The core of observation is the behaviour of categories of individuals, with the category 'young person' featuring prominently. The link between human behaviour and ill-health/social problems is meticulously analysed. The outcome (including problem drug taking) is seen to result from a complex interaction of psychosocial and cultural factors. Policies have to be, it is argued, well informed about these complex interactions if they are to have any chance of being effective. The aim is a rational, scientific approach to policy-making.

Whether such views actually inform policy-making will reflect the extent to which rational, scientific discourse is well regarded and respected in policy-making circles. In the mid-twentieth century (on the whole the high point of the scientific-managerialist approach to policy) the views of professionals and experts weighed quite heavily in the process, albeit always subject to constraint from other influences. With the end of the welfare state era, one effect, seen in Britain particularly, has been the relative decline in the influence of such technical experts and scientific discourse, compared to the rising influence of other forces, with the mass media being the most important growing influence on policy through its direct impact on the ideas and priorities of politicians and civil servants in an era of mass electoral politics.

SOCIOLOGICAL EXPLANATIONS

> There are two drug problems in America. One is the drug problem of the affluent . . . The other one is the drug problem of America's have-nots. (Currie, 1993: 3)

Sociological accounts at present focus on the problems of the 'inner city poor'. To say drug misuse is endemic is to say that it is 'deeply entrenched in a population and stubbornly resists eradication' (Currie, 1993: 4). In his recent book on social policy and drugs, Currie castigates American drugs policy because it has been based on a false reading and analysis of the problem. He argues that 'drug abuse on the American scale reflects deeper structural problems in our economy and society' (1993: 4). He stresses that drug abuse is far worse in the US than in any other country in the developed world (cf. Pearson, 1995). The scale of the problem should be at the centre of attention: a problem of this magnitude cannot be explained adequately in terms of individuals' malfunctioning. Serious drug abuse runs along the fault lines of society: 'it is concentrated among some groups and not others and has been for at least half a century. Recognising these realities is the first step in coming to grips with the drug crisis in America,' argues Currie (1993: 5).

Drug use is a social problem: to address it, policy has to confront its social roots. Currie argues that the search for quick-fix solutions is self-defeating and wasteful and observes that a high proportion of prisoners in America's gaols are there simply because of the 'war on drugs'. Other social critics in America (Priven and Cloward, 1993; Gans, 1995) have seen such policies as part of wider wars on welfare and on the poor. Some political activists have gone so far as to describe these practices as constituting a genocidal war on the black race.

The structural roots of drug problems are those associated with the collapse of inner city neighbourhoods: the consequences are decay, lawlessness, drug-related violence, crime and gun warfare. Other features highlighted in numerous sociological 'social problems' accounts are the links between drug use and AIDS and the strain on the American criminal justice system – 'the largest and most costly apparatus of surveillance and confinement in the world' (Currie, 1993: 14). 'Today the United States incarcerates a larger proportion of its citizens than any other country, having surpassed South Africa and the Soviet Union by the end of the 1980s' (1993: 14) an achievement partly propelled by the escalation of the criminal justice response to drugs, both 'hard' and 'soft': (the implications of the 'three strikes and you're out' policy is that a drug offence can result in incarceration). The massive imprisonment of the disadvantaged young that has accompanied this trend means that 'nearly one in four black men and one in ten Hispanic men between the ages of twenty and twenty-nine are behind bars, on probation, or on parole . . . In New York, two young black men are in prison for every one in college' (1993: 19).

These trends reflect a new urban reality in the USA. Placing stress on this fact dramatically distinguishes the sociological approach from the medical approach. The medical explanation focuses, in spite of various qualifications and niceties, on issues of 'maladjustment'. Currie's account, like that of other major American sociologists (W.J. Wilson being the leading figure here), concentrates on the central role of social and economic forces. Material poverty plays a part but a greater influence is that of the 'inner city subculture' – the surrounding values and social practices which socialise young people into customs and habits that encourage drug use and crime.

W.J. Wilson emphasises the importance of paying attention to these environmental factors, which have been given insufficient attention in recent years, he argues, as the behaviourist approach has come to dominate discourse and policy (in large part under the influence of writers like Charles Murray and the ensuing debate about an 'under-class', characterised by pathological behaviours, teenage pregnancy, male unemployment, crime and drug use: Murray, 1984, 1990). Liberal and left-leaning sociologists have been afraid to speak out about these realities for fear of being accused of racism, since any value-statements about right and wrong behaviour, desirable and undesirable styles of life might be interpreted as an attack on poor black people (Wilson, 1987). Sociologists, argues Wilson, have to be prepared to describe these cultures honestly and not leave the field to racists and right-wingers. But, at the same time, they need to *explain* the emergence of these cultures in jobless ghettos, to show how they arise because of structural transformation and the disconnection – increasing detachment – of areas of these cities from mainstream institutions, particularly from the regularities and patterns associated with the world of paid labour.

In his latest book *When Work Disappears* (1996) Wilson describes, from detailed studies conducted in Chicago, how the drugs economy moves into the vacuum left by the disappearance of regular formal employment. The central coordinates of social life – time and space – are patterned differently in jobless ghettos than they are in neighbourhoods more closely linked to the dominant capitalist-industrial economy. In describing how these jobless neighbourhoods had 'gone down', increases in drug trafficking and drug consumption figured large in residents' narratives. The brazenness of drug taking was commonly remarked upon as a key change: 'when drugs start flowing in, people start having drugs fights and you couldn't sleep because there were cars coming up and down the street all night long' (quoted in Wilson, 1996: 10). 'The decline in legitimate employment opportunities among inner city residents has increased incentives to sell drugs' (1996: 21). Increasing use of crack-cocaine is linked to rises in violent crime. Joblessness and weak social organisation are at the root. It is not poverty *per se* that causes these social problems but the changes in social organisation (and values and habits) that go along with extensive joblessness (long-term and high rates of unemployment in a given neighbourhood).

Such sociological explanations bear some resemblance to the medical ones in that they describe social trends which cause stresses and strains, to which communities have to respond. Like individuals, communities are here seen as being more or less resilient, and able to varying degrees to withstand or cope with these pressures. Those communities which are least resistant, most vulnerable to drug addiction and its associated crime and violence, are those with weak social organisation: the most important cause of weak social organisation is extensive joblessness.

The culture associated with employment in large-scale manufacturing and the values of discipline, respectability, thrift and hard work, individual responsibility and care for your neighbour which went towards the 'making of the working class' (Thompson, 1963) has been eroded with the loss of this way of work and community organisation. Where long-term unemployment is concentrated in males, their loss of social position and respect weakens family structures and alters the balance of power between men and women. A crisis of masculinity appears: strong women and weak men are a feature of many communities where drug and alcohol use has become entrenched. For young men, the choices available are extreme – social failure or adoption of violent, aggressive, extreme forms of masculinity (Campbell, 1993).

In such neighbourhoods, the flashy drug dealer is an attractive role model for young men. Cloward and Ohlin's thesis of limited opportunity structures remains relevant (Cloward and Ohlin, 1960). Cloward himself has recently appeared to despair of the social reformist stance taken by Wilson. He has argued that the only way social change can be brought about is when the authorities begin to fear riots and social disorder (in a comment in a discussion at ASA annual conference, Washington 1995). Here we can see other similarities between the medical and some sociological approaches. Writers in each school believe in the power of evidence, of reasoned, scientific, soundly based argument, to persuade policy-makers to implement much-needed social reforms. Acceptance of either set of evidence-based explanations would encourage policies aimed at increasing employment, education and training for young people, especially those in disadvantaged neighbourhoods, improved attention to education, youth work and supports for families (to encourage good parenting and provide child care) etc. A wide range of other fairly conventional social policies (those which seemed unarguably right in the heyday of the welfare state) would follow logically from acceptance of these sets of arguments and the evidence on which they rest.

The problem is that these reasonable arguments, with all their accumulated evidence, fall on deaf ears in an era characterised by the widely-held assumptions that public expenditure must be contained, that voters won't vote to increase taxes, that voters don't trust the state to deliver good public services, and that societies can, after all, get along with high levels of unemployment, crime and drug taking without actually falling apart. Once the spectre of social breakdown recedes (something very much dependent on which images are purveyed through the media) and when it seems possible to dump social problems on one separate stratum of society (especially if it is also spatially segregated, out of sight and out of mind) even if this means increased spending on prisons and policing, arguments for social reformist social policies find it difficult to gain a hearing.

Currie's list of appropriate policies would seem eminently sensible and very familiar to British and other northern European readers. It is very similar to the lists emerging from Wilson's various publications. Currie argues for fundamental change and a pragmatic approach, one which adds up to a 'strategy of inclusion' (Currie, 1993: 282). He proposes such staple items as:

- expanding the opportunity structure:
  This would involve job creation in inner city areas; better training and education, especially for disadvantaged youth; schools-jobs compacts; a serious apprenticeship system (encouraging attachments to new peer groups and role models); a higher minimum wage (i.e. a 'solidaristic' approach to jobs and earnings); improving wages and skills; initiatives like the old Jobs Corps program, programmes combining housing, schooling and work – public works schemes.
- revitalising public health care:
  This would involve introducing something like the NHS into the USA – a universalistic, comprehensive scheme.
- supporting families:
  This would be a real not rhetorical family policy, involving child-care schemes, better housing, paid family leave, playgroups and accessible treatment and rehabilitation for drug-using mothers.
- assuring shelter:
  This requires policies to cut homelessness and increase affordable, low-rent public housing.
- rebuilding the infrastructure:
  Policies here would include public works, public employment and a national youth employment policy, focused on improving roads, bridges and the environment.

It is important to keep stating the facts, to keep voicing these arguments and offering such lists. Failure to do so is to give up on the battle of ideas. Cloward's despair is understandable if unacceptable. To call for riot and disorder is arguably irresponsible and counterproductive, since it will result only in further crack-downs and incarcerations of the poor (it is less likely that academics will be locked away). The extensive riots and rising crime of the 1980s have not resulted in fairer and more equitable social policies in the USA or the UK. On the contrary, in these societies, poverty and inequality have increased more rapidly than in other advanced industrial societies (McFate et al., 1995). However, it must be admitted that political conditions in late twentieth-century capitalist societies are not favourable to social reform.

MORAL EXPLANATIONS

We have seen that two of the main approaches to explaining drug misuse – the medical and the sociological – share some features but differ on others. The final approach to be discussed here – the moral argument – is one which differs radically from these others. Its attractiveness in certain policy circles lies in its being able to justify policies of neglect and segregation, containment, separation and confinement. These arguments have not as yet been related directly to illicit drug use. But they do see crime and deviance as explicable in terms of inherent biological tendencies, concentrated in particular races or classes (the degenerate underclass). They lead ultimately to social hygienist and eugenic social policies.

The logic would be to reduce the reproductive capacity of deviant anti-social groups. Arguments to curtail support for welfare mothers, or to punish mothers on welfare who become pregnant again, have been implemented in some US cities (sometimes involving pressure to accept sterilisation or long-term contraception) and have been flirted with by some commentators and local administrations in Britain.

The most prominent recent example of this approach is Herrstein and Murray's The Bell Curve (1994). While this book does not deal directly with drug use, it mirrors an extensively held view in the USA that blacks are more crime-prone than whites (Gordon, 1994: 151). The image of the drug user promoted in many countries (especially in the USA but also in Britain and other European countries) is that drug use and drug dealing are particularly associated with young black men (and even some black single mothers).

Murray's writings on the underclass have also helped to develop this stereotype. 'The interaction of public opinion, media portrayals of heroin largely as an inner-city drug, and law enforcement attention laid the foundation for the coded message that a tough drug law would help contain unruly blacks' (Gordon, 1994: 152).

Gordon argues that 'the drugs problem' has provided the codifier for signifying minority groups as the new 'dangerous classes' in American society. This perception has shaped the American 'war on drugs' which has provided the justification to reverse progressive policies on affirmative action, equal opportunities, welfare and educational reform, and has led to that incarceration of disadvantaged youth abhorred by Currie and Wilson. 'Resistance to race and gender equality, greater emancipation of youth, and civil liberties would be limited to the authoritarian fringe if it could not assume the cloak of righteous containment of identifiably dangerous people' (Gordon, 1994: 126).

The aim of late twentieth-century social policy in the USA, which has drugs policy at its core, is to tame the untamed, regiment, restrain and inhibit the marginalised and excluded. 'Partnership' policies, growing in prominence in many countries, could be the kinder, gentler face of this policy paradigm – the velvet glove within which hides a tougher, punitive response to those who fail to be tamed and included.

SOCIAL POLICY REGIMES AND APPROACHES TO THE DRUGS QUESTION

A key question to ask is whether policies on drugs reflect, parallel or fit with wider principles and approaches to social policy in a society, or is drugs policy usually the odd one out in the policy panoply? The answer may be 'sometimes it does, sometimes it doesn't'. What then explains these differences? Is it the extent and character of drug taking in a society? Who take what drugs, in what ways, how often and with what effects? Are these patterns much the same as they have always been or has there been recent change, causing alarm and fear of breakdown of control? Are the remedies adopted ones which have grown out of conventional approaches to social policy (they fit, make sense, have meaning in that society) or are they imports, transplants, solutions borrowed from elsewhere?

Very little systematic research on these questions has been conducted. The evidence available is overwhelmingly from advanced industrial societies, particularly dominated by the United States. There is information from Canada, Britain, Scandinavia, Australia and some European countries but thereafter it fizzles out, with patchy information at best on other countries. This in itself reflects the extent to which 'drugs' are perceived as a 'problem' to which social policies have to respond. But it also reflects the strength of social research in a society, which relates to the extent to which structures of surveillance exist. Social science has grown alongside the technical-managerialist state. Where a state of this shape does not exist, or has only recently emerged, the extent of available information is similarly less.

Policies which aim to reduce demand for drugs rest on the premise that certain patterns of use of certain drugs/substances are in fact harmful to an individual's health and to the safety of others. Acceptance of this assumption is fundamental and prior to discussion of what kinds of social policy should be pursued, and also prior to attempts to discover which policies work best. Those who adopt a totally relativist position on health and safety would stop at this point. But those who, either from common sense or from deeper social, historical and humanistic analyses, refute 'anything goes' approaches then move on to review the evidence on policy and practice, where choices range rather narrowly with varying degrees of stress on or combinations of treatment and punishment.

Key distinctions are those between societies of the erstwhile first, second and third worlds. The post-industrial economies of the USA and UK, particularly in their old rust-belt cities, differ from the turbulent economies of south-east Asia. Western and Eastern traditions clash in interpretations of individualism or social hierarchy: the strength of liberal values is a key indicator of the shape of social policies. Cultures vary in the meanings they give to the role of the family and community, and to informal support structures based on mutual exchange of favours *vis-à-vis* public law, public provision and regulation. Roman or common law, inquisitorial or adversarial legal systems, all influence the shape and direction of policy, modes of service delivery and methods of financing services. Sub-Saharan Africa, still coming to terms with the effects of colonialisation, wars of independence and civil war and off the map as far as international capitalism is concerned, presents a quite different scenario from that found in other regions of the world – China, Latin America, Europe, the former Soviet Union and North America. Catholicism or Protestantism, English speaking or Hispanic speaking, the legacy of authoritarian socialism, the impact of structural adjustment policies, the influence of the snake-oil medicines of neo-liberal economics or new managerialism, demographic contrasts (ageing or youthful societies), etc. etc. – the list goes on and on. All these and other huge differences produce varieties of patterns of drug use, receptivity to drug trafficking, and social policy responses which defy easy generalisation.

Comparative social policy analyses can produce generalisations which are at best trivial and at worst misleading if the attempt is made to review too many societies of widely varying difference. Construction of typologies may help, but only preliminary classifications have been made with regard to drugs policies and these too tend to be banal. Clearly there are differences between societies which condemn alcohol use and those where alcohol use is part of everyday life; between those where certain substances like cannabis, beer or wine have a long history and have traditionally been controlled by complex webs of custom; between societies undergoing profound and rapid social transformation, producing breakdown of traditional controls and severe problems of migration, lawlessness, homelessness and destitution (as in the former Soviet Union) and those which are relatively stable (most countries in Western Europe in the latter but certainly not in the early or mid-twentieth century). And so on.

Such an enterprise might be attempted and might produce some insights. However, it is as likely to produce distortion. All attempts at typology construction produce criticisms from those who would give higher priority to different key variables in the explanation (religion rather than the level of GNP, gender rather than class or race, for example).

Broadly, different policy regimes can be characterised. In Britain, for example, over the twentieth century the model has moved through five phases:

1 a phase covering the nineteenth century to the 1920s, in which the availability of opiate drugs was gradually brought under professional control;
2 from the 1920s to the 1960s when the British system prevailed and medical prescribing was a key characteristic;
3 1960s to the 1980s, with the establishment of the clinics, the growth of multi-disciplinary work and the rise of the voluntary sector, especially in rehabilitation and street agencies;
4 the 1980s, the phase of the expansion of community-based services, with harm-reduction becoming the leitmotif under the impact of AIDS and a growth in the number of syringe exchange schemes;
5 finally the 1990s, when a new phase of community partnerships arrived with greater stress on prevention and tighter funding regimes for services in health and social care.

The key processes influencing the shape of drugs policy and practice in Britain in these five phases can be divided into three sub-areas. These three sets of influences may be used to analyse drugs policy regimes cross-culturally as well as historically. First there is the issue of how we talk about the problem. The language of debate and especially principles applied to construction of definitions of *illicit* drugs and of drugs *misuse* are important. Secondly and not to be underestimated are data on the *real* base of the social phenomenon – it is not all simply a matter of perceptions. The characteristics of drug users, the size of the problem and the social and physical location of the drugs problem are crucial. Thirdly we can consider how policies are implemented. What is done by whom, to and for whom – i.e. who are the key players? what are the major interests involved? Questions to answer here would relate to who is given responsibility for dealing with drug users, for treatment, care or punishment: are professionals involved at all and if so who are the *key* professionals, and what is the form and content of service provision?

In recent years it is the latter aspect which has changed most markedly with the retreat from state and public services in many countries. This has had a major impact on the shape of drugs policy and service provision.

Regime types may crudely be divided into those which are relatively pragmatic (as in Britain and the Netherlands) and those which are more moralistic or ideological (e.g. the USA). They differ in their stress on harm-minimisation or abstinence. They differ as to whether they are strongly or weakly interventionist: this reflects the strength of liberal values and the relative power of the state *vis-à-vis* other institutions. They differ in the extent to which they sign up to and implement international agreements on drugs policy. They differ in the mode of service delivery, whether located in a public health system or one in which private, charitable or family care plays a larger role. This latter affects especially the extent to which people of different backgrounds are treated in similar ways or whether there are major divisions in the treatment accorded to relatively comfortable or relatively disadvantaged groups (especially the poor, black people and stigmatised groups). They differ especially in the relative balance in the system between care and control, whether drug users are dealt with through a health and social care system or mainly through prisons and the criminal justice system. The socio-medical approach, compared to a strongly penal approach, has given more weight to caring and compassion. The balance struck between understanding and condemning (to echo one of John Major's epithets) varies over time and between societies.

PREVENTION AND PARTNERSHIP APPROACHES

As globalisation has taken the place of the Cold War as the overarching all-purpose explanation of social issues, more attention has been given to the 'global habit' of drug misuse (Stares, 1996). While not wanting to exaggerate the phenomenon of globalisation (cf. Hirst and Thompson, 1996) the evidence on the world-wide phenomenon of drug taking cannot be overlooked. The evolution of a global market for drugs has gathered pace in the twentieth century and, as the twenty-first century approaches, looks set to be a well-established feature of international political economy. International trade in illicit drugs ranks high and matches that in arms and oil. The expanding global economy facilitates the production and distribution of illicit drugs: increasing poverty, inequality and social breakdown encourage receptivity to the use and misuse of drugs.

International agencies (like WHO, UNDCP and UNESCO) now take it for granted that drug abuse can no longer be explained as an individual problem. The basic premise which guides their shared approach is that drug abuse has become a societal phenomenon, one which is seen as tending to weaken the economic, political and cultural fibre of communities. The policy response promoted is one in which 'society as a whole' is encouraged to take responsibility for promoting a life in which drug abuse has no place. Linked to this prescription is another taken-for–granted commonplace of international social policy discussion, that the root cause of this (and other social problems) is 'social exclusion'. Social exclusion in these explanations is linked to poverty and inequality but more importance is given to inadequate education, and the consequent inability of some sections of society to participate actively in the life of democratic polities. Along with drug abuse, the unhealthy tendencies produced by social exclusion also encourage violence, social disorder and uncontrollable eruptions into chaos (cf. Commission on Narcotic Drugs, Thirty Ninth Session, Vienna 16–25 April 1996).

This set of assumptions guides debate in influential international policy circles and can be seen at work in the development of international agreements, attempts to develop a common European approach to drugs policy (EMCDDA, 1995) and in the statements of national governments, regional and local administrations, as policy packages are adopted, agreed to with some adaptation and implemented in a wide range of situations and conditions.

Why has this become accepted as the right approach for the 1990s and the new century? The main reason is the recognition that drug problems are more widespread. But it is partly because drug abuse is an 'apple-pie' social issue. Almost all governments and political parties can agree that the death and degradation of young people are undesirable. All agree that the state's authority and sway is challenged by the activities of organised and disorganised crime (which by definition is part and parcel of the use of illicit drugs).

In the post-Cold War world, 'drugs' has risen higher on the international policy agenda because it can serve as the glue which anti-communism previously provided: new parties, new alliances can be welded together with the flame of anti-drugs rhetoric. Not only this, but new structures of governance can be actively promoted and developed through anti-drugs and drugs prevention initiatives.

Of course, the international promotion of a common strategy on drugs has been present throughout the twentieth century, largely as a result of American interest in the issue. What has changed has been the growing awareness that 'supply-side' policies have failed and, since the late 1980s, there has been more active promotion of demand-reduction.

> Making international drug control policy more effective must begin with a restatement of its principal goals and priorities. The primary objective should be to minimise the consumption of psychoactive substances that are deemed harmful to one's health and to the safety of others . . . Attaining these pragmatic goals requires both a major shift in policy emphasis and a more discriminating use of resources. (Stares, 1996: 112)

In addition, as drug misuse has become endemic and more widespread, the dominance of the medical-scientific paradigm in explaining drug dependence has waned, allowing more room for multi-disciplinary, multi-agency approaches, drawing in a wider array of professions and institutions, who are encouraged to work together in 'partnership'. These ideas are the latter-day heirs of the earlier public health tradition, which contained concepts of medical policing, quarantine and notification. Features of surveillance run in a straight line from this tradition through to contemporary ideas of partnership.

The development and implementation of these models has taken place in a global context characterised by the collapse of the 'socialist alternative', the decline of the welfare state paradigm, the increased power of international agencies, including their ability to impose structural adjustment policies, the dominance of neo-liberal economics, moves to decentralisation and privatisation, and the divesting by states of their responsibility for social programmes and the promotion of ideas of local solutions to local problems. Drugs prevention policies have been prominent in the development of such new locally based arrangements. In many countries, private–public partnerships are being promoted and the relationship between government and non-government organisations is being transformed. This has profound implications for the shape and direction of social policy, including drugs policy.

The greater attention now paid to prevention echoes earlier concerns of the temperance movements (Burnham, 1993). It is not accidental that this focus has re-emerged along with concern about degeneracy and social decay (encapsulated in the contemporary use of the term 'underclass': Murray, 1990; Morris 1994). As in the early twentieth century, education is once again seen as the remedy. Drugs education and better processes of socialisation (better parenting, community involvement) are now central features of policy responses as the century draws to a close. It is also noteworthy that the new paradigm which has emerged in the post-welfare-state world so closely mirrors features of pre-welfare-state social policies. Ideas of the greatest non-welfare state on earth – the USA – have particular force but are being challenged by ideas emanating from the newly industrialising countries with their more authoritarian, strictly disciplined, communitarian approach. In most places, alternative policies believed to be tainted by 'socialist ideas' remain profoundly discredited.

The shift away from a primarily medical response to alcohol and drugs towards a community-based partnership approach has much to do with 'the changing class and range of drug-takers and desires to find low-cost solutions' (Berridge, 1990: 11). Thus drugs policy responses have moved closer in form and direction to responses to other 'social problem' groups, as drug misuse has ceased to be a marginal and eccentric activity.

The new public health approach 'with its emphasis on primary care, individual life-style, health planning; and health indicators and·information' (Berridge, 1990: 12) now informs a wide range of social policies, including those on drugs and alcohol, HIV/AIDS, sexual behaviour and mental illness. A distinctive feature of the new partnership approach however is the closer working together of the criminal justice system and other socio-educational-medical agencies.

The partnership alliances which have developed in US communities are seen by Gordon as 'a formidable constituency for culturally conservative policy positions' (Gordon, 1994: 131). Drug Action Teams have been established in a top-down manner in England and Wales and similar initiatives are under way in Scotland, Eire and Northern Ireland. Zimbabwe has implemented a system of Drug and Alcohol Action Committees and this model may be extended to other countries in southern Africa. It is not obvious that such alliances will automatically be culturally conservative. This remains to be seen.

Drugs prevention policies based on multi-agency, community involvement *may* effectively steer the majority of young people away from harmful use of illicit drugs. What is to be done with the 'hardcore' who continue to misuse? Studies show an increasing divide between young people who do not use or who may experiment only once or twice with relatively harmless drugs and those who go on to become involved as regular illicit drug users.

For problem drug users, the rise of locally based partnership approaches to drugs social policy could increase rather than decrease their social exclusion. The partnership may include those who fit with the dominant values and attitudes but it may provide no place for those who do not conform. A new stratum of vagrants excluded from each parish's social provision could emerge. Their place in society might be in a grey underworld or in segregated jobless ghettos or in prisons.

CONCLUSION

We have seen that drugs policies reflect varying definitions of the 'drugs problem'. Three types of explanation have been present throughout the twentieth century, stressing variously the medical dimension, the role of customs and values, or moral fibre. All three operate at the same time but one or other can be seen to be more influential in different places and at different times. Throughout, however, the medical approach has largely informed social policy. As the twenty-first century approaches, there is a clear shift in many countries towards stress on multi-agency, partnership approaches and on communities taking responsibility for policies in their local areas. Voices are heard emphasising the need for less liberal and pragmatic social policies and more influence for explicitly moral positions in shaping public policy. There are dangers in the rise of these moralistic assertions, as they coincide with an unwillingness to pay for social programmes, especially those which meet the needs of those categorised as disadvantaged and undeserving. Scientific evidence from either a public health or a social environmental position stresses the need for more intervention and support for vulnerable individuals and communities. But these would need to be paid for by raising revenue from the more comfortably off. Only when these groups are moved by a combination of persuasive argument, well-mobilised evidence, compassion, a sense of shared experience and fear of a common threat will current trends to neglect and segregation be reversed.

REFERENCES

Berridge, V. (1990) 'Dependence: historical concepts and constructs', in G. Edwards and M. Lader (eds), *The Nature of Drug Dependence*. Oxford: Oxford University Medical Press.

Burnham, J.C. (1993) *Bad Habits: Drinking, Smoking, Taking Drugs, Sexual Misbehaviour and Swearing in American History*. New York: New York University Press.

Campbell, B. (1993) *Goliath: Britain's Dangerous Places*. London: Methuen.

Cloward, R. and Ohlin, L. (1960) *Delinquency and Opportunity*. New York: Free Press.

Commission on Narcotic Drugs (1996) Thirty-ninth session. Vienna: 16–25 April.

Currie, E. (1993) *Reckoning: Drugs, the Cities and the American Future*. New York: Hill & Wang.

Effectiveness Review (1996) *The Task Force to Review Services for Drug Misusers: Report of an Independent Review of Drug Treatment Services in England*. Department of Health PO Box 410 Wetherby LS23 7LN UK.

EMCDDA (European Monitoring Centre for Drugs and Drug Addiction) (1995) *Annual Report on the State of the Drugs Problem in the European Union*. Lisbon: EMCDDA.

Gans, H.J. (1995) *The War against the Poor*. New York: Basic Books.

Gordon, D.R. (1994) *The Return of the Dangerous Classes: Drug Prohibition and Policy Politics*. New York: W.W. Norton.

Herrstein, R.J. and Murray, C. (1994) *The Bell Curve: Intelligence and Class Structure in American Life*. New York: Free Press.

Hess, L.E. (1995) 'Changing family patterns in Western Europe: opportunity and risk factors for adolelescent development', in M. Rutter and D.J. Smith (eds), *Psychosocial Disorders in Young People: Time Trends and Their Causes*. Chichester: Academia Europaea, Wiley. pp. 104–93.

Hirst, P. and Thompson, G. (1996) *Globalisation in Question*. Cambridge: Polity Press.

Kurdek, L.A. and Sinclair, R.J. (1988) 'The adjustment of young adolescents in two-parent nuclear, stepfather and mother-custody families', *Journal of Consulting and Clinical Psychology*, 56: 91–6.

McFate, K., Lawson, R. and Wilson, W.J. (eds) (1995) *Poverty, Inequality and the Future of Social Policy.* New York: Russell Sage Foundation.

Morris, L. (1994) *Dangerous Classes: The Underclass and Social Citizenship.* London: Routledge.

Murray, C. (1984) *Losing Ground: American Social Policy 1950–1980.* New York: Basic Books.

Murray, C. (1990) *The Emerging British Underclass* (Choice in Welfare Series, no. 2). London: Health and Welfare Unit, Institute of Economic Affairs.

Pearson, G. (1995) 'City of darkness, city of light: crime, drugs and disorder in London and New York', in S. MacGregor and A. Lipow (eds), *The Other City: People and Politics in New York and London.* Atlantic Highlands, NJ: Humanities Press. pp. 85–113.

Piven, F.F. and Cloward, R.A. (1993) *Regulating the Poor: The Functions of Public Welfare,* new edn. New York: Vintage.

Rutter, M. and Smith, D.J. (eds) (1995) *Psychosocial Disorders in Young People: Time Trends and Their Causes.* Chichester: Academia Europaea, Wiley.

Silbereisen, R.K., Robins, L. and Rutter, M. (1995) 'Secular trends in substance use: concepts and data on the impact of social change on alcohol and drug abuse', in M. Rutter and D.J. Smith (eds), *Psychosocial Disorders in Young People: Time Trends and Their Causes.* Chichester: Academia Europaea, Wiley.

Single, E. (1996) 'The concept of harm reduction and its application to alcohol'. The 1996 Dorothy Black Lecture, Centre for Research on Drugs and Health Behaviour, Charing Cross and Westminster Medical School, 23 October.

Smith, D.J. and Rutter, M. (1995) 'Introduction', in M. Rutter and D.J. Smith (eds), *Psychosocial Disorders in Young People: Time Trends and Their Causes.* Chichester: Academia Europaea, Wiley. pp. 1–6.

Sonnedecker, G. (1962) 'Emergence of the concept of opiate addiction', *Journal Mondiale Pharmacie,* 3: 275–90.

Stares, P.B. (1996) *Global Habit: The Drug Problem in a Borderless World.* Washington, DC: Brookings Institution.

Thompson, E.P. (1963) *The Making of the English Working Class.* Harmondsworth: Penguin.

Wilson, W.J. (1987) *The Truly Disadvantaged.* Chicago: University of Chicago Press.

Wilson, W.J. (1996) *When Work Disappears: The World of the New Urban Poor.* New York: Alfred A. Knopf.

6

DRUGS AND POLICING IN EUROPE: FROM LOW STREETS TO HIGH PLACES

Nicholas Dorn and Maggy Lee

Policy debates on drugs, policing and related phenomena have now become routine features of our everyday lives. Recent examples might include concerns over open and visible drug dealing, high-profile police 'zero tolerance' operations to 'take back the streets', public health fears, the politicisation and privatisation of drug enforcement, and representations of the 'fight' against drugs (in the policy discourse of the European Union) and the drug 'war' (in American parlance). Yet, behind these rhetorical smokescreens, the aims and objectives of drug policies and strategies are beginning to be reformulated in less 'total' ways, and perhaps in more practical and potentially achievable ways. In short, in more *manageable* ways – as this chapter will demonstrate, with particular reference to British localities, the national level and the European Union.

LOST COMMUNITIES AND NEW CONTROLS: HARM REDUCTION IN BLUE

In Britain, despite a tough stance on law and order by the Conservative government, the 1980s witnessed a continuing increase in crime (Hough and Mayhew, 1985; Mayhew et al., 1989; Mayhew and Maung, 1992). In England and Wales in 1992, there were 5.2 million crimes recorded by the police, equivalent to 620 per hour (Audit Commission, 1993). It has been cogently argued that the state's expenditure on criminal justice has not prevented crime, deterred criminals, protected people, eradicated fears, helped victims or reformed offenders (Savage, 1989). Whether this is a fair assessment or not, it is certainly the case that the perception of crime running out of control has challenged what Garland (1996: 448) has described as 'one of the foundational myths of modern societies: namely, the myth that the sovereign state is capable of providing security, law and order, and crime control within its territorial boundaries'.

What is the general response of the state, when it is acknowledged that 'criminality is not confined to a small minority, but is evident at some time in the lives of many' (Audit Commission, 1993: 6)? The response has been to normalise crime, and to 'manage' the problem. Crime is no longer perceived as an exceptional event requiring explanation and exculpation – but an everyday risk to be assessed and managed (Garland, 1996: 447–8), in the same pragmatic way that we deal with, say, road traffic. This trend can clearly be seen in relation to drugs and drug control. Despite increases in the number of arrests of drug sellers, and the burdens such 'success' places on the caseload of the criminal justice system, drug dealing continues to be a major economic activity for many young males especially in inner city areas. Self-report studies reflect an upward trend in the use of drugs (ISDD, 1994) and some police sources continue to consider drugs a major cause of crime (but see Dorn et al., 1995). The failure of drugs control is perceived as a failure of the courts, the prisons and, above all, the police. The apparent rising crime rates and falling detection rates, when combined with well-publicised allegations of police corruption and mishandling of informants in high-profile drugs-related cases (McLaughlin, 1991: 131; *Guardian*, 3 February 1997: 1; 8 February 1997: 3), dealt a further blow to the credibility of the police, as far as their ability to fight drug trafficking is concerned.

One way in which the police have reacted to the pressure to deliver 'results' is by scaling down expectations, redefining their aims, and modifying the criteria by which success is judged. In the early 1990s, senior police officers floated the idea that it was time to 'think the unthinkable' (Grieve, 1993), which triggered a renewed interest in the decriminalisation debate. Increasingly, the police define their mission in terms of being responsive to the expressed needs of local communities, creating a 'consistent' and 'coordinated' response to the drugs problem, and measuring their performance based on a 'realistic' assessment of the scale of the problem (ACPO, 1995), rather than winning a 'war against drugs'. Using the 1990s language of new managerialism, local communities are the customers for policing. Hence the restructuring of police roles and responsibilities (including devolution of routine policing to self-contained local command units), and the practice of conducting customer surveys, to identify and meet local needs. In the context of drug enforcement, such thinking is most apparent in the ACMD Report, *Police, Drug Misusers and the Community* (1994) and in *Tackling Drugs Together* (HM Government, 1994).

These developments have several implications. Firstly, the police are asked to accept that, since the elimination of the drugs trade seems impossible, and 'containment' is the best that can be achieved, they have to minimise the various harms associated with drug misuse. The 'community damage limitation' approach aims to reduce fears of drug-related crime; levels of drug dealing; and threats to public health. Ironically here, we seem to be seeing a return to the historical origins of the idea of policing, which included fire-fighting, life-saving and preserving the general health of the city. This idea narrowed during the course of the nineteenth century, to focus on anti-crime activities. But now, as the millennium approaches, police work again widens in scope, encompassing many forms of 'good work' perceived to have some beneficial impact on the locality – for instance, improving public health and the physical appearance of a locality by reporting litter and graffiti to the local authority. In relation to drugs, under the approach of 'community damage limitation', successful policing is redefined:

> If, for example, a crackdown on dealing in a public place leads to dealers switching their business operations to a private house and drug availability and consumption remain undiminished, this may be regarded as a failure in enforcement terms. But the other outcome may be to restore a public amenity for the benefit of the wider community, in which case the police should be given the credit. (ACMD, 1994: 27)

Secondly, policing strategies are to be developed in 'partnership' with the most appropriate local agencies that bring together various responsibilities and areas of concern. Drug Action Teams have been formed to 'tackle drugs together' (HM Government, 1994) in the light of local needs and priorities, generally involving senior representatives of education, health and local authorities, the police and other criminal justice agencies. In this development, a new division of labour between the police and the community can be conceptualised. Operation Welwyn in King's Cross, London, has been described as being the nearest expression of the ideal of 'community damage limitation' in strategy terms.[1] The police supported local councils in their efforts to carry out environmental improvements such as better street lighting, boarding up derelict buildings and sealing off railway arches, which in turn were linked to police efforts to 'return areas to normality'. 'Good' results in drug enforcement no longer need to be defined in the conventional sense of drug seizures or court-based punishments, as long as local councils are prepared to use their planning powers to evict suspected drug dealers or to close down a crack house (Lee, 1996).

Thirdly, this orientation towards community damage limitation has also led to a redefining of the *ownership* of the drugs problem. This involves the police seeking to impact upon crime not only in a direct way (for instance, through detective investigation), but also by activating statutory and non-statutory agencies and the public. This is the essence of the 'new community emphasis' emerging within Home Office thinking since the 1980s, typified by the Five Towns Initiative and Safer Cities Project (cf. Hope and Shaw, 1988; Tuck, 1991; Crawford, 1994). By promoting 'practical ways to crack crime' as an essential part of the daily routine for the whole community (Home Office, 1988), Home Office ministers were reinforcing the importance of self-reliance, initiative and self-discipline within the context of a free market economy as the only way of achieving 'the good life' (King, 1991).

Such principles are reflected in the carefully delineated role of 'the community' in anti-drugs policing matters. The community is given a crime prevention role through emphasis on physical measures to 'design out crime' and situational strategies to reduce opportunities for drugs selling and buying. 'Place managers' in fast food restaurants and betting shops can be trained to be aware of drug dealing in such popular meeting places and transaction sites and take remedial measures (for instance, by discouraging long-stay customers, installing blue lighting in toilets to make injection of drugs more difficult). Phone boxes can be located under direct surveillance of place managers to discourage in-coming calls to drug dealers (Edmunds et al., 1996). Members of the community are to share in the responsibility for reducing drug-related crime by meeting their moral obligations as 'good' parents and teaching their children to say no to drugs. The public as 'active citizens' have also been mobilised to cooperate with the police in the fight against drug-related nuisance, for instance as informants or by calling drug hotlines. The community can also help police their own neighbourhoods by paying for private and quasi-private security patrols (Lee, 1995; Jones and Newburn, forthcoming).[2]

'Community' is, of course, not an unproblematic concept. As Cohen (1979: 609) has argued, a 'new mode of deviancy control' premised on the presence of community is advocated 'just at the historical moment when every commonplace critique of "technological", "postindustrial" or "mass" society mourns the irreplaceable loss of community'. High-profile police operations such as Operation Welwyn and other community safety strategies are often based on the working assumption of a homogeneity of community interests. In reality, they occupy a place at the intersection of multiple interests and sometimes competing demands within the community. In King's Cross, the local council restricted the licences of local fast food outlets to facilitate drug enforcement: 'so that prostitutes and "dealers had nowhere to duck into". This did not go down well with some local businesses and they looked set to challenge the council's curfew through the courts' (Lee, 1996: 48). Some residents in nearby estates also complained that the police operation had displaced drug activities to their 'backyard' and demanded the employment of private security guards, video cameras and entry-phones on some council estates, whilst 'others want to build an eight-foot wall around their estate to keep the drug users away' (Lee, 1996: 49).

The 'them and us' division that conventional crime prevention strategies can create has been well documented (South, 1987; Currie, 1998; Walklate, 1996). In what Mike Davis (1990) has described as the ongoing process of segregation in the city of Los Angeles (or 'Fortress LA'),

homeowners in well-off neighbourhoods have taken the extreme measure of erecting barriers on public streets to exclude non-residents from
the area and employing private security guards to set up guard stations
or a 'Checkpoint Charlie' as a deterrent to drug buyers and other
undesirables. 'Residential areas with enough clout are thus able to
privatize local public space, partitioning themselves from the rest of the
metropolis, even imposing a variant of neighbourhood "passport control" on outsiders' (Davis, 1990: 246). What has received less academic
attention is the complex and seemingly contradictory nature of community attitudes towards policing in inner cities. In the United States,
'public support for aggressive enforcement is the strongest among
persons *most likely* to be the target of that enforcement, namely African
Americans, Hispanics, low income residents, renters, and persons of
limited education' (Rosenbaum, 1993: 76, emphasis added). While
American research surveys have shown that minorities are strongly
opposed to police use of excessive force – more so than whites (Rosenbaum, 1993), the same groups of these most disadvantaged residents may
call upon the police 'to do whatever it takes' to remove the local drug
problem.

The notion of 'community' conceals all kinds of contradictions and
conflicts. If this critique is extended to include ethnic, gender and age
divisions, then the concept of the community becomes even more
problematic in terms of realising any drugs control policies premised
upon it. Nevertheless, the politics of community occupies a powerful
position in the discourse of criminal justice because 'it dispels the idea
that crime is the problem of government, to be dealt with away from the
community's gaze' (Lacey and Zedner, 1995: 305). As Clarke (1987: 387)
has argued:

> part of the attractiveness of community solutions to crime and policing lies
> not in the effectiveness of such schemes in reducing the actual incidence of
> offences ... but in the development through revived community institutions of
> a sense of control of crime and of security deriving from an understanding that
> collective resources, formal and informal, are being directed at those kinds of
> conduct which are held to be most offensive.

Thus, intensive police activities and zero-tolerance operations to remove
drug dealers from the streets, to curb 'cycling on the footways and
obstruction by traders', to 'clear away beggars, prostitutes, drunks,
pickpockets and vandals, either by warning them off or seeing them out
of the area' have been launched (and justified) on the basis that such
actions would 'make local people feel better and safer' (*The Times*, 19
November 1996: 5). This is despite recognition by some senior police
officers that the zero-tolerance approach to tackling low-level disorder
and incivilities is 'narrow, aggressive and uncompromising and, by its
very nature, targets people rather than addresses the underlying problems' (NACRO, 1997: 18).

What this all amounts to is an increasing emphasis on the *management* of crime. The multi-agency/community line of strategy and practice provides a neat solution to the problem of trying and failing to reduce drug supply *per se* by altering the forms of response. As we shall argue below, this adaptation to the failure of drug control – the widening of policy goals, so as to be at least partially achievable – is also reflected at the two other levels of analysis we address in this chapter – the national and the European.

LOST WARS AND NEW INTERPRETATIONS: PERFORMANCE INDICATORS

The reconstruction of drug control strategies that has become so visible in localities throughout Britain is also found in developments at national level. Here too, policy failure has been avoided by changing the terms of engagement – from winning the war, to managing it:

Today's record [drug] seizure figures are a credit to Customs and Police – a real demonstration of the value of the enforcement agencies working together. I am also announcing further measures which will strengthen that partnership – two new performance indicators on drugs law enforcement which will apply to both Customs and Police. I hope these new targets will give added impetus to their efforts. (Tony Newton, Chair of Ministerial Committee on Drug Misuse, HM Customs and Excise press release, 17 March 1997: 2)

The interpretation of drug seizure data and arrest statistics has generally been regarded as problematic, by the enforcement agencies themselves, government, press reporters and independent commentators. When the figures go up, does this mean that the agencies are being overwhelmed by increases in imports, supply, possession, and so it would be difficult not to make more seizures? Or could it be a reflection of greater resources being applied to drug enforcement? Or does it reflect short-term successes following the introduction of new techniques, in the periods before most traffickers understand what is happening and develop counter-measures – as may have been the case with amphetamine producers, in a period in the 1980s in which precursor monitoring was relatively new? Or could 'success' be real, as the Minister suggests: control agencies becoming so much more efficient that they exert sufficient downward pressure on the drug market as to cause its diminution? If so, the impact on the drug market is rather dramatic: Customs seized more synthetic drugs than ever before, and their seizures of cannabis were up by 46 per cent compared with the preceding year.[3]
  Another strand in explaining the coexistence of diverse interpretations may lie in a Performance Indicator (PI) applied by Customs:

Customs and Excise smashed nearly 100 major drugs smuggling operations during 1996 and made a record number of seizures, Exchequer Secretary Phillip Oppenheim said today [. . .]: 'These figures demonstrate the success of Customs' strategy of using more and better intelligence to combat drug smuggling . . . A major achievement has been the dismantling of 96 commercial drug smuggling operations. These are organised criminal gangs who make a profit out of this evil trade. Smashing their organisations will continue to be a key objective for Customs'. Dick Kellaway, Chief Investigation Officer, said: '[. . .] Customs carried out high-quality investigations into the most significant trafficking groups operating in the UK. We dismantled 96 organisations in 1996 by arresting people *or otherwise disrupting* those responsible for the purchase, shipment and profit laundering elements of their drug trafficking.' (HM Customs and Excise press release, 17 March 1997: 1, emphasis added).

In this interpretative context, where increases in seizures are placed alongside the 'disrupting', 'dismantling' and 'smashing' of trafficking organisations, through an intelligence-led approach, such increases can come to be viewed in positive terms. Additionally, if 'dismantling organisations' can be done by means other than arrests – basically, by disrupting them, messing them up though misinformation, and so on – then it could make sense to count such activities as valuable outputs of enforcement agencies. Incidentally this approach sets the scene for a more central role for those other agencies which are very good at 'messing people up', even though they do not have the power of arrest: the security services. And it is possible that, with a higher level of cooperation between agencies, a mix of uniformed frontier-manning, intelligence-led operations, and purely disruptive techniques, many trafficking (importing) organisations could be put out of business. Such an amalgam of efforts could, conceivably, make the risks to established drug importers and distributors, and the prospects so unpalatable for new entrants to the business, that Britain's drug markets could go into decline. Time will tell, but meanwhile the authors will not be holding their breath.

In any event, the UK government's decision to implement 'two new performance indicators on drugs law enforcement which will apply to both Customs and the Police' (HM Customs and Excise press release, 17 March 1997: 2) is important for our understanding of drug enforcement. One of these indicators is a version of the existing 'organisations disrupted' measure, already applied by Customs. The wider use of this PI will further dilute the traditional focus on seizures *per se*, and introduce more scope for enforcement agencies to have 'successes'. Even in a future scenario in which seizures might go up again – and again, and yet again – the agencies will be able to interpret this in the light of the 'disruption' and 'dismantling' of trafficking organisations.

The development at national level of criteria and strategies other than seizures and arrests parallels the new 'community' strategies at local level. In both cases, new goals are being constructed, in a sense retrieving the enforcement agencies from their posture of apparent defeat in the drug war. The new approaches, aiming to reduce harm which may be associated with drug trafficking (unsafe streets, troubled communities, organised crime, violence, laundering of super-profits, etc.), provide a basket of indicators – some of which may be expected to be encouraging even if others turn out not, in any particular year. This development signals a real widening of the aims and techniques of drugs enforcement: not simply the development of multi-agency goals and harm-reduction methods in relation to drug users, but equal innovation in relation to trafficking. Parallel to the ACMD's (1994) guidance on community harm reduction in policing at local level, we see the emergence of what might be called 'national harm reduction' in policing at national level.

An initial speculation on future trends in Britain is now in order, following Labour's sweeping win in the parliamentary elections in May 1997. The Swedish criminologists Lenke and Olsson (1996) have argued that, while in opposition, conservative parties 'talk up' drug problems within a law and order discourse, identifying a 'need for repression' which strikes a chord with sectors of the population and helps their election prospects. But, when in power, conservatives turn out to be relatively liberal in their drugs policy – no longer needing to pose issues in a 'repressive' way. Cautiously, Lenke and Olsson go on to say:

> If this relationship holds for the future, then any political shift that brings to power more conservative parties in Europe could tilt the balance of drug policies, away from repression . . . Correspondingly, if conservative parties lose power, we might yet see more repressive drug policies. (1996: 116)

This pattern may indeed have been seen in Britain during the long period in power of the Conservative Party (1979–97), when we consider the government's acceptance of harm reduction for drug users. It was only in the mid-1990s, as the Conservatives suffered a loss of political support and were faced with the possibility of defeat, that the Home Secretary came to adopt a populist stance on drugs and crime. What, then, might be the consequences of the Labour win in relation to drug enforcement? What if the Conservatives, finding opposition uncongenial, should seek to 'talk up' law and order issues by arguing that any future increases in drug arrests or seizures are not at all 'a credit to Customs and Police', nor a credit to the Labour government of the day? In those circumstances, we might find that, just as the debate on drugs policy generally becomes politicised for the first time since the 1960s (as distinct from the bipartisan approach of the 1980s; see Dorn and South, 1987), so political debate might focus upon the widened set of performance indicators recently put into place for drug enforcement at national level (rather as indicators of the health of the national economy may be debated between political parties).

That is to say, there might be real controversy about performance indicators, methods and objectives of drug enforcement. Any such opening up of debate will find echoes in the European arena, our third and final sphere of exploration.

LOST SOVEREIGNTY AND THE NEW EUROPE: LAWS AND LIMITATIONS

Controversies over the development of the European Community – the rights and wrongs of its transition from what was primarily an economic community, concerned with the free movement of capital, goods, services and labour (citizens), into a Union with a common currency, a common foreign and security policy, and a functioning policy on justice and home affairs – provide the scene for arguments about the extent of harmonisation of the drug policies of EU Member States (see for example O'Keefe and Twomey, 1994).

In brief, already relatively highly harmonised are those drugs controls that fall within the Community's single market policies. The European Court of Justice some years ago ruled that, in the context of free movement of labour within the EU, a Member State may not expel citizens of another on the grounds that they have broken a national law, for example have trafficked in drugs: a serious and imminent threat to public health, public safety or public security is required before expulsion is possible. More recently, regulation of the financial services industry has provided a context for harmonised measures to prevent and detect money laundering; regulation of the chemical industry frames common legal measures against diversion of precursors.[4] At the other end of the spectrum, not being harmonised at all, are national arrangements regarding drug-related education, prevention, early intervention and treatment: in these policy areas, every state and, in those in which such policies are determined at a more local level, every local administration, does as it pleases. In these non-harmonised areas, the European Community facilitates cross-fertilisation of information about health problems and responses, and facilitates cooperation on a programme-by-programme basis.

None of these measures has provoked much controversy, other than on technical points. But political sensitivity of a high order attaches to the issue of convergence or harmonisation of the laws of EU Member States on drug use/possession, and on drug trafficking. The debate concerns two issues: (a) approximation and (b) harmonisation of laws.

Just how close would national laws have to be approximated (made similar) in order to avoid an uneven control space – which might attract drug trafficking, stimulate drug tourism, and undermine legitimacy of laws by making them appear to be a matter of 'relative morality'? On this issue, the Council of Ministers agreed in 1996 that:

Member States shall undertake to cooperate fully in the fight against drug addiction and shall endeavour to approximate their laws to make them mutually compatible to the extent necessary to prevent and combat illegal drug trafficking in the Union.[5]

This begs a question, since 'the extent necessary' of compatibility of laws is not self-evident.

On the second issue – whether at some point in the future to go further than approximating laws, to harmonise them (make them identical) – the jury may remain out for some time, while the EU undertakes an 'examination of the extent to which harmonisation of Member States' laws could contribute to reducing the consumption and supply of drugs in the European Union'.[6]

During the first half of the 1990s such issues were political 'hot potatoes' in the EU, with what we might call the 'normal' level of angst about drug trafficking being exacerbated by a row between France and the Netherlands, the former accusing the latter of undermining drug control, though the operation of the well-known cannabis cafés. This conflict exposes fundamental difficulties underlying the implementation of approximation and the evaluation of harmonisation: just who is going to change their legislation, in order to approximate or harmonise it with that of another country?

The issues raised by approximation and by harmonisation proposals are not just about cannabis (or other substances) – they are fundamental legal and constitutional issues. EU Member States' laws do differ.[7] As far as anti-trafficking measures are concerned, there may exist a degree of consensus between governments that penalties should be high, rather than trivial[8] – but after that is said it becomes difficult to be specific. Is there a self-evidently right level of penalty for selling 100 grams of hashish? In relation to 'simple' drug use/possession (insofar as that can be delineated), the differences in laws between EU Member States are not just a matter of the degree of constraint, they also concern the very forms of control: various mixes of criminal law (sometimes with 'aggravated offences'), administrative-penal approaches, other administrative measures, and/or *laissez-alley*, with an emergent civil law dimension.[9] Furthermore, within Member States, different cities and regional administrations may in some cases develop rather different judicial policies and guidelines about the borderline to be set between trafficking offences and possession for personal use. Such local or regional determinations may be constitutionally appropriate.[10]

It is politically conceivable for all Member States together to adopt a new type of legal measure, as an 'add-on' (for instance, regulatory measures and criminal penalties to prevent money laundering). But for one Member State to trade in its existing legal forms and traditions for those of another is obviously much more problematic. It is hardly likely to happen under conditions of duress. Therefore, advocates of rapid top-down harmonisation of drug laws either do not appreciate what it is they are demanding, or else their proposals are more a matter of display than substance, or they may be settling in for a bumpy ride on a very long road.[11]

What does all this mean for political accountability, for public debate, for the images of drug enforcement that are available to the citizens of the European Union? The continuation of a disparate and uneven crime control space at the European level means that cooperation between judicial systems, Customs and police will remain legally and bureau-cratically elaborate for the foreseeable future (cf. Dorn, 1993). Judicial systems are set for a series of exchanges of personnel, Customs services are under pressure from several sources to find ways of cooperating more closely,[12] and Europol, the European Police Office set up after the Treaty of European Union, seems likely to continue to have very complex tasks thrust upon it. To say that the resulting control space is not very transparent (to use a vogue EU term, meaning roughly clarity of pro-cedures) is an understatement; there are also arguments to the effect that it is not all that efficient.[13]

If the central argument of this chapter is correct, then soon we should witness the development at EU level of the kinds of definitions of crime problems, counter-measures and performance indicators that do more to flatter police and judicial cooperation – and less to draw attention to its shortcomings. Why such a delay then, between the impact of manage-rialism at local and national levels, and its impact at EU level? It is simply that the inter-state realm of high politics and diplomacy is penetrated more slowly by managerialist practices and thinking than the lowlier local and national levels.

What does this 'importation' of the European dimension into the usually nationally circumscribed frame of thinking of criminology imply for the propositions that the late modern context is characterised by a failure of criminal justice (Savage, 1989), and by a collapse of the 'foundational myth' that a 'sovereign State' can provide security for all, within its territorial boundaries (Garland, 1996)? First of all, the question of efficiency (more starkly, success or failure) cannot be grasped in the implicitly nineteenth-century terms of *prevention* of crime, *reformation* of offenders, etc., which nostalgic critics invoke. The goalposts have moved rather too radically for that familiar game of policy-making and policy-critique to continue. Indeed, as we have argued throughout, the defini-tional issue is paramount and the *management* of crime involves the essential step of construction of indicators that can be addressed through policing.

Secondly, considering the attention being paid to local and European as well as national dimensions of crime, these issues cannot be captured by a hackneyed discourse on territorial boundaries and sovereignty. Within the debates on the development of the European Union, the construction of a pan-EU zone of 'freedom, security and justice' is an accepted goal (even if the details remain fuzzy, at the time of writing). Following the 1997 Intergovernmental Conference, it is expected that cooperation on justice and home affairs will move further in this direction and, within five years, provide enhanced roles for the European Union institutions – the European Court of Justice, the Commission, the Parliament ('Noordwijk clears the path to summit agreement', *Financial Times*, 26 May 1996: 2). The expansion of the judicial oversight of the Court and the possibility of some extent of political oversight by the Parliament can only be welcomed, given the underdevelopment of such forms of oversight in relation to cross-border (and sometimes national and local) policing.

In a wider perspective, this enhanced pan-EU dynamic on justice and home affairs, coming from 'above', will be meeting with a current from 'below', insofar as local and regional administrations of the Member States are becoming almost as much a part of the political fabric of the EU as the already less than sovereign national authorities. Within the UK, at least, this evolution is assisted by the trouncing of the Euro-sceptical right in the 1997 elections by a cautiously pro-devolution Labour government. In this context, sociological/criminological reten-tion of the early modernist category of the 'sovereign State' surely has (or should have) reached its limits – not only for policy-makers and judges, but also for academic commentators. Purely national analyses of and ruminations on crime control have passed their sell-by date.

CONCLUSION

During the 'nervous 1990s', states have been grappling with a sense of crisis of criminal justice agencies, and a sense of the limits of their capability to regulate conduct and prevent crime – internationally, across Europe, in national settings and in the everyday lives of citizens. It seems that one response has been to settle for modest improvements at the margin: the better management of risks and resources, reduction of the fear of crime, reduction of criminal justice expenditure and greater support for crime's victims. These have become the less than heroic policy objectives which are replacing the idea of winning a war against crime. Transformations in official perceptions of the problem of drugs, redefining criteria for 'success' in drug enforcement, provide a vivid illustration of such adaptations.

In summary, 'manageability' of crime and drugs problems replaces the more heroic but politically risky 'war' stance. Welcome as this may seem to some observers, especially those for whom the war phase was offensive to human rights and/or inherently distasteful, a query never-theless needs to be placed over the prospect of depoliticisation of drug policies. Can it really be desirable that the enforcement agencies are able to utilise managerialism to reconstruct their objectives, to construct indicators of achievement such that their tasks become more 'do-able', their achievements more apparent, and their budgetary claims more appealing? Where is the element of external scrutiny in this process? Let these issues not be left to the enforcement agencies themselves, their lobbyists, managers and supporting experts. Policy debates on crime generally and on drug enforcement specifically should animate not only national parliaments, but also regional assemblies, city councils, local forums, the Committee of the Regions and the European Parliament.[14] Maybe the forms taken by the politicisation of drugs and crime issues have sometimes been unpalatable, but its replacement by depoliticised, technocratic and self-serving forms of PI chasing is a mixed blessing. In short, we can say goodbye to the drug wars, but have yet to get the measure of their successor. And, shocking though it may appear, we look forward to a democratic repoliticisation of drugs and crime issues.

NOTES

1.   Operation Welwyn, which brought together a special squad of Metropolitan Police officers from four neighbouring police divisions, started in 1991. It went through at least three different phases: phases 1 and 2, both of which were described by senior and frontline officers as 'straightforward' anti-drug operations, arguably had limited impact on the open, visible drug market. It was phase 3 of the Operation – involving 'partnership' between key individuals within the police, local councils and other local agencies – that was hailed as a success by local resident groups, council leaders, the Metropolitan Police Commissioner, Labour Party politicians (*King's Cross News*, 3, spring 1994) and the then Conservative Prime Minister (*Tackling Drugs Together*, White Paper, 1994).
2.   In 1994, for instance, the District Council of Sedgefield set up a Community Force and employed twelve civilian staff to patrol the streets of the whole district. The pictorial images of the community force officers dressed in police-lookalike uniform in publicity material are designed to illustrate the force's stated aims of providing a visible deterrent to prospective criminals or those who might indulge in anti-social behaviour, and serving as 'eyes and ears for the public Police' (I'Anson and Wiles, 1995).
3.   For a contrasting interpretation of the rise in police seizures, see Keith Hellawell, Chairman of Association of Chief Police Officers' Drugs Sub-Committee, ACPO press release, 17 March 1997: 1. (Mr Hellawell has since become new drug czar for the British government, tasked to consult and lead government policy and initiatives in the response to drugs. The post follows the American example.)
4.   Precursors are those chemicals which are in widespread use in industry, but also have a role in illicit drug production: many common substances are implicated, and chemical companies are required to report purchasers that appear not to fit an expected pattern of trade.

5. Joint Action of 17 December 1996, adopted by the Council on the basis of Article K.3 of the Treaty on European Union concerning the approximation of the laws and practices of Member States to combat drug addiction and to prevent and combat illegal drug trafficking, Article 1; *Official Journal of the European Community*, L 342 of 31 December 1996.

6. Council Resolution of 14 October 1996 laying down the priorities for cooperation in the fields of justice and home affairs for the period 1 July 1996 to 30 June 1998.

7. The situation is too complex to summarise here, there being variations within many EU Member States as well as between them, and considerable (albeit little understood) variations in application of measures in practice. See for example Leroy, 1992. More recently updated but less accessible sources include European Commission, 1995, also De Ruyver et al., 1995.

8. Joint Action (see note 5, above).

9. In fact these various forms of control can be found in relation to aspects of trafficking and public order, as well as use/possession, in some Member States. Cf. 'Drug enforcement in the EU: towards a European Civil Space?', a study funded by the European Commission (Directorate General) and coordinated by ISDD, London. For further information and publication details, contact by e-mail nicholas@isdd.co.uk and see Dorn, 1998.

10. See for example, for Germany: Leitsätze zum Beschluß des Zweiten Senats vom 9 März 1994.

11. For a relatively sophisticated but still problematic step upon that road, see Delmas-Marty, 1997.

12. EU Member States 'shall endeavour to make the practices of their police, customs services and judicial authorities more compatible with each other' (Joint Action, see note 5, above) See also European Parliament, 1997.

13. Because of the timing of this book, we do not address issues current at the time of writing in the EU's Intergovernmental Conference (IGC), on justice and home affairs and related matters. For updates on the IGC, see the WWW IGC database provided by the European Commission at http://europa.eu.int/en/agenda/igc-home and European Union, 1997.

14. The European Union's Committee of the Regions (COR), appointed to represent regional government, mayors and similar figures throughout the EU, issued an opinion on drugs in 1996. This calls for exchanges between agencies concerned with drug demand and drug supply, the development of multi-regional and multi-local-authority exchange networks, and asks the European Council and the Commission to consult Parliament and COR 'to ensure that all actions are properly coordinated' (Committee of the Regions, 1996).

REFERENCES

Advisory Council on the Misuse of Drugs (ACMD) (1994) *Drug Misusers and the Criminal Justice System, Part II: Police, Drug Misusers and the Community.* London: HMSO.

Association of Chief Police Officers (ACPO) (1995) *ACPO Drugs Strategy.* London: ACPO.

Audit Commission (1993) *Helping with Enquiries: Tackling Crime Effectively.* London: HMSO.

Clarke, M. (1987) 'Citizenship, community and the management of crime', *British Journal of Criminology,* 27 (4): 384–400.

Cohen, S. (1979) 'Community control in a new utopia', *New Society,* 15 March: 609–11.

Committee of the Regions (1996) *Opinion on the Communication from the Commission to the Council and the EP on a EU Action Plan to Combat Drugs (1995–1999), Official Journal of the European Communities,* 96/C 100/10.

Crawford, A. (1994) 'The partnership approach to community crime prevention: corporatism at the local level?', *Social and Legal Studies,* 3 (4): 497–519.

Currie, E. (1988) 'Two visions of crime prevention', in T. Hope and M. Shaw (eds), *Communities and Crime Reduction.* London: HMSO.

Davis, M. (1990) *City of Quartz.* London: Vintage.

Delmas-Marty, M. (1997) *Towards a European Legal Area: Corpus Juris introducing Penal Provisions for the Purpose of the Protection of the European Community* (Study carried out at the request of the European Parliament under the aegis of the Directorate General for Financial Controls at the European Commission, document XX/29/97–EN). Brussels: European Commission.

De Ruyver, B., Van Daele, L., Vermeulen, G., Van der Beken, T., Soenens, A. and Serlippins, A. (1995) *Drug Policy in the European Union: Possibilities Offered by Article K.1(4) of the Union Treaty.* Ghent: University of Ghent. Mimeo.

Dorn, N. (1993) 'The quiet harmony of the police: enforcement, welfare and Single Market perspectives on policing in Europe, with special reference to illegal drugs', in A. Skretting, P. Rosenqvist and J. Jepsen (eds), *Drug Politics: International Perspectives.* Helsingfors, Finland: NAD. pp. 93–109.

Dorn, N. (ed.) (1998) *Regulating European Drug Problems.* The Hague: Kluwer.

Dorn, N. and South, N. (eds) (1987) *A Land Fit For Heroin?: Drug Policies, Prevention and Practice.* London: Macmillan.

Dorn, N., Baker, O. and Seddon, T. (1995) *Paying for Heroin.* London: ISDD.

Edmunds, M., Hough, M. and Urquia, N. (1996) *Tackling Local Drug Markets* (Police Research Group Crime Detection and Prevention Series, paper 80). London: HMSO.

European Commission (1995) *Comparative Study on Drug Legislation in Europe,* prepared for Conférence sur la politique des drogues en Europe, Bruxelles (Justice and Home Affairs Task Force), December. Mimeo.

European Parliament (1997) *Committee of Enquiry into the Community Transport System, Draft Final Report (Preliminary Version)* (PE 220.895). Strasbourg: European Parliament.

European Union (1997) *Consolidated Versions of the Treaty on European Union and the Treaty Establishing the European Community.* Luxemburg: Office for Official Publications of the European Communities.

Garland, D. (1996) 'The limits of the sovereign state – strategies of crime control in contemporary society', *British Journal of Criminology,* 36 (4): 445–71.

Grieve, J. (1993) 'Thinking the "unthinkable" ', *Criminal Justice Matters,* 12. (summer).

HM Government (1994) *Tackling Drugs Together – A Consultation Document Strategy for England 1995–1998.* London: HMSO.

Home Office (1988) *Practical Ways to Crack Crime*. London: HMSO.

Hope, T. and Shaw, M. (eds) (1988) *Communities and Crime Reduction*. London: HMSO.

Hough, M. and Mayhew, P. (1985) *Taking Account of Crime: Key Findings from the 1984 British Crime Survey* (Home Office Research Study 85). London: HMSO.

I'Anson, J. and Wiles, P. (1995) *The Sedgefield Community Force: the Results of a Survey of the Public's Response to the Introduction of the Force*. Sheffield: University of Sheffield, Centre for Criminological and Legal Research.

Institute for the Study of Drug Dependence (ISDD) (1994) *Drug Misuse in Britain*. London: ISDD.

Jones, T. and Newburn, T. (forthcoming) *Private Security and Public Policing*. Oxford: Clarendon Press.

King, M. (1991) 'The political construction of crime prevention: a contrast between the French and British experience', in K. Stenson and D. Cowell (eds), *The Politics of Crime Control*. London: Sage.

Lacey, N. and Zedner, L. (1995) 'Discourses in community in criminal justice,' *Journal of Law and Society*, 22 (3): 301–25.

Lee, M. (1995) 'Across the public-private divide? Private policing, grey intelligence and civil actions in local drugs control', *European Journal of Crime, Criminal Law and Criminal Justice*, 3 (4): 381–94.

Lee, M. (1996) 'London: community damage limitation through policing', in N. Dorn, J. Jepsen and E. Savona (eds), *European Drug Policies and Enforcement*. London: Macmillan.

Lenke, L. and Olsson, B. (1996) 'Sweden: zero tolerance wins the argument?' in N. Dorn, J. Jepsen and E. Savona (eds), *European Drug Policies and Enforcement*. London: Macmillan.

Leroy, B. (1992) 'The European Community of twelve and the drug demand. Excerpt of a comparative study of legislations and judicial practice', *Drug and Alcohol Dependence*, 29: 269–81.

McLaughlin, E. (1991) 'Police accountability and black people – into the 1990s', in E. Cashmore and E. McLaughlin (eds), *Out of Order? Policing Black People*. London: Routledge.

Mayhew, P. and Maung, N.A. (1992) *Surveying Crime: Findings from the 1992 British Crime Survey* (Home Office Research and Statistics Department, Research Findings 2). London: HMSO.

Mayhew, P. Elliot, D. and Dowds, L. (1989) *The 1988 British Crime Survey* (Home Office Research Study 111). London: HMSO.

National Association for the Care and Resettlement of Offenders (NACRO) (1997) *Criminal Justice Digest*, 92. (April). London: NACRO.

O'Keefe, D. and Twomey, P. (eds) (1994) *Legal Issues of the Maastricht Treaty*. Colorado Springs: Chancery Law Publishing; Chichester: Wiley.

Rosenbaum, D. (1993) 'Civil liberties and aggressive enforcement: balancing the rights of individuals and society in the drug war', in R. Davis, A. Lurigio and D. Rosenbaum (eds), *Drugs and the Community*. Springfield, IL: Charles Thomas.

Savage, S. (1989) 'Crime control: the law and the community', *Talking Politics*, 2 (1).

South, N. (1987) 'The security and surveillance of the environment', in J. Lowman, R. Menzies and T.S. Palys (eds), *Transcarceration: Essays in the Sociology of Social Control*. Aldershot: Gower.

Tuck, M. (1991) 'Community and the criminal justice system', *Policy Studies*, 12 (3).

Walklate, S. (1996) 'Community and crime prevention', in E. McLaughlin and J. Muncie (eds), *Controlling Crime*. London: Sage.

7

CONTROLLING DRUGS IN SPORT: CONTRADICTIONS AND COMPLEXITY

Ross Coomber

'Talking past' one another is an activity employed by many who take differing stances on a whole variety of social issues. The issue of drug control in sport is no different. Advocates of prohibition (of those drugs deemed to be *performance enhancing*) often relate marginally to those who would advocate less extreme control or even the complete removal of controls, and vice versa. This is also true in the non-sporting world where debate around drug control is more advanced and contended more fiercely. The aim of this chapter is not to convince the reader of one side or other of the argument but to present the *complexity* of the issue and show how simple accounts arguing for or against the prohibition of drugs in sport, which may serve as good rhetoric, have little real policy value other than as symbolic positioning.

Simple prohibition and severe punishment of those caught, currently the primary approach to the use of performance enhancing drugs (PEDs) in the sporting world, as in the non-sporting world, has not been effective even in its own terms. Moreover, it has even been argued that an unintended effect of existing policy may be that it works against some of the principles upon which it is based and seeks to maintain, such as the health of the competitor (Coomber, 1993). Thus, stressing the real life complexity of the problem as it is currently defined as well as the complexity of resolving such concerns will hopefully contribute to a broader debate on the control of drugs in sport. We need to recognise, however, that the acknowledgement of complexity in an issue makes people uncomfortable (so they often do not do it) for it also means they have to acknowledge that the current approaches to dealing with the matter are of limited utility. Rhetoric is clean; reality and everyday life are messy.

UNDERSTANDING THE BASIS UPON WHICH DRUGS IN SPORT ARE CONTROLLED

This is not the place to undertake a full history of how drugs in sport came to be controlled but it is necessary to provide some background to, and contextualisation of, its emergence. The controls, or relative absence of them, which exist over drugs (all drugs) at any one time are contingent upon the particular socio-historical context which is being considered. Tea and coffee have both been illegal drugs and vilified, as is alcohol today in Saudi Arabia and a number of other Muslim countries. Cannabis and other psychedelics (both natural and synthesised) as well as certain stimulant drugs have been and continue to be not only legal in some parts of the world but also an important aspect of the culture in which they are used (Evans Schultes and Hofmann, 1992; Rudgley, 1993; Goodman et al., 1995). Heroin is a controlled drug (not an illegal one) prescribed as a painkiller by doctors in the UK whereas in the US, where heroin *is* illegal, the prescribing of heroin has, in the past, led to the imprisonment of medics. The control, and more specifically the banning, of drugs in sport is a very recent phenomenon. It is only in the last thirty years or so that any concerted effort to control the use of so-called performance enhancing drugs has been made. Prior to 1963, and for hundreds if not thousands of years, the seeking of advantage through potions, plants or drugs was part and parcel of the general seeking of sporting advantages in whatever way possible (Prokop, 1970; Yesalis, 1993) which in large part constitutes the very nature of competitive activity. In fact, concerns around doping in sport used to centre not on performance enhancement, but, in relation to horse and greyhound races for example, on *diminished* performance: a doped animal would be prevented from performing well, making a race more predictable for gambling purposes (Donohoe and Johnson, 1986). A number of events, however, conspired to alter how drug use for performance enhancement was perceived and thus understood in the second half of this century, from being one of many forms of advantage seeking to the most heinous of forms.

Initial calls for control did not focus on notions of unfair advantage, although debate about this did go on, but upon potential health problems, particularly from drugs such as amphetamine. Early concerns were highlighted by the death of the Danish cyclist Knud Jensen during the 1960 Rome Olympics, and the International Federation of Sports Medicine lobbied for controls on PEDs (Donohoe and Johnson, 1986). Other high-profile sporting deaths have since galvanised opposition to PEDs (despite a relative paucity of absolute numbers) and controls have been widened and punishments increased. A simple reading of sporting drug controls, which have slowly gathered steam from the early 1960s, would have us believe that the impetus came solely from within sport. Whilst it is true that technology and medicine now provide the opportunity to speculate on the dangers of drug use for performance enhancement, the gaze on drugs in sport in the 1960s cannot be separated from concerns about drugs and drug users in the non-sporting world.

The 1950s and 1960s were periods of high-velocity change for Western societies in general. Many conventions, traditions and norms were being challenged by emergent youth cultures. Recreational and addictive drug use was widely associated (although this was often wildly overstated) with many of these fashions and cultures. In general, drug use, whether it was by jazz musicians, mods and rockers or hippies, became associated with a relatively deviant way of life, and with people who were less committed to the conventions of society. It, and they, were thus perceived to represent a threat to society in general. In the non-sporting world much has been written about the unsound and morally based rationales which provided the impetus and grounding for drug controls there (cf. Saper, 1974; Musto, 1987; Coomber, 1997a). Much of this (ir)rationality inevitably found its way into the formation of early sporting controls as well. It would be naive to believe that those governing sport sought to 'clean up' sport (amphetamines for example, were being used in and outside of sport), merely to protect the competitor. The protection of the image of sport was also paramount. Concerns around drug use in sport were thus, in part, transformed by the concerns around drugs in society in general and not solely by issues of fair play and safety, and the history of drug controls in sport cannot be divorced from this fact.

The emergence of doping regulations is therefore a recent phenomenon and not unrelated to non-sporting drug use outside the sporting community. A shift in attitudes took place towards the use of particular substances: from being considered one of a vast range of potential, and not necessarily inappropriate, attempts to enhance performance, to being considered an improper means.

THE PROS OF CONTROLLING DRUGS IN SPORT

The policy rationales for controlling drugs in sport are firmly put in terms of offsetting harm, whether physical or moral. In other words the pros of controlling drugs are considered to outweigh the harm which is believed would result by not controlling them. Fraleigh (1985) for example, in reviewing the ethical debate, concludes that if there were no restrictions then the amount of aggregate harm befalling athletes and 'society' as a result of drug use would be greater than at present, which justifies the restriction of the choice to use drugs. As discussed elsewhere (Coomber, 1993), the primary justifications for the banning of certain drugs in sport are to help ensure that competition takes place on a 'level playing field', i.e. that no competitor or competitors have unfair advantage over others and that the health of those competing in sport is protected. Moreover, many of the ideals upon which Baron Pierre de Coubertin revived the Olympic Games, with which most modern sport officials (particularly those at the forefront of doping control), declare their affinity, also underlie the particular version of fair play which is adopted. Taken at face value, there is little wrong with these rationales. It is relatively uncontentious that a sporting body should seek to protect its members from harm, at least when it comes from ingested or administered substances.[1] It is also reasonable to ask competitors to compete within the rules that are laid down for respective sports in the name of fairness. Preserving 'fair play' in sport however also elevates sport to something more, to an example and model of what ought to be: nations and individuals competing at ever greater levels but with a spirit which embodies that 'what is important is the taking part – not the winning'. The ideal of modern sport is a hearty mix of magnanimity and competition, or an example of and manifestation in abstract form of a kind of benevolent (and friendly) capitalism. Preventing these ideals from being undermined, in the best traditions of paternalistic policy, thus protects both competitor (individual) and society from itself. That sport feels threatened by drugs is evident from the extent of efforts to eradicate their use and the pronouncements of some of its leading spokespersons, e.g. 'It is a sad fact of life that doping has become a deadly threat to sport but thankfully our sport has recognised the problem of doping and is sparing no expense or effort to bring it under control' (Ljungqvist, 1993: 3). It is not the intention of this chapter to question the ideals of fair play: that sport should protect its competitors or that it should wish to encourage something more than 'winning' as the essence of sporting endeavour. Indeed, this author believes that such ideals are laudable. The assumed pros of contemporary approaches to drug control in sport however are undermined in a number of significant ways mainly because the precepts upon which they are based are either more complex than assumed or are confronted by other contradictory, if not hypocritical practices which themselves are not prohibited. The rest of this chapter will concern itself with the two essential areas that present real and ongoing problems for the achievement of drug-free sport. To begin with it will consider the actual 'hands-on' problems of successfully carrying out a sporting war on drugs and preventing the use of performance enhancing drugs, and secondly, it will discuss a number of ethical and rational problems presented by the current trajectory of drugs control policies.

WINNING THE WAR ON DRUGS IN SPORT

The main weapon that sporting authorities employ to prevent the use of PEDs is that of urine testing to detect the use of banned substances.

Testing however produces varying results. It may be reasonably argued that the fact that no competitors in the 1995 World Athletics Championships in Helsinki tested positive for doping is more of a testament to the *failure* of drug testing than to its success. I do not intend to rehearse this argument at great length in this chapter (see Coomber, 1993 for further discussion); suffice it to say that there are few officials with responsibility for doping controls, athletes, coaches or journalists attending the Championships who will believe that a significant number of those athletes competing in Helsinki were not PED users. Testing as a means to detect drug use is seriously problematic for various reasons. Firstly, there are a number of substances and practices which are difficult to test for or cannot be tested for (Ferstle, 1993; Duncan, 1995). This is particularly true when the substances, such as human growth hormone (HGH) or erythropoetin (EPO) are also naturally produced by the human body. Although drug testing laboratories can *detect* such substances they cannot prove that they were unnaturally administered as opposed to naturally produced (Duncan, 1995). This creates serious and currently irresolvable problems for testing. Athletes who may once have used androgenic anabolic steroids (AAS), or stimulants such as amphetamine, may now be using HGH or EPO, and in the case of insulin growth factor 1, its use by athletes may be even 'more prolific than the use [prescription] by specialist clinicians' for appropriate medical conditions (Parry, 1996: 48). Testing at the World Championships would not have produced positive results for these competitors. Even if tests become available for these substances it is likely that new substances problematic for testing will emerge as they have historically done to date. In the 1996 Atlanta Olympics a new 'stimulant' was detected in a number of Russian athletes but as the substance was unknown to the International Olympic Committee (IOC) at this time (despite its use by the Russians for some years) no action was taken against the athletes (Woodhouse, 1996). Athletes employ various techniques to outsmart the testing system, including switching from drugs which can be tested for to those for which testing is not yet available or to drugs which are yet to be banned, and to the use of various masking agents. There is no evidence to suggest that athletes will not stay one step ahead of new technologies and new testing strategies.

The practical problems of actually preventing the use of PEDs through testing are further compounded by the fact that even when a positive test *is* recorded a simple outcome is far from certain. Litigation arising from problems relating to positive and false-positive tests continues to plague national and international sporting authorities and perhaps even threaten their bankruptcy. Numerous cases involving positive tests have been contested in recent years in the courts. Testing by non-IOC-accredited laboratories has been shown to be fallible (Uzych, 1991), and problems with the administration of samples have even led to IOC-accredited laboratories being subject to question, and in extreme cases, the athlete being exonerated.[2] The testing procedure itself is thus, on occasion (but increasingly so), being called into question and challenged in court. Each time a decision goes against a sporting authority a blow is struck against the effort to prevent drug use and, importantly, scarce funds are used up.

Even when a positive finding is successfully translated into a ban on the individual competing in further sporting activity, that ban, imposed through the sporting authorities rules and regulations, may be overturned by national courts on the basis of broader employment laws which take precedence in the country of which the competitor is a citizen. This poses particular problems for leading international sporting authorities such as the IOC, the International Amateur Athletic Federation (IAAF) and the Federation of International Football Associations (FIFA), among others, who may find that their decisions are effectively overturned by domestic legislation.

Something called 'harmonisation' is the goal of bodies like the IOC. Harmonisation would entail the consistent application and implementation of rules, regulations and punishments relating to PEDs not only across sports but also across nations and continents. Unfortunately, even if such harmonisation were possible at the level of stated policy, the chances of expensive and reliable testing regimes being carried out around the globe is, in the near future, simply fantasy. The very many developing countries which participate in major sporting events have important demands on scarce resources that will take precedence over developing the kind of extensive (and expensive) testing regimes in place in countries such as the UK. Harmonisation will in practice mirror (to some extent) the efficacy of the various international drug conventions of the non-sporting world. Many of those countries who have ratified the international drug conventions are also foremost in producing illicit drugs, such as heroin, cocaine and cannabis, and have neither the resources nor often the will to combat production and trafficking in practice. Perhaps half the sporting world will, for the foreseeable future, also have insufficient means or political will to try to ensure drug-free competition.

As in the non-sporting world, the evidence to date suggests that the war on drugs cannot be won, and that simple prohibition of drugs, pursued primarily through enforcement measures, does not, and is not able to, prevent their use. The response to this of course may be simply to spend more and more time and resources on improving the systems already in place, arguing that not enough has yet been done. This has certainly been the position of drug war advocates in the non-sporting world. To date, however, there is no evidence to suggest that simple enforcement and harsh punishment strategies – even when relatively well funded – have been successful in preventing the general escalation of drug use over the last twenty years in the US where such policies have been pursued with great vigour (Bullington, 1998).

What hope is there for preventing the use of PEDs in the sporting arena? It would seem very little, and this is a practical problem that has to be faced up to and not rejected out of principled idealism. Trotting out aphorisms which would suggest that this is 'giving in to' or 'going soft on' drugs is missing the point that at present the means to prevent their use are not at hand and are unlikely to be so. Moreover, much of that principled and indignant idealism arguably manifests itself in the way it does (outright prohibition and strong-armed enforcement at all costs) because of a lack of understanding of drug issues more broadly and the belief that the specific issue of drug use in sport is a *simple* matter, in the sense that drug use is cheating and must be prevented. If the very harsh penalties which attach themselves to the crime are any indication, it is certainly conceived of as a form of cheating far worse than most others. But is it *really* that simple?

ISSUES OF EFFICACY

The general mood in the 1990s regarding the efficacy of PEDs, particularly anabolic steroids, is that they do indeed work (WHO, 1993). To suggest otherwise lays one open to derision. This represents a stark change to the mood of the 1960s and 1970s when most sporting, medical and other scientific authorities tended to deny PEDs' performance-enhancing abilities (Donohoe and Johnson, 1986; Van Helder et al., 1991; Lycholat, 1993; WHO, 1993). Science, however, was saying one thing but the body-builders and athletes taking the drugs were saying another. In the eyes of the people they were trying to influence, those who were taking PEDs, the scientific community lost credibility. Those using them argued that they were experiencing and seeing improvements in musculature and/or performance and that research was failing to prove this because research ethics prevented studies from using the very large doses of PEDs that were being taken outside of experiments (in the 'real' world) and/or in the ways that they were taken – e.g. the use of a number of different drugs at the same time. Although continued research has not been able to prove that PEDs, especially anabolic steroids, do actually enhance performance (see Stone and Wright, 1993)[3] the need (conscious or unconscious) to recapture public and sporting credibility has meant that few sports scientists, medics or sporting authorities now question that PEDs do work. However, even leading authorities such as the IOC, the IAAF and the UK Sports Council are hesitant and selective in their pronouncements on performance enhancement:

There is little evidence to support the belief that Anabolic Steroids alone can increase muscle strength; development is very much dependent upon an appropriate diet and exercise programme. However, studies have shown that muscles tend to look bigger, but this is probably due to water retention. It is more likely that the androgenic effect of steroids – increased aggression and competitiveness – which makes people train harder and enables them to recover more quickly, increases strength. (Sports Council, 1990: 3)

The last sentence is the one that pays lip service to those who claim that the benefits of AASs are meaningful. Unfortunately, distinguishing such effects from those produced by *expectation* of drug effects is difficult to achieve and whilst athletes claim AAS use helps heal injuries quicker there is also evidence to suggest that using steroids may lead to recurring injuries which may be said to negatively affect training and performance (Freeman and Rooker, 1995; Hang et al., 1995). Charlie Francis, the coach of Ben Johnson, has stated that he believes that steroids represented at least 1 per cent of performance, a figure so low that working out whether the improvement was due to a placebo effect (through expectation or raised confidence) or from the use of AASs is impossible. Moreover, we have to accept that huge improvements in performance across all sports and athletic disciplines are not in fact uncommon and that drug use is not suspected in many cases – but, how do you tell the difference between the two? A greater correlation between exceptional performance and suspicion of drug use, arguably, often has far more to do with politics and geography than proof. When the Ethiopian (Ethiopia being a world leader in distance running), Haile Gebrsilassie 'demolished' the 10,000 metres world record by a massive nine seconds in 1995 one television commentator was moved to exclaim 'if I hadn't seen it with my own eyes I wouldn't have believed it' and yet no media (and thus confident peer) suspicion was evident in the aftermath of the race. Similarly, when the British athlete Jonathan Edwards (a man known to hold strong Christian beliefs) improved his triple jump performances to lengths far beyond those previously known in this event (but suspected probable by his own previous performances) his character was un-questioned. Both of these performances were in the region of amazing improvement but neither athlete came under suspicion even though most world records often deemed to be the result of drug use entail no more than minor incremental improvements. Conversely, when Michelle Smith, a swimmer from Dublin, won three gold medals in the Atlanta Olympic Games in 1997, despite being ranked world number one the previous year in one of the events and having showed steady improve-ment in her times in general, she suffered the extreme media pressure of suggestions that she had used steroids. There was no evidence that Smith had done so other than her not being considered pre-event favourite. But she was from a country which had never previously won a swimming gold medal. Likewise, when China started to produce world records in distance running and swimming in the early 1990s, emphasis on the extent of improvement raised suspicions of the use of steroids (a reaction partly reflecting suspicion of a communist nation), as opposed to the training schedules and lifestyle which led one top Western athlete who had witnessed the difference from Western regimes to declare it not so surprising (Wightman, 1993).

There is a distinct lack of consistent application when it comes to the commonsense (or even 'specialist') notions of the kind of level of improvement that is expected from the use of drugs. The improvement is often expected to be phenomenal, and in that way 'detectable' – as we have seen however, this applies only to those vulnerable to such suspicion, for other 'phenomenal' feats are simply accepted as evidence of great athleticism. There are also inconsistencies in expectations about the speed at which drug use can produce improvements. Whilst there is little, if any, evidence, to show that tremendous improvements can be made through the simple use of PEDs there is ample evidence to show that level of confidence and the right or wrong frame of mind can produce great improvements in performance or hinder it despite an athlete's relative physical conditioning (Feltz and Landers, 1983; May and Asken, 1987; Turner and Raglin, 1996).

WHY 'PICK' ON DRUG USE?

Even if we accept for the moment that it could be demonstrated that the use of PEDs is effective in enhancing performance we would still have to ask why this has been elevated to a position of such concern that competitors are publicly humiliated and castigated and then given comparatively severe punishments? The issue here is to understand why the evil of drug use as a means of gaining advantage is a greater problem than other means used to gain advantage. It is not due to clear and consistent evidence that drug use provides either fail-safe or, necessarily, even any advantage. In fact when a myriad of offences is considered in a whole variety of sports it appears that many other illegitimate techniques may offer greater potential advantage than the use of drugs, but are punished far less severely. In motor racing in 1994 the Benetton team was given relatively light penalties for cheating (in ways which gave them clear, measurable and predictable improvements in performance) on two separate occasions in one season (Henry, 1994), and yet its driver Michael Schumacher went on (and was permitted) to win the World Championship in that same year. In the 1998 Football World Cup finals numerous players were booked for 'diving', attempting to convince the referee that a foul had been committed, sometimes looking for a penalty, at other times positional advantage. Shirt pulling and other 'professional fouls' were commonplace. This is part and parcel of football matches all around the world. In ice hockey as in football and rugby, violence (and the 'taking out' of key players with over the top tackles (football) or 'stamping' (rugby) – potentially career threatening actions) is commonly punished (rewarded?) with little more than a caution or time in the 'sin-bin' whereas in other sports it would result in lengthy bans. Each sport has its techniques and methods of cheating which arguably offer as much in the way of advantage as drug use, none represent positive role models of behaviour, each in its own way brings its sport into disrepute – yet the punishment is minor. There are also of course techniques which, whilst not illegal, stretch the spirit of the game unreasonably: tennis players who habitually argue during games, often at key moments, thereby unsettling their opponents; managers who seek to 'psych-out' the competition by using the press to make carefully calculated statements; or even the calculated failure to actually bowl towards the batsperson in cricket.[4] Significant advantage can be achieved through foul and unfair means but relatively little is made of this. Sometimes these advantages may threaten the health and well-being of others, sometimes they just offer significant potential advantage. What they mostly attract though is relatively minor censure and forms of punishment far less severe than those applied in cases of the use of drugs, which, in terms of performance enhancement, may merely enhance the ability to train longer and harder.

Not only do other forms of cheating provide equal or perhaps more significant levels of advantage, but the very arena of *normal* sporting activity also provides numerous examples of legal methods of advantage seeking which nonetheless leave some competitors at a very great disadvantage. The very notion of a level playing field, and the notion of policy as an attempt to ensure it, is one of the greatest myths of the modern sporting environment. Some nations seek advantage by systematically providing their competitors with better environments and arrangements for training and practice competitions. These may range from centres of excellence providing top-rate coaches, accommodation and state-of-the-art training regimes to simply providing adequate sponsorship for full-time and appropriate training. Some nations can afford to do this; others cannot. Some individuals, such as Steffi Graf, Boris Becker, Ayrton Senna, Jose-Maria Olazabel and Alberto Tomba, were born into families with resources that provided them with the relative advantages that money can offer from the earliest of ages to enable them to reach the very heights of their respective sports. In boxing and weight-lifting, some attempts are made to provide weight-based categories but in the high jump, unless you are tall, then forget it. Why? Records are broken year in, year out, but some of those records are broken under conditions that were not provided to the competitors whose records have been broken. Faster tracks (some tracks are fast for sprinters, some for distance runners), faster pools, more efficient javelins, better poles in the pole vault, better running shoes, better skis . . . the list is endless. Some of these advantages, which may confer riches and status, or simply opportunities to continue competing, may provide no real superiority over the effort they have been said to have superseded, yet one competitor may suffer whilst the other may reap the dividends offered by technology.

This is an unfair advantage external to the ability of the competitor yet is sanctioned and encouraged by the sporting powers that be. We must also ask: if drugs offer no simple route to performance enhancement, then why is it deemed legitimate and unproblematic for competitors to improve their levels of confidence, ability to endure pain and discomfort for longer periods, or increase aggression in training and competition, through recourse to hypnosis, meditation or techniques of sport psychology which are ways of adjusting and improving the natural (and sometimes) fragile state of mind of a competitor? Is it fair that some squash players have access to experts able to provide techniques for improving ball-to-eye coordination, and that some competitors have access to other ergogenic (performance enhancing) aids, when others do not?

If other forms of illegal and legal advantage seeking which undermine the hallowed level playing field are attempted and practised regularly, and secure significant advantages yet go relatively unpunished, why are drug users scapegoated? Again, we probably need to look more closely at what goes on in the non-sporting world.

GOOD DRUGS, BAD DRUGS

As in the non-sporting world, much of the prohibition of drugs is predicated on the idea that there are good drugs which are not banned (and which are of medical utility) and bad drugs, which are. The specific drugs of primary concern in sporting and non-sporting worlds are different but the basic underlying rationale is often the same. The bad drugs are considered bad because they are a threat to health and in addition, in the sporting world, because they supposedly provide an unreasonable and unequal route to artificially enhanced performance. In the non-sporting world this performance enhancement may also have its parallels in the sense that having a 'good time' through recourse to non-socially sanctioned artificial as opposed to natural ('I don't need drugs to enjoy myself') or socially sanctioned means (such as alcohol) is frowned upon.

The 'good' drugs are not generally considered to be bad because they are taken under medical supervision and are not therefore considered to present comparable health risks. Moreover, as prescribed medication they are not considered to provide artificially induced improvement to performance. As in the non-sporting world, though, this distinction between good and bad is not very useful, nor is the way in which such a distinction is made. To begin with, many of the prescribed drugs may also present dangers or risks comparable to, or in excess of, many of those that are banned. They may produce cardiac disorders, convulsions, a range of other side-effects and even death if not used appropriately

(Donohoe and Johnson, 1986). Addiction may also result from use of certain groups of drugs if these are not used carefully; some require a carefully managed withdrawal to avoid serious health consequences (Favre, 1996). Withdrawal from corticosteroids may even lead to the development of adrenal deficiency and the condition known as Addison's disease (Donohoe and Johnson, 1986). Although these drugs may be prescribed and their use condoned by sporting authorities, those using them may choose to compete or take part in sporting activity only because they are *enabled* to do so by use of a drug. In the short or long term this may lead to serious injury. Without the drug, competing would not have been possible, although taking part arguably would have. Prescribed drugs therefore may not only facilitate participation in competition but also enable a level of performance to be achieved that would have been unlikely without the drug. Granted, the sporting competitor may not be able to perform to their normal level but without the drug they might not have performed at all. So the good drugs can, and sometimes do, cause harm, and arguably also enhance performance. For the sporting authorities the issue is firmly that there is a qualitative distinction between 'enabling' and 'performance enhancing' drugs, but is there? Take two hypothetical athletes, with similar capabilities under normal conditions, but with similar injuries. One runs without the use of painkilling drugs and is comparatively inhibited, the other, using painkillers, is able to perform close to their norm, uninhibited by the discomfort of the injury and the constant psychological messages to 'protect it' (the injury) which may result in minutely (or greatly) changed gait or stance. Therefore, one athlete's performance is potentially enhanced beyond that of the other, and as such an *advantage*, occasioned by the use of drugs is the possible result, as is further harm to the injury.

Significantly, many of the drugs banned do not, despite common representation, present too great a danger to health. Many of the widely reported dangers of androgenic anabolic steroids for example are reversible shortly after use has stopped and others are exaggerated (cf. Windsor and Dumitru, 1988; Van Helder et al., 1991; Stone and Wright, 1993; Yesalis, 1993). Likewise in the non-sporting world the dangers of drugs such as cocaine, amphetamine and heroin are often unreasonably exaggerated (Kaplan, 1983; Alexander and Wong, 1990; Miller 1991; Bean, 1993; Ditton and Hammersley, 1994; Greider, 1995; WHO/UNICRI, 1995; Coomber, 1997b). Almost regardless of substance, a large list of fearsome-sounding side-effects and potential harms can be reported regarding its use, particularly its use to excess. Caffeine for example can cause 'insomnia, muscle tremor, abnormally elevated heart rate and breathing . . . vomiting and diarrhoea . . . to delirium. Death from overdose is possible' (ISDD, 1993: 43). Even water, taken in excess over a short period of time, can cause intoxication, headaches and a condition called hyponatremia, a swelling of the brain which may result in death. Yet we give relatively little concern to these dangers, and rightly so because the risk is small, and often managed. Merely to list the health risks of androgenic anabolic steroids and other PEDs without reference to context and without regard to an understanding of *relative* risk is thus problematic. It is not my intention here to disregard the risks of taking AASs in large doses, as the taking of many substances in excess is risky. We need to be aware though that many of the reported dangers are exaggerated or quite simply unproven (see Van Helder et al., 1991; Stone and Wright, 1993; Windsor and Dumitru, 1988; Friedl, 1993). It is not unusual for such a situation to occur when a drug has been demonised for other reasons (being illegal as in the case of amphetamines and cocaine, and undermining fair play, and thus sport, in the case of AASs). The reporting of drug dangers in general may be massively overstated. Alexander and Wong (1990) have shown how the reporting of health risks for cocaine, even in respected medical journals, is often imprecise and misleading with a tendency to overstate *potential* risk at the expense of the probable or common risks involved. Most cocaine use is in fact moderate, and presents few health risks, whilst reporting of health risks tends to emphasise those that result from excessive use. The general impression gained of the riskiness of cocaine is therefore an exaggerated and distorted one. The press on AASs has at times been similarly sensational. Scares over 'Roid-Rage', a supposed steroid-induced aggression, as well as other scares linking steroids to various problems from cancers to heart disease, have been and continue to be emphasised by sporting authorities and the media as a major part of their campaign to prevent drug use in sport. As with fears of drugs in the non-sporting world (see Chapters 1, 2, 3 and 4 in this volume), the scares around PEDs suggest a danger out of proportion to reality. Studies demonstrating links with aggression are often weak in research design (Stone and Wright, 1993), may show no direct link between aggression and steroids, fail to take into consideration the expectations of the users that steroids increase aggressive tendencies, and report that those involved in weight-lifting and body-building who are not taking steroids have higher levels of recorded aggression anyway. This is not a new issue to those of us who research on drug effects more broadly. Many drugs in the non-sporting world have long been associated with violent behaviour, but once you control for expectation of drug effects, previous violent disposition of the individual concerned, the context in which the violence occurs, and the choices available to the individual to avoid violence, the picture is much more blurred (MacAndrew and Edgerton, 1969; Falk, 1994; Potter, 1989; Fagan, 1990). For some drugs, such as heroin, the association with violence is in fact *lower* than for the non-drug-using population (cf. Tonry and Wilson, 1990). We have to remember that steroids are commonly used to help treat numerous medical conditions and that, contrary to popular beliefs, steroid users are not dropping down dead all over the place despite many decades of high-level use. As in the non-sporting world, the distinction between what is a good drug and what is a bad drug is largely a construction based upon muddy thinking and moral positioning around what is considered 'medication' and what is considered 'abuse'.

In terms of protecting athletes' health (a stated rationale for the banning of the bad drugs), it is far from clear that outright prohibition of PEDs prevents more harm than would a policy where drugs were not banned but appropriate and well-managed information and guidance on drug use operated.

SHOULD 'INTENT' TO CHEAT BE PUNISHED?

The question of whether PEDs work or not is an important one for a number of reasons. For example, if PEDs do not work, should athletes actually be punished? If they do work but do not provide as much advantage as other forms of cheating, should the athletes be punished at the levels currently set? Should the intent to cheat, even if it provides little advantage, be punished? In football, an identified attempt to deceive the referee into giving a free kick or penalty is punished, but relatively lightly. If intent alone is to be punished, at what level should the punishment be set? If we cannot prove that PEDs improve performance should we even be banning them? Should policy which aims to control behaviour and punish transgressors, as in the case of PED controls in sport, precede the proof that what is being punished has actually taken place? This latter point is not a purely hypothetical issue. Some sports regulations accept that competitors may not have intended to cheat and either punish lightly or not at all when intent cannot be proved; others state that a positive finding is sufficient to impose the standard ban even while recognising that 'intent' is often difficult to prove. Discretion in the application of the rules is widespread in various areas of sporting decision-making involving 'intent' and attempts to 'cheat', e.g. a defender (accidentally) handling a ball in the penalty area in football.

WHAT IS WRONG WITH DRUGS THAT AID TRAINING AND HEALING?

One of the supposed problems with some PEDs like the AASs is that they are deemed to aid a faster healing of injuries for the athlete or competitor using them; some studies appear to support this (Stone and Wright, 1993: 15). This may or may not be true. As with other issues relating to the efficacy of AASs, separating out the effects of expectation from what would have been a 'normal' recovery is simply not possible without the implementation of rigorous controlled trials.[5] Even then, as with trials to detect performance enhancement, expectation of effects is almost impossible to prevent. If, however, drugs such as AASs *are* able to prevent sports injuries and/or enable faster healing, it is not clear why this should be deemed a problem. Surely, it points towards the *controlled* use of such drugs for the benefit of health and sport alike? Millar (1996) (on the strength of one medically controlled programme) has suggested that side-effects from steroids can be minimised, whilst benefits to performance enhancement may still be gleaned.[6]

WHAT IS A PED? FOOD, MEDICINES AND UNFAIR ADVANTAGE

If the primary advantage gained by the use of drugs such as anabolic steroids is its enhancement of training – and even then only when it is part of a hard rigorous training programme and specialised dietary regimes, as opposed to some artificial 'quick fix' akin to turning on the turbo on a racing car – how is it to be distinguished from other training aids? What, objectively, constitutes a drug and what constitutes a food or food supplement is far from straightforward (Goodman et al., 1995) and may in fact by IOC doping criteria represent a real ethical problem (Williams, 1994). A professional athlete may legally take the food supplement creatine (which is naturally produced by the body, as is testosterone) as a training aid in order to increase strength and endurance.[7] Carbohydrate loading, the technique whereby an athlete would load up (and thus store reserves) of carbohydrates by eating large portions of pasta and other foods high in carbohydrate in the days before an endurance event, is now a commonly accepted use of the food and dietary approach to competition. Added to this simple dietary process may be the completely legal use of refined carbohydrate pills or drinks, even during activity, which likewise may help optimise the amount of energy going to the muscles. Without carbohydrate loading, the simple act of internally storing appropriate high-grade fuel for the muscles, an athlete can expect to endure less well than if they had not prepared in this way (Bjorkman et al., 1984; Coggan and Coyle, 1989; McConell et al., 1996). The use of vitamin supplements is permitted and yet these supplements may cause harm if too high a dosage is taken, although their proper use may also aid speed of recovery from vigorous training and injury or perhaps maintain or even enhance performance (Bird et al., 1995; Clarkson and Haymes, 1995; Dekkers et al., 1996). The distinction between a food and a drug is not a scientific one (see South, and Ruggiero, Chapters 1 and 8 in this volume). Modern sports competitors legally use many highly refined dietary aids where the purpose is to enhance the ability to train harder, last longer, recover quicker and compete more effectively. These may come in the form of tablets and be unavailable, and unlikely to be used, as normal foodstuffs. Perhaps what should be of primary concern is the *safe* use of performance enhancing aids, whatever their arbitrary scientific classification, rather than continuing to force prohibited and potentially harmful use underground.

TOWARDS THE FUTURE

For the near future, the likely trajectory of drug control policy in sport is in the direction of 'more of the same'. Concerns continue to focus on 'getting it right' (testing, uniformity of practice, the traversing of awkward legal fences) and pursuing PED users with acrimony. If anything, controls will become ever wider and inclusive. A number of sports now punish competitors for recreational drug use under the guise of 'help', even in cases where the police would not have taken action. Many national sporting bodies are lobbying for PEDs to be brought under stricter control or included in existing national drug laws where they are not already covered. However, the direction of drug use and drug control in sport are likely to mirror the concerns and problems of the non-sporting world. The ever-increasing rewards of success in modern sport, and the rising numbers able to reap such rewards, are factors likely to ensure that drug use continues to grow. Getting control right will simply mean drug-using competitors staying one step ahead of the testers. They always have; they probably always will.

NOTES

1. It is not a completely uncontentious concern that a sporting authority should seek to control behaviour and even participation in the interest of the competitor. Individual and concrete cases often belie the simplicity of abstract formulations and ideals such as these. There are numerous examples, at all levels of many sports where non-participation in an event may be to the obvious health benefit of the competitor involved yet no action is taken to prevent that individual taking part. In the 1996 Atlanta Olympic Games, Kelly Holmes was allowed (although she had been advised against it) to run on a hairline fracture above her ankle despite this fact being widely reported and the long-term potential damage being significant. Many athletes over-train, and many endurance competitors maintain diets which leave them undernourished. The potential harms for each and any of these examples can be serious and long term yet the idea of formal controls on them seems unreasonable.
2. In the case of Dianne Modahl, a top British athlete initially found guilty of a positive test for testosterone, it was found, after further investigation, that

the procedures taken by the IOC-accredited laboratory in Lisbon allowed the sample to deteriorate (producing unusually high levels of testosterone). The athlete was finally cleared by both the British Athletics Federation and the International Amateur Athletics Federation of any doping infringement (Bierley, 1996).

3. Proof is sometimes a difficult thing to achieve. In particular, in relation to research on anabolic steroids, it has proved difficult to distinguish between actual effects and those resulting from the research subjects' expectations relating to the use of anabolic steroids. Even for those subjects on double-blind studies the particular side-effects which those on steroids experience mean that the subjects who are receiving the active substance (as opposed to the placebo) are soon aware that this is the case. When this occurs, 'improvements' directly attributable to the anabolic steroids are almost impossible to discern. Improvements are generally small in any case and in some studies the placebo group has even out-performed the group taking the steroids.

4. During a recent international cricket Test match Zimbabwe prevented England from winning the match by effectively not bowling within reach of the England batsmen (*Guardian*, 23 December 1996) regularly enough to prevent too rapid scoring. If they had, they would have been easily beaten. In the end the game ran out of time and was formally drawn. In some senses they literally didn't compete, but they stayed within the rules.

5. Recovery rates for all sorts of health-related problems, from addiction to other chronic illnesses, have often been demonstrated to improve comparatively more quickly for patients who experience either positive encouragement from their practitioner and/or are given treatment (even placebo or 'passive' treatment) than for those who are given little attention or no treatment. Thus we might anticipate that for athletes who expect AASs to heal them more quickly and/or to enable enhanced training, this would commonly result.

6. Improvement is a difficult thing to measure but however it comes about this is what the competitor is after. Appropriately controlled prescribing regimes working hand in hand with medical specialists may provide a safer alternative than *laissez-faire*, non-intervention prohibition.

7. As with anabolic steroids, creatine has been credited with 'providing immediate and significant improvements to athletes involved in explosive sports' (Greenhaff, 1993) through both anecdotal and 'scientific' study. Such claims, however, have recently become less convincing and the level of significance has been reduced to within what might be potentially achieved through expectation. In some instances double-blind trials report no improvement (Murjika et al., 1996).

REFERENCES

Alexander, B.K. and Wong, L.S. (1990) 'Adverse effects of cocaine on the heart: a critical review', in A. Trebach and B. Zeese (eds), *The Great Issues of Drug Policy*. Washington: Drug Policy Foundation.

Bean, P. (1993) 'Cocaine and crack: the promotion of an epidemic', in P. Bean (ed.), *Cocaine and Crack: Supply and Use*. London, Macmillan.

Bierley, S. (1996) 'Modahl verdict leaves IAAF furious with testing laboratory', *Guardian*, 26 March: 24.

Bird, S.R., Wiles, J. and Robbins, J. (1995) 'The effect of sodium bicarbonate ingestion on 1500-m racing time', *Journal of Sports Sciences*, 13 (5): 399–403.

Bjorkman, O., Sahlin, K., Hagenfeldt, F. and Wahren, J. (1984) 'Influence of glucose and fructose ingestion on the capacity for long term exercise in well trained men', *Clinical Physiology*, 4: 483–94.

Bullington, B. (1997) 'America's drug war: fact or fiction?' in R. Coomber (ed.), *The Control of Drugs and Drug Users: Reason or Reaction?* Amsterdam: Harwood.

Clarkson, P.M. and Haymes, E.M. (1995) 'Exercise and mineral status of athletes: calcium, magnesium, phosphane, and iron', *Medicine and Science in Sports and Exercise*, 27 (6): 831–43.

Coggan, A.R. and Coyle, E.F. (1989) 'Metabolism and performance following carbohydrate ingestion late in exercise', *Medicine and Science in Sports and Exercise*, 21: 59–65.

Coomber, R (1993) 'Drugs in sport: rhetoric or pragmatism', *International Journal of Drug Policy*, 4 (4): 169–78.

Coomber, R. (1997) 'Vim in the veins – fantasy or fact: the adulteration of illicit drugs', *Addiction Research*, 5 (3): 195–212.

Coomber, R. (ed.) (1998) *The Control of Drugs and Drug Users: Reason or Reaction?* Amsterdam: Harwood.

Dekkers, C., van-Doornen, L.J.P. and Kemper, H.C.G. (1996) 'The role of anti-oxidant vitamins and enzymes in the prevention of exercise-induced muscle damage', *Sports-medicine*, 21 (3): 213–38.

Ditton, J. and Hammersley, R. (1994) 'The typical cocaine user', *Druglink*, November/December: 11–14.

Donohue, T. and Johnson, N. (1986) *Foul Play: Drug Abuse in Sports*. Oxford: Basil Blackwell.

Duncan, J. (1995) 'Test loopholes leave room for drug cheats', *Guardian*, 4 August: 6.

Evans Schultes, R.E. and Hofmann, A. (1992) *Plants of the Gods: Their Sacred, Healing and Hallucinogenic Powers*. Vermont, VT: Healing Arts Press

Fagan, J. (1990) 'Intoxication and aggression', in M. Tonry and J.Q. Wilson (eds), *Drugs and Crime*. Chicago: Chicago University Press.

Falk, J.L. (1994) 'Drug dependence: myth or motive?' in R. Coomber (ed.), *Drugs and Drug Use in Society: A Critical Reader*. Dartford: Greenwich University Press.

Favre, B. (1996) 'Bitter pill: packer Brett Favre tells SI how the pain of playing in the NFL led to his addiction to painkillers and, nearly, his death', *Sports Illustrated*, 84 (21), 27 May: 24–30.

Feltz, D.L. and Landers, D.M. (1983) 'The effects of mental practice on motor skill learning and performance: a meta analysis', *Journal of Sport Psychology*, 5: 25–57.

Ferstle, J. (1993) 'Evolution and politics of drug testing', in C.E. Yesalis (ed.), *Anabolic Steroids in Sport and Exercise*. Champaign, IL: Human Kinetics.

Fraleigh, W. (1985) 'Performance enhancing drugs in sport: the ethical issue', *Journal of the Philosophy of Sport*, 11: 23–9.

Freeman, B.J.C. and Rooker, G.D. (1995) 'Spontaneous rupture of the anterior cruciate ligament after anabolic steroids', *British Journal of Sports Medicine*, 29 (4): 274–5.

Friedl, K. (1993) 'Effects of anabolic steroids on physical health', in C.E. Yesalis (ed.), *Anabolic Steroids in Sport and Exercise*. Champaign, IL: Human Kinetics.

Goodman, J., Lovejoy, P.E. and Sherratt, A. (eds) (1995) *Consuming Habits: Drugs in History and Anthropology*. London: Routledge.

Greenhaff, P. (1993) 'Update – creative ingestion and exercise performance', *Coaching Focus*, 23, summer: 3–4.

Greider, K. (1995) 'Quieting the crack-kid alarm', *Drug Policy Letter*, summer: 16–21.

Hang, D.W., Bach, B.R. and Bojchuck, J. (1995) 'Partial Achilles tendon rupture following corticosteroid injection: A caveat to practitioners', *Physician and Sports Medicine*, 23 (2): 57–66.

Henry, A. (1994) 'Benetton win one, lose one', *Guardian*, 8 September: 19.

Institute for the Study of Drug Dependence (1993) *Drug Abuse Briefing*, 5th edn. London: ISDD.

Kaplan, J. (1983) *The Hardest Drug: Heroin and Public Policy*. Chicago: University of Chicago Press.

Ljungqvist, A. (1993) Preface to *Procedural Guidelines for Doping Control*. Horsham, West Sussex: International Amateur Athletic Federation.

Lycholat, T. (1993) 'Who says they don't work?', *Coaching Focus*, 23, summer: 9–10.

MacAndrew, C.R. and Edgerton, B. (1969) *Drunken Comportment: A Social Explanation*. Chicago: Aldine.

McConell, G., Kloot, K. and Hargreaves, M. (1996) 'Effect of timing of carbohydrate ingestion on endurance exercise performance', *Medicine and Science in Sports and Exercise*, 28 (10): 1300–4.

May, J.R. and Asken, M.J. (eds) (1987) *Sport Psychology: The Psychological Health of the Athlete*. New York: PMA.

Millar, A.P. (1996) 'Anabolic steroids – a personal pilgrimage', *Journal of Performance Enhancing Drugs*, 1 (1): 4–9.

Miller, R.M. (1991) *The Case for Legalising Drugs*. New York: Praeger.

Murjika, I., Chatard, J., Lacoste, L., Barala, F. and Geyssant, A. (1996) 'Creatine supplementation does not improve spring performance in competitive swimmers', *Medicine and Science in Sports and Exercise*, 28 (11): 1435–41.

Musto, D.F. (1987) *The American Disease: Origins of Narcotic Control*, expanded edn. New York: Oxford University Press.

Parry, D.A. (1996) 'Insulin-like growth factor 1 (IGF1). A new generation of performance enhancement by athletes', *Journal of Performance Enhancing Drugs*, 1 (2): 48–51.

Potter, E. (1989) 'Differential diagnosis of physiological, psychoactive and sociocultural conditions associated with aggression and substance abuse,' *Journal of Chemical Dependency Treatment*, 3 (1): 37–59.

Prokop, L. (1970) 'The struggle against doping and its history', *Journal of Sports Medicine and Physical Fitness*, 10 (1): 45–8.

Rudgley, R. (1993) *The Alchemy of Culture*. London: British Museum Press.

Saper, A. (1974) 'The making of policy through myth, fantasy and historical accident: the making of America's narcotics laws', *British Journal of Addiction*, 69: 183–93.

Sports Council (1990) *Doping Control Information Booklet, No. 1: Anabolic Steroids*. London.

Stone, M.H. and Wright, J.E. (1993) 'Literature review: anabolic-androgenic steroid use by athletes', *National Strength and Conditioning Association Journal*, 15 (2): 10–28.

Tonry, M. and Wilson, J.Q. (eds) (1990) *Drugs and Crime*. Chicago: University of Chicago Press.

Turner, P.E. and Raglin, J.S. (1996) 'Variability in pre-competition anxiety and performance in college track and field athletes', *Medicine and Science in Sports and Exercise*, 28 (3): 378–85.

Uzych, L. (1991) 'Drug testing of athletes', *British Journal of Addiction*, 86: 25–31.

Van Helder, W.P. Kofman, E. and Tremblay, M.S. (1991) 'Anabolic steroids in sport', *Canadian Journal of Sports Science*, 16 (4): 248–57.

WHO (1993) *Drug Use and Sport: Current Issues and Implications for Public Health*. Geneva: World Health Organisation.

WHO/UNICRI (1995) *Cocaine Project: Summary Papers* (March). Geneva: World Health Organisation.

Wightman, G. (1993) 'No dopes in the long run', *Observer*, 24 October: 8.

Williams, M.H. (1994) 'The use of nutritional ergogenic aids in sports: is it an ethical issue?' *International Journal of Sport Nutrition*, 4 (2): 120–31.

Windsor, R.E. and Dumitru, D. (1988) 'Anabolic steroid use by athletes: how serious are the health hazards?', *Postgraduate Medicine*, 84: 37–49.

Woodhouse, C. (1996) 'Arbitration: a necessity for sport?' Conference address at Tackling Ethical Issues in Drugs and Sport, Covent Garden Exhibition Centre, London, 30 October.

Yesalis, C.E. (1993) 'Introduction', in C.E. Yesalis (ed.), *Anabolic Steroids in Sport and Exercise*. Champaign, IL: Human Kinetics.

8

DRUGS AS A PASSWORD AND THE LAW AS A DRUG: DISCUSSING THE LEGALISATION OF ILLICIT SUBSTANCES

Vincenzo Ruggiero

There are no drugs in nature. There are natural poisons, some of which are lethal. The concepts of 'drug' and 'drug dependence' are produced by socially institutionalised definitions. These definitions are based on culture, history, judgement and norms grounded in an elliptic or explicit rhetoric. With this premise, Jacques Derrida (1989) sets off for his journey through the contemporary drug phenomenon, revealing a mixture of curse and blessing, an amalgamation of destruction and *joie de vivre*. Indeed, though it is possible to identify the *nature* of a toxic substance, it must be recognised that not all toxic substances are defined as drugs. The concept of 'drug' cannot genuinely claim scientific status, as it is grounded in political and moral evaluation. In this respect, the word 'drug' conveys a notion of norm and interdiction; it alludes to something from which we intend to distance ourselves: it indicates a social separation. For this reason 'drug' is not a descriptive but an evaluative concept: it is a *password* automatically implying a prohibition.

The fact that in English there is also a medical use of the word 'drug' does not concern me here. Firstly, because this double use, to my knowledge, is not found in any other European language. Secondly, because I am concerned with the relationship between law as an artefact and 'drugs' as a password. When the penal law uses this password, the social separation which the concept of drug entails is exacerbated: the impact can be tremendous. Let us bear in mind Kelsen's (1975) notion of the law as a locus which is devoid of any ontology, an artificial domain where values can never claim universal validity. In the analysis of Kelsen, law is the arena where strategies are devised with a view to impeding forms of violence from emerging. Law is therefore the place where 'claims to peace' can be asserted through injunctions which are peaceful, as law differs from violence. However, law may well resemble that which it claims to regulate, and thus become another form of violence. Girard (1980, 1987) argues that law thrives on a specific form of *disregard*, which is apparent in the inability of society to recognise its own violence. This self-deception manifests itself in the exclusion, separation and social exile of some of its members: all expressions of the sacrificial practices prevailing in modern societies.

The ambivalence of law, which takes the risk of causing damage while trying to avoid or respond to the causation of damage, is associated by Resta (1992) with the ambivalence of violence itself. Violence destroys and renovates, condemns and saves, kills and cures at the same time. This combination is conveyed by the Greek term *pharmakon*, which designates both a poison and an antidote, a drug which causes illness and cures simultaneously. This *pharmakon* or 'drug' allows society to look at its own violence without recognising it as such, its ambivalence making self-deception possible. How the law lacks reflexivity is exemplified by environmental disasters: 'The society that we want to cure is the same that we are destroying; the technology that destroys is the same with which we want to revive it' (Resta, 1992: 18).

I believe that the encounter between 'drug as a password' and 'law as a drug' constitutes the drug problem as we know it today. In the following discussion of drug legalisation and prohibition, the above concepts will be regarded as the inescapable backdrop against which freedom of choice and the causation of harm, which form an apparent antinomy within the drug phenomenon, can be examined. This chapter will chart the key aspects of the legalisation-versus-prohibition debate. It will then discuss the drug issue in relation to individual freedom and social harm. Finally, it will sketch a proposal of drug rehabilitation as a form of compensation to users. Let us first summarise the most relevant arguments of legalisers and prohibitionists respectively (see also South, 1995: vol. 1).

LEGALISERS

Legalisers include conservative, liberal and radical commentators who in one way or another oppose drug-prohibition laws. While all seem to be inspired by the principle that governments should not interfere with individual choice, conservatives emphasise freedom within the market, whereas liberals and radicals focus on the sphere of personal freedom within the broader social context. In an overview provided by Nadelmann (1991), legalisation strategies are located within a wide spectrum which is delimited by two extremes. At one extreme is the view that no institutional control should be imposed on the production and marketing of any drugs, and that the only prohibition should regard the sale of drugs to children. At the other extreme are advocates of total government control on the quality and quantity of drugs produced and of agency monitoring of commercial or state-organised sale. In between lies a strategy in which 'Government makes most of the substances that are now banned legally available to competent adults, exercises strong regulatory powers over all large-scale production and sale of drugs, makes drug-treatment programmes available to all who need them, and offers honest drug-education programmes to children' (Nadelmann, 1991: 19).

Underpinning most legalisation strategies is the belief that drug-related problems such as acquisitive crime, violence, and to a degree 'addiction' itself, are to a large extent the result of drug prohibition rather than drug use *per se*. The availability of natural euphoriants in many Asian countries, it is stressed, did not cause addiction until these countries 'learned' to use them in the way they are used in the developed countries. It is contended that legalising drug use would not increase but reduce drug-related problems. Quality control of the type of drugs made legally available would also foil 'cutting' and dilution with dangerous additives by dealers.

Legalising drug use is consistent with the principle that individual conduct which does not cause harm to others should not be penalised (Manconi, 1991). Moreover, legalisation would spare drug users the experience of prison, which in many cases accelerates drug-using careers, and provides a boost to dealing and trafficking careers (Ruggiero, 1992). As for acquisitive crime fostered by habitual drug use, legalisers argue that if drugs were legal, 'the price would drop dramatically, and most of those who steal and cheat in order to pay for [them] would not have to do so, and some of the worst racketeers in the world would go out of business' (Graham, 1991: 254). It is argued that this was the outcome of the repeal of the US alcohol prohibition laws, an important precedent with which legalisers augment their arguments (Behr, 1995).

Several models of drug legalisation have been suggested. Among these is the idea that producing countries could sell their raw materials to developed countries, with a benefit to the former in terms of employment and profits. 'The establishment of cannabis, opium, and coca as domestic cash crops might eliminate the need for costly farm subsidies, while providing employment for farmers, unskilled labourers, pharmacists, chemists, and retailers' (Karel, 1991: 90). Nevertheless, legalisers agree that advertising of currently illegal drugs should be prohibited. In his study of passive marketing, for example, Caballero (1989) argues that drugs should not be subject to the customary market mechanisms which impose encouragement of demand in order to increase profits. A passive market implies discreet use, strict government control of production and distribution, and prohibition of advertising.

Most of the arguments used by legalisers, however, do not translate into practical proposals as to how legalisation could be structured and brought to bear, but are confined to the elaboration of a number of arguments against prohibitionism. Among the effects of prohibition, for example, legalisers pinpoint the development of a 'barrier strategy'. This strategy imposes on users the consideration of their drug use within a dichotomy separating legal and illegal drugs. This separation renders the hierarchy of risks indistinct, and users are prevented from grasping the significance of the diversity of substances generically labelled as drugs; the diversity of risks related to the ways they administer them; and the diversity of contexts in which they use them (Arnao, 1991). For example, when the United Nations (1987) suggested that the expression 'respons- ible use of drugs' be banned from the official vocabulary, the possibility for users to identify, control and avoid the risks of abuse was implicitly denied or impeded. The barrier strategy delimiting legal and illegal drugs made all the latter equally dangerous, irrespective of quantity, quality, context and mode of administration. One could suggest that such a strategy aims to cause damage to users, who can therefore act as living warnings to young people and novices to stay away from drugs.

Drug prohibition is also viewed as possessing a shadow agenda, in that, for example, the war on drugs gives politicians the opportunity to appear caring and protective, and to manipulate racist and xenophobic fears. Prohibition is said to mobilise activists and to trigger crusades to protect individual or group interests. For example, 'ordinary citizens who take up the drug-control banner can find meaning in political life by participating in reviving what many feel is a threatened moral con- sensus' (Gordon, 1994: 17). In this view, drug prohibition is a political resource or a hidden social programme which transcends the object of its apparent preoccupation. Finally, there are suggestions that the war on drugs is in reality a war declared against the ethnic minorities inhabiting the inner city areas of Western countries, and that racial discrimination is endemic to drug prohibition. In the US, 'The fact that drug dealing in the city, unlike that in the suburbs, often goes on in public areas guarantees that law-enforcement efforts [are] directed at young black and Hispanic men' (Miller, 1996: 81).

PROHIBITIONISTS

In their case against legalisation, Inciardi and McBride (1991) contest the 'enslavement theory' of addiction whereby the illegality of the drug market contributes to the increase in price, thus pushing users into committing property crimes. These authors endorse research which finds that drug use tends to intensify and perpetuate established offending behaviour, rather than initiating criminal careers: 'the evidence suggests that among the majority of street drug users who are involved in crime, their criminal careers were well established prior to the onset of either narcotics or cocaine use' (1991: 55). Against the argument that legalisation would not cause a substantial increase in use, prohibitionists pinpoint the extraordinary power of market systems to create, expand and maintain high levels of demand for any legitimate good.

The assumption that drug use would increase with legalisation leads some prohibitionists to evaluate the potential outcomes in terms of violence, if a free market of what are at present illicit drugs were to be established. According to Goldstein (1985, 1986), there are three types of drug-related violence: the psycho-pharmacologic, the economically compulsive, and the systemic. The first derives from drug use itself, and is part of the effects of some specific drugs, be they legal or illegal. The second type of violence emerges when economically oriented crime committed by drug users becomes increasingly difficult because of property protection and target hardening, forcing users to engage in armed robberies and muggings. The third type of violence is believed to be intrinsic to drug markets, where interactions between suppliers, between users, and between users and suppliers, are said to be embedded in violent forms of regulation. Violence, in sum, is said to be a common sanction for failure to honour contracts that by definition cannot be legally enforced, and is threatened or used to deter fraud, betrayal, theft and dishonesty (Arlacchi, 1996). Prohibitionists embrace these categories and argue that drug legalisation would perhaps cause a decline in systemic violence, which is associated with the illegality of markets, but it would increase psycho-pharmacologic violence, because more people would be using psychoactive drugs. It is also argued that, unless legalisation made drugs freely available to users, property crime would not decline because users would still need funds to buy supplies.

While assuming that drug use is concentrated in inner city areas, prohibitionists argue that this is hardly a reason to legalise drugs, but instead a reason to reject all legalisation proposals. 'Within this context, the legalisation of drugs would be an elitist and racist policy supporting the neocolonialist views of underclass population control' (Inciardi and McBride, 1991: 65). Legalisation, therefore, would be tantamount to a programme of chemical destruction of youth and minorities.

As for the aspects concerning individual freedom of choice, prohibitionists respond to legalisers by adopting the ethical framework provided by John Stuart Mill (1859) and his concepts of liberty and legitimate bases for government intervention. Ironically, these concepts, when applied in a different fashion, can also reinforce the arguments of legalisers, as we shall see later. Prohibitionists stress that government intrusion into personal choice is justifiable when such choice causes harm to others. Acquisitive crime to procure the money necessary to buy drugs is an example of such harm, while legalisation would result in more harm

being suffered by society in general, in terms of physiological, psychological, and private safety costs. 'Society already pays a rather high tariff
as a result of the public health, safety, and violence problems associated
with drug use – both legal and illicit. This would necessarily increase
when levels of drug consumption increase through legalisation' (Inciardi
and McBride, 1991: 69). Against the argument that alcohol and tobacco
cause more deaths than heroin and cocaine, prohibitionists argue that
these legal substances are so lethal precisely *because* they are legal, and
that illegal drugs made more readily available would have the same
effect.

Among prohibitionists, there are various authors who claim that
coercion into drug treatment is likely to be more successful than voluntary treatment (Leukefeld and Tims, 1988). Some of these authors call for
the criminal justice system to intervene at demand level, namely against
users and street dealers. Intervention at street level by law enforcement
agencies is justified by the argument that it is here that small-scale
distribution and user–dealer interactions occur, and that illicit drug use
spreads. Institutional response, in this perspective, is charged with the
task of stopping new users from entering the market and experimenting
with drugs. Moreover, low-level drug enforcement could play a major
role in encouraging users to seek treatment. 'Stated bluntly, it is about
stacking the odds through the threat of penal sanctions so that the drug
user is more likely to recognise that entering some form of treatment is a
rational choice: forcing people to be free, in fact' (Gilman and Pearson,
1991: 117).

As I have argued earlier, the encounter between 'drugs as password'
and 'law as a drug' constitutes part of the drug problem as we know it
today. Embedded in this problem is a selective understanding of the
concept of individual rights on which societies rest. It comes, therefore,
as no surprise that the classics of liberal democracy and liberal law still
inspire most discussions related to prohibitionism and legalisation. It is
exactly in these classics that the root of such selective understanding can
be located.

JOHN STUART MILL: WHOSE LIBERTY?

'The only purpose for which power can be rightfully exercised over any
member of a civilised society against his will is to prevent harm to
others' (Mill, [1859] 1910: 123). In reading this passage, attention should
be focused not so much on the political incorrectness of the word *his* as
on the pompous adjective *civilised*. We shall return to this key word,
which captures in a nutshell the self-infatuation of liberalism, particularly in the Anglo-Saxon world, and whose longevity is as astonishing as
it is unmerited.

The prohibitionist argument relies heavily on Mill's general principle cited above. However, this principle lends itself to a range of interpretations and has affiliates also among legalisers. Let us see why.

Writing during the period of the first alcohol prohibition experiment, promoted by temperance campaigners and conducted in the USA in the 1850s, Mill described the prohibition law as a gross usurpation of the liberty of private citizens and 'an important example of illegitimate interference with the rightful liberty of the individual' ([1859] 1910: 143–5). Nobody, he stressed, should be punished simply for being drunk. The desire to penalise other people's private conduct was viewed by Mill as monstrous, because such desire is propelled by pure resentment of conduct which some regard as distasteful (Zimring and Hawkins, 1992). The legalisers' endorsement of Mill's thought appears to stop here. There are in fact exceptions to Mill's principle, the first of which pertains to children and young persons. Freedom of choice, according to the father of liberal thought, is granted exclusively to human beings in the maturity of their faculties. The other exception, which is implied in the original formulation of the principle, applies to specific individuals who may infringe on the well-being of others as a result of their conduct. The example cited by Mill regards those whose state of inebriety triggers excitement which results in offending behaviour against others. Finally, Mill's principle is suspended in cases in which people sell themselves into slavery, a practice which should be prevented through state intervention.

It should be clear how prohibitionists find an authoritative ally in John Stuart Mill and his general principle. For example, once drug use and violence are indicated as being closely associated, the intervention of the state can easily be advocated on grounds that individual choice leading to drug use has a harmful impact on others (De La Rosa et al., 1990). One has to assume that violence, here, indicates physical harm against others rather than against users themselves, though prohibitionist thought on this issue is far from clear. Prohibitionists may also find support when the second exception to Mill's principle is referred to. This exception applies to persons who are regarded as incapable of free choice, and who must therefore be protected from the harmful behaviour of others whose choice affects them. In this respect, think of the way in which children suffer the consequences of their parents' drug use, or of the potential effect on young persons of drug legalisation. The exception pertaining to individuals selling themselves into slavery can also be mobilised by prohibitionists, particularly if drug abuse is likened to a condition of slavery (as 'addiction') against which institutional intervention is warranted (Kaplan, 1983). Moreover, the prohibitionist perspective is guided by what seems a crucial economic argument, namely that the harm caused by illicit drugs is also to be found in the health expenses to which the state is subjected by users in need of care and therapy, and in the material damage caused by those who finance their drug habit through acquisitive crime. In this perspective, individual choice turns into a burden to others.

There are, finally, important implications in the recourse to Mill's analysis which may explain its appeal to prohibitionists. At the beginning of this section I highlighted the word *civilised* because it is of crucial importance for the understanding of Mill's 'map of liberty'. The author describes and delimits 'who' deserves liberty, and establishes a border between the deserving, namely the civilised, and the undeserving, that is the barbarians. Civilisation distinguishes wealthy and populous nations from savages; it is the opposite of rudeness: 'In a narrow sense, it refers to the ontology of a place – Europe generally, and Great Britain in particular' (Passavant, 1996: 307). It also refers to specific groups and individuals, namely those who are able to engage in a dialogue and pursue 'truth' collectively. Inability to perform dialogically entails the incapacity to exert self-control, to bend impulses to calculation: all characteristics of barbarians. 'The judge, the soldier, the surgeon, the butcher, and the executioner constitute an anomalous category to mediate between civilisation and barbarism; to protect civilisation from its own barbarity' (Passavant, 1996: 309). Hence the justification of state intervention in individual choice: despotism is a legitimate way of dealing with barbarians. Among the circumstances which warrant this legitimacy is the association of illicit drugs with violence, which deserves a brief but specific discussion.

THE 'VIOLENT' METAPHOR

The cause–effect relationship between drug use and violence is extremely difficult to establish, and often violent behaviour is associated less with the choice of using drugs, or with the market in which drugs are available, than with the lifestyle of persons prior to their involvement in the drug economy (Fagan and Chin, 1990). Research findings about the drugs/violence nexus are contrasting and inconclusive, and while in some cases they seem to prove that violent behaviour is related to a state of acute intoxication (Brody, 1990), in others it would appear that the capacity to adopt violent behaviour is a prerequisite for access to drug markets (Hamid, 1990). Violence can also be viewed as one of the elements which are linked less to a drug-using career than to 'street lifecycles', which entail a defensive worldview and a perception of society as exploitative, a place where one is either aggressor or victim (Fleisher, 1995). Violence and drugs, in this perspective, have no cause/effect correlation, but are two of the narrow options available in street lifecycles. Finally, even studies devoted to notoriously violent drug gangs seem to prove that familiarity with violence is achieved outside drug markets, and is sometimes acquired through involvement with institutional politics rather than with psychoactive substances (Gunst, 1995).

However, leaving aside contradictory research findings on this question, the very reason why the drug/violence nexus is so forcibly put forward in many quarters deserves interpretation. This nexus has gained a status of certainty in academic circles, to the point where there seems to be no need for further discussion. Christie (1996) attributes such cases of perfect consensus to the over-socialisation of criminologists within their own discipline. However, looking at how the drugs/violence link is also predominant among the worst of media representations of drug problems, one is faced with a unique example of intellectual consensus between scholars and media representatives, who mutually reinforce their convictions. These convictions can be questioned when the relationship between drugs and firearms is examined. This relationship is viewed with such automatism that it resembles a sociological syllogism, whereby from a logical premise an illogical generalisation is drawn. A similar syllogism was prevalent in the 1960s, when drug use was associated with sex, particularly with orgiastic sex. Examples of this illogical procedure are also offered by Sutherland (1983), who remarked that the study of young offenders from a deprived social environment may lead to the conclusion that white-collar criminals are a figment of people's imagination, because white-collar offenders do not have a deprived background. By the same token, in studying forms of security and of property and business protection, one must reasonably conclude that workers in the world of business have more familiarity with guns than drug dealers. In fact, the possession and use of weapons is indicative of the perception of risk prevailing among different groups, rather than being suggestive of any automatic association of their business activity with them. The use of arms in drugs markets should be examined against the background of the increase in armaments available in society at large. Moreover, it should be borne in mind that the development of the drugs economy was initially hailed by armed robbers as a long-awaited occasion to do away with arms, and that, in a sense, the drug culture may be adopting a gun culture which is also developing elsewhere, at the general level (Campbell, 1990; Ruggiero, 1996a). If concern about the increasingly destructive behaviour of armed dealers is genuine, one wonders why the 'war on drugs' has not been turned into a 'war on arms' (Ruggiero and South, 1995).

The analysis of violence in one specific group cannot be extrapolated from the general context in which 'violence as a resource' is distributed within a society. An assessment of the degree of visibility of the specific type of violence used by different groups, and examination of the benefits that each group gains from the use of its specific form of violence (Levi, 1994; Ruggiero, 1996b) would perhaps put in a different perspective the use of firearms in the drugs economy.

THE *SOCIUS* IMPOSED AND DENIED

Underlying the penalisation of drugs is the tendency to impute to drug misuse all the unpleasant features of contemporary societies. We have seen the example of firearms. It should be added that penalisation also entails a pre-established notion of the public–private dynamic. Users are, in a sense, imputed with the incapacity to engage constructively in the public sphere. Mill regards the capacity to engage in a dialogue as one of the traits of civilised human beings. It is drug users' repetitive behaviour, which does not lead to a dialogical search for truth, that renders them deserving of punishment. Their behaviour leads to irresponsibility and oblivion, which are the exact contrary of the qualities belonging to a disciplined self (Smart, 1984). These qualities, according to Mill, are achieved through work, particularly through the acceptance and internalisation of the division of labour prevailing in manufacturing: the great school of cooperation. However, the uncooperative nature of drug use is imposed by the very definitions of drug and drug dependence. These definitions enter the private sphere of individuals because their choices are charged with a heavy social burden: users' behaviour *must* have implications for others. The variables crime, violence and damage are the artefacts which allow official intervention to impose a *socius* on drug users. In fact, what is prohibited is a type of pleasure which is solitary and desocialising, and which therefore contaminates the *socius*. 'It is pretended that, if that pleasure were purely private, if drug users confined themselves to the use of the sacred right of property on their body and soul, then pleasure, even the most threatening, would be legitimate' (Derrida, 1989: 51). But this is denied *a priori*, because as customers or dealers in the drug market, users' private acts are nonetheless placed in the public sphere. In fact, the public character of drug use is predominant in its forced association with crime and violence, and is implied in the very definition of 'illegal drug', which alludes to a prohibition. However, while the *socius* is imposed on users, it is denied when institutional intervention takes place. In penalising users and dealers, one takes them away from the social arena because they are incapable of engaging in the Platonic pleasure of public dialogue. This reminds us of Robespierre's execution in one of Molière's plays, when the revolutionary asks why he is being punished. The answer is 'because you lack grace'. In other words, Robespierre is executed because he is not a well-formed person (Moore, 1993). He lacks the *socius*, which was never given to him, and which is taken away from him for ever.

PATERNALISM AND HARM

According to Ferrajoli (1989, 1991), drug prohibition promotes a political use of the criminal justice system which is apparent in its propaganda symbols. These symbols are aimed at the mobilisation of consensus, and are less effective in preventing harmful behaviour than in satisfying 'expressions of disapproval' among sections of society. Moreover, the solemnity of the official stigma against drugs shows how the law, which implies a notion of individualism and individual responsibility, is incapable of dealing with those who take individual choice to the extreme. Hence the imposition of an artificial social dimension to unmanageable individual choices.

The prevalence of the symbolic aspect of the law in relation to illicit drugs is based on the notion of harm which, directly or otherwise, is linked to a judgement about the wrongness of drug use. It is also based on a specific hierarchy of harm implying a judgement of values. Behind the condemnation of illicit drugs for the harm they cause to others, lies a condemnation of drug use *per se*. The notion of harm utilised in drug prohibition, in other words, is a 'normative' one, which promotes ideals rather than protecting rights (Feinberg, 1986, 1988). This normative aspect is linked to a particularly paternalistic view of the law which can be detected in proposals for forced treatment of drug abusers.

In a definition suggested by Dworkin (1989), paternalism posits a political community in which individuals are responsible for the well-being of others. Paternalism, therefore, is not inspired by the authoritarian notion which associates law with the will of the majority, and consequently conflates 'the community' with the majority. The paternalist argument is not a winner-take-all argument, but one which appeals to the idea of the community in a more genuinely democratic sense. However, paternalism can be distinguished in two practices and philosophies. Dworkin (1989) suggests that 'volitional paternalism' views coercion as a form of help given to individuals in order for them to achieve what they already want to achieve. 'Critical paternalism', instead, supposes that 'coercion can sometimes provide people with lives that are better than the lives they now think good, and coercion is therefore sometimes in their critical interests' (Dworkin, 1989: 485). The intervention of the criminal justice system against drug abusers is of the second type. However, threats of punishment may corrupt rather than enhance critical judgement in users, as the metaphor of 'law as a drug' discussed above implies. Penal threats may, in fact, persuade individuals that the life they live is better, and that the 'improvement' that such threats allegedly promise are not to be regarded as an improvement at all. It is not easy to justify making people do things against their will. In an example provided by Nagel (1987), if someone wants to pray for the salvation of someone else's soul, the beneficiaries of such prayers cannot complain on the ground that they would prefer a subscription to *Playboy*. The problem arises when someone is forced to attend church and pray instead of staying at home reading *Playboy*. The author distinguishes between two kinds of disagreement: 'one whose grounds make it all right for the majority to use political power in the service of their opinion, and another whose grounds are such that it would be wrong for the majority to do so' (Nagel, 1987: 231).

COMPENSATION AS REHABILITATION

The 'disagreement' of official society with illicit drugs is expressed by its resort to the law which, as suggested at the beginning of this chapter, requires the use of violence in order to counter violence. This sacrificial mechanism is reproduced by popular participation in contemporary societies through the mass media. Canetti (1962) argues that sacrificial murder still involves the participation of crowds, though executions are made public only via newspapers and TV. This makes things easier. Large gatherings are no longer necessary, and crowds can now hide behind the law in order to divide and arrange human beings into opposing groups. The password of 'drugs' seems to respond to such a profound need to divide and oppose. At its root lies the urge to identify and categorise hostile groups and, ultimately, the desire to declare war on some of them (see South, Chapter 1).

The 'disagreement' of official society with 'illegal' drugs appears, also, to be based on a naturalistic view of humans: prohibitionists posit a pure, uncontaminated individual who achieves happiness without resorting to artificial euphoriants. However, such a naturalistic view is, in a sense, shared by legalisers, especially those who would support a 'supermarket model' of legal drug sale whereby drugs are purchased like chocolate. These types of legalisers regard mood-altering substances as part and parcel of human needs, these substances being known, in one form or another, to all traditional societies. Surely, when the social effects of both drug misuse and drug prohibition are examined, these compatible views sound inappropriate. Against this background of the debate between legalisation and prohibition proponents, I would like to propose a model of *compensation* due to users.

In most European countries, we are now faced with a situation in which it is not so much drug use which is penalised, as drug intoxication. This is so because many users escape institutional attention and tend to retain their drug-using habit undetected for years, some of them for a lifetime. Users who are known to official agencies are generally unable to manage their drug use in a safe environment, or to combine such use with other commitments which, in a sense, would dilute their using career. The accumulation of a number of social disadvantages leads them to intoxication, and hence to increasing involvement in the illicit market of drugs, and inevitably to penalisation. They are apprehended, and often punished, because of the cumulative effect of such disadvantages, because of their visibility and vulnerability. They are punished for their state of intoxication, and for their low status in the drugs economy, rather than for their acts.

Compensation should be devised for such users, in the form of a range of possibilities open to them. These should include resources to establish self-managed projects aimed to redress the balance caused by their disadvantages. Options should include the possibility of obtaining voluntary therapy, to decide independently to abstain, but also to receive drugs on a maintenance basis. These self-managed projects should be regarded as something which is due to vulnerable users because of the shared societal responsibility for causing their vulnerability. Official society would otherwise be indictable for crimes of omission, as in other cases where vulnerable individuals are denied vital help. I am talking here of giving such users the resources to make decisions about themselves and, as in the 'volitionist' approach described above, *giving them help to achieve that which they already want to achieve.*

This proposal is an implicit rejection of a political use of the law, and presupposes that legislative intervention should elevate social conflicts to the level of non-violent processes (Ricoeur, 1995). Legislation should be inspired by the notion of *capacity*, namely it should make individuals capable of acting, choosing, speaking, and taking responsibility for their own actions. In other words, legislation should aim to provide drug users with the capacity to recognise the effects of their actions as their own, and thus to recognise themselves as agents. This notion of the law excludes punishment, by definition. If those involved in the drug scene are to gain a dialogical capacity to identify the effects of their own actions, they also 'need continuous forms of mediation in their interpersonal relationships and some forms of institutional representation which give them the real power and the related rights' (Ricoeur, 1995: 33). Currently, punishment annuls this dialogical capacity, it constrains interpersonal relationships and eventually abolishes institutional representation to which rights are ultimately linked. Drug abusers should be compensated for having acquired their state, by the restitution of this capacity.

REFERENCES

Arlacchi, P. (1996) 'Some observations on illegal markets'. Paper presented at ESRC Crime and Social Order in Europe Conference, Manchester, 7–10 September.

Arnao, G. (1991) 'Perché legalizzare la droga significa ridurne la pericolosità', in L. Manconi (ed.), *Legalizzare la droga. Una ragiovevole proposta di sperimentazione.* Milan: Feltrinelli.

Behr, E. (1995) *L'Amérique hors-la-loi. La folle épopée de la Prohibition.* Paris: Plon.

Brody, S.L. (1990) 'Violence associated with acute cocaine use in patients admitted to a medical emergency department', in M. De La Rosa, E.Y. Lambert and B. Gropper (eds), *Drugs and Violence: Causes, Correlates, and Consequences.* Rockville, MD: National Institute on Drug Abuse.

Caballero, F. (1989) *Droit de la drogue.* Paris: Précis Dalloz.

Campbell, D. (1990) *That Was Business, This is Personal: The Changing Faces of Professional Crime.* London: Secker & Warburg.

Canetti, E. (1962) *Crowds and Power.* London: Victor Gollancz.

Christie, N. (1996) 'Four blocks against insight. Notes on the oversocialisation of criminologists', *Theoretical Criminology,* 1 (1): 13–23.

De La Rosa, M., Lambert, E.Y. and Gropper, B. (eds) (1990) *Drugs and Violence: Causes, Correlates and Consequences.* Rockville, MD: National Institute on Drug Abuse.

Derrida, J. (1989) *Rhétorique de la drogue.* Paris: Autrement.

Dworkin, R. (1989) 'Liberal community', *California Law Review,* 77 (3): 479–87.

Dworkin, G. (ed.) (1994) *Morality, Harm and the Law.* Boulder, CO: Westview Press.

Fagan, J. and Chin, K. (1990) 'Violence as regulation and social control in the distribution of crack', in M. De La Rosa, E.Y. Lambert and B. Gropper (eds), *Drugs and Violence: Causes, Correlates and Consequences.* Rockville, MD: National Institute on Drug Abuse.

Feinberg, J. (1986) *Harm to Self.* New York: Oxford University Press.

Feinberg, J. (1988) *Harmless Wrongdoing.* New York: Oxford University Press.

Ferrajoli, L. (1989) *Diritto e ragione.* Rome and Bari: Laterza.

Ferrajoli, L. (1991) 'Proibizionismo e diritto', in L. Manconi (ed.), *Legalizzare la droga. Una ragiovevole proposta di sperimentazione.* Milan: Feltrinelli.

Fleisher, M.S. (1995) *Beggars & Thieves: Lives of Urban Street Criminals.* Wisconsin: University of Wisconsin Press.

Gilman, M. and Pearson, G. (1991) 'Lifestyles and law enforcement', in D.K. Whynes and P. Bean (eds), *Policing & Prescribing. The British System of Drug Control.* London: Macmillan.

Girard, R. (1980) *La violenza e il sacro.* Milan: Adelphi.

Girard, R. (1987) *Il capro espiatorio.* Milan: Adelphi.

Goldstein, P.J. (1985) 'The drugs–violence nexus: a tripartite conceptual framework', *Journal of Drug Issues,* 15: 493–506.

Goldstein, P.J. (1986) 'Homicide related to drug traffic', *Bulletin of the New York Academy of Medicine,* (June) 62: 509–16.

Gordon, D.R. (1994) *The Return of the Dangerous Classes: Drug Prohibition and Policy Politics.* New York: W.W. Norton.

Graham, G. (1991) 'Criminalisation and control', in D.K. Whynes and P.T. Bean (eds), *Policing & Prescribing. The British System of Drug Control.* London: Macmillan.

Gunst, L. (1995) *Born Fi' Dead: A Journey through the Jamaican Posse Underworld.* Edinburgh: Payback Press.

Hamid, A. (1990) 'The political economy of crack-related violence', *Contemporary Drug Problems,* 17: 31–78.

Inciardi, J.A. and McBride, D.C. (1991) 'The case *against* legalisation', in J.A. Inciardi (ed.), *The Drug Legalisation Debate*. Newbury Park, CA: Sage.

Kaplan, J. (1983) *The Hardest Drug: Heroin and Public Policy.* Chicago: University of Chicago Press.

Karel, R.B. (1991) 'A model legalisation proposal', in J.A. Inciardi (ed.), *The Drug Legalisation Debate.* Newbury Park, CA: Sage.

Kelsen, H. (1975) *La dottrina pura del diritto.* Turin: Einaudi.

Leukefeld, C.G. and Tims, F.M. (eds) (1988) *Compulsory Treatment of Drug Abuse: Research and Clinical Practice.* Rockville, MD: National Institute on Drug Abuse.

Levi, M. (1994) 'Violent crime', in M. Maguire, R. Morgan and R. Reiner (eds), *The Oxford Handbook of Criminology.* Oxford: Clarendon Press.

Manconi, L. (1991) 'Limitare la sofferenza. Per un programma di riduzione dei danni', in L. Manconi (ed.), *Legalizzare la droga. Una ragionevole proposta di sperimentazione.* Milan: Feltrinelli.

Mill, J.S. ([1859] 1910) 'On Liberty', in *Utilitarianism, Liberty and Representative Government.* New York: Dutton.

Miller, J.G. (1996) *Search and Destroy: African–American Males in the Criminal Justice System.* Cambridge: Cambridge University Press.

Moore, M. (1993) *Act and Crime: The Philosophy of Action and its Implications for Criminal Law.* Oxford: Clarendon Press.

Nadelmann, E.A. (1991) 'The case for legalisation', in J.A. Inciardi (ed.), *The Drug Legalisation Debate.* Newbury Park, CA: Sage.

Nagel, T. (1987), 'Moral conflict and political legitimacy', *Philosophy and Public Affairs Journal*, 16 (3): 215–34.

Passavant, P.A. (1996) 'A moral geography of liberty: John Stuart Mill and American free speech discourse', *Social & Legal Studies*, 5: 301–20.

Resta, E. (1992) *La certezza e la speranza: saggio su diritto e violenza.* Rome and Bari: Laterza.

Ricoeur, P. (1995) *Le Juste.* Paris: Esprit.

Ruggiero, V. (1992) *La roba: economie e culture dell'eroina.* Parma: Pratiche.

Ruggiero, V. (1996a) *Economie sporche: l'impresa criminale in Europa.* Turin: Bollati Boringhieri.

Ruggiero, V. (1996b) 'Falling revenues of violence', *Science as Culture*, 5 (25): 627–31.

Ruggiero, V. and South, N. (1995) *Eurodrugs: Drug Use, Markets and Trafficking in Europe.* London: UCL Press.

Smart, C. (1984) 'Social policy and drug addiction: a critical study of policy development', *British Journal of Addiction*, 79: 31–9.

South, N. (ed.) (1995) *Drugs Crime and Criminal Justice Vols 1 and 2.* Aldershot: Dartmouth.

Sutherland, E. (1983) *White-Collar Crime: The Uncut Version.* New Haven, CT: Yale University Press.

United Nations (1987) *The UN and Drug Abuse Control.* New York: United Nations.

Zimring, F.E. and Hawkins, G. (1992) *The Search for Rational Drug Control.* Cambridge: Cambridge University Press.

CONCLUSION

9

TAKING TEA WITH NOEL: THE PLACE AND MEANING OF DRUG USE IN EVERYDAY LIFE

Michael Shiner and Tim Newburn

In 1932 Aldous Huxley detailed his vision of the future. His was a world turned upside down, a World State where the privileged elite were conditioned into the virtues of a powerful hallucinogen called soma. In this world;

> if ever by some unlucky chance such a crevice of time should yawn in the solid substance of their distractions, there is always *soma*, delicious *soma*, half a gramme for a half holiday, a gramme for a weekend, two grammes for a trip to the gorgeous East, three for a dark eternity on the moon. (Huxley, 1932: 49)

Time has blunted the revolutionary nature of Huxley's vision. Apparently ever increasing levels of use have challenged the traditional image of drugs as something associated with subterranean cultures and, as we approach the end of the current millennium, some have been tempted into suggesting that we are witnessing the emergence of a 'Rave new world' (Paphides, 1997). Certainly, there is an emerging orthodoxy among some academics, policy-makers and other social commentators which emphasises the extent to which drug use has become a 'normalised' activity for young people. It has even been suggested that this process of normalisation reflects the development or emergence of a new, postmodern, social order.

This chapter presents a critique of this view. In challenging the link that is often made between drug use and postmodernity, we will argue against the claim that illicit drug use has become a normalised feature of everyday life for young people. Throughout the chapter the focus is on youth. This, as we will see, reflects both the nature of current debates and the realities of contemporary drug use: young people are, without doubt, the prime users of illicit drugs.

THE NORMALISATION OF DRUG USE

When considering the place and meaning of drug use in the late twentieth century, the events of January 1997 provide a useful starting point. The New Year revelry had barely died down when Brian Harvey, then a member of the British band East 17, decided to speak openly about his drug use, expressing the view that Ecstasy was a safe drug 'which makes you a better person' (*Evening Standard*, 31 January 1997). There was an immediate backlash against Harvey. He was criticised by the Prime Minister in the House of Commons, furiously condemned by much of the media, and isolated by the pop-music establishment. East 17's records were banned by several radio stations and Harvey was sacked by the group. Having a sex, drugs and rock'n'roll lifestyle is one thing; suggesting that it might actually be good for you appears to be quite another.

Although the official reaction to Harvey's comments was swift and retributive, there was an alternative view. Amidst the fulminating rage and condemnation, Noel Gallagher, pop icon and mastermind of super-group Oasis, made the following statement to the press:

> As soon as people realise that the majority of people in this country take drugs, then the better off we'll all be . . . Drugs is like getting up and having a cup of tea in the morning. (*New Musical Express* 29 January 1997)

The response to this statement was mixed. On the one hand there were those predictably outraged voices who, whilst refusing to pay attention to what Gallagher actually said, condemned him as yet another pop star abusing his status as a hero to the young. Thus, perhaps understandably following the Ecstasy-related death of his daughter, Leah Betts' father argued:

> There are no ifs and buts about this. People in his position, who are looked upon as gods by young people, can't go around making these sort of remarks. It means more young people will grow up thinking taking drugs is perfectly acceptable and normal. (*Evening Standard*, 31 January 1997)[1]

In addition to the outrage, however, Gallagher also received considerable support for his intervention, some of it from unlikely quarters. In an article in the London *Evening Standard* (31 January 1997) entitled 'Why Noel is right about drugs', A.N. Wilson, the normally conservative commentator, wrote:

whatever we would like to be the case, what he says is actually right. For the generation under the age of 40, drug-taking *is* normal. You do not need to watch 'concerned' television documentaries about housing estates in the North of England where tabs of LSD change hands for less than a small round of drinks, nor to watch police raids at 'raves' where the dancers have all taken Ecstasy, to know this is the case.

Though using rather different language, both Noel Gallagher and A.N. Wilson were articulating what has become a standard discourse about young people and drug use. Such a discourse is by no means the exclusive property of pop stars and iconoclastic journalists who operate outside the mainstream. It reflects a view which has, in recent years, emerged as a virtual orthodoxy among many academics and professionals working in the drugs field.

NORMALISATION AND POSTMODERNITY

As the key contributors to the development of the 'normalisation thesis', Howard Parker and colleagues have offered what is perhaps the most telling observation in the recent sociology of drug use. The most straight-forward summary of their thesis was provided by the claim that 'for many young people taking drugs has become the norm' and the prediction that 'over the next few years, and certainly in urban areas, non drug-trying adolescents will be a minority group. In one sense they will be the deviants' (Parker et al., 1995: 26).

The process of normalisation has been viewed as a relatively recent phenomenon and one which is indicative of the emergence of a post-modern era. In this context the concept of postmodernity:

> is concerned with whether 'advanced' post-industrial societies such as the UK are reshaping into a new formation that is so different from that which was the UK in the 1960s and 70s that we can usefully talk about the end of an epoch rather than the evolution and development of the same sort of social structure. (Parker et al., 1995: 23)

According to these authors Britain, as a postmodern state, has become characterised by the fracturing of moral authority, increasing global-isation, an emphasis on consumption rather than production, and a reshaping of class and gender relationships. The perceived growth of middle-class drug use and the narrowing of the gender gap in drugs consumption have led them to the conclusion that:

> perhaps drugs *consumption* best depicts what is under way; for illegal drugs have become products which are grown, manufactured, packaged and mar-keted through an enterprise culture whereby the legitimate and illicit markets have merged. (Parker et al., 1995: 25)

While the main proponents of normalisation have drawn on a rich seam of social theory, they have been fairly narrow in their focus. For authors, such as Lyotard (1984), who have developed the notion of postmodernity, the abandonment of grand narratives, the declining power of the nation-state and the development of new, more atomised communities represents a significant break with the past. Other commentators, while recognising that significant changes have taken place, are more sceptical of the notion of a 'postmodern society'. Reluctant to posit a radical departure from modernity, they talk, for example, of 'high' or 'late modernity' (Giddens, 1990, 1991) or 'reflexive modernisation' (Beck, 1992; Beck et al., 1994). For these authors it is not appropriate to talk of revolutionary or epochal social change. Kumar (1995) has argued, however, that there is an underlying consensus among these authors about the key features of contemporary industrial societies and that this makes some of the debate about the status of the transformation – the idea of historical stage or period – less crucial. While we have some sympathy with this view, the debate about the nature of social change is relevant to the debate about youthful drug use. As it has been constructed the normalisation thesis rests on the idea of fundamental social change. Thus, if the idea of a radical break, or epochal change, is questioned, this immediately raises doubts about how significant or radical consequent changes in drug use may have been.

In order to locate the place and meaning of drug use in everyday life, we shall focus on three questions. Firstly, how common is illicit drug use? Secondly, how have levels of illicit drug use changed over time? And, thirdly, what are people's attitudes to illicit drug use? In challenging the normalisation thesis we will suggest that claims about the extent, and the normative context of, youthful drug use are exaggerated and inaccurate. In this regard, we suggest that Pearson's (1983) notion of 'respectable fears' – longstanding fears of moral degeneracy associated with young people – provides a useful framework from which the discourse about 'normalisation' can be understood.

THE DATA

In this chapter we draw on four surveys, two from Britain and two from the United States of America:

The 1994 British Crime Survey (hereafter BCS): is a nationally representative survey covering the population of England and Wales aged 16 and above (Ramsay and Percy, 1996).

The 1992 Youth Lifestyle Survey (hereafter YLS): is based on a nationally representative sample of young people in England and Wales aged 14–25 (Graham and Bowling, 1995).

The 1995 National Household Survey on Drug Abuse (hereafter NHSDA): is based on a nationally representative sample of the United States population aged 12 and above (Gfroerer et al., 1996).

The 1995 Monitoring the Future Study (MTF): is a school-based survey based on a representative sample of eighth-, tenth- and twelfth-grade students in the United States (ISR, 1996).

This strategy was developed for two principal reasons. Firstly, employing multiple sources of data for each country afforded us greater confidence in identifying general patterns. As Gfroerer et al. (1996) noted, 'the interpretation of the NHSDA data is best made when studied in conjunction with other available data sources, taking into account the strengths and limitations of each source'. It is also worth noting their view that, despite the different samples, 'the NHSDA results are consistent with the results of the Monitoring the Future Study'. Secondly, in thinking about the broader questions raised by theories of postmodernity, making use of data from Britain and America allowed us to move our focus beyond the boundaries of one nation-state and to consider the extent to which transnational or global processes are visible. In addition, as will become clear, in one very important respect, the American data go well beyond the British data and allow a more thorough evaluation of the link between theories of postmodernity and drug use. In using British and American data we do not wish to suggest, however, that they provide the basis for reliable, detailed comparison between the two countries. The surveys were conducted independently of each other and were not designed to allow cross-cultural comparison. They do, nevertheless, enable us to talk confidently about broad patterns of drug use in the two countries.[2]

PATTERNS OF ILLICIT DRUG USE BY YOUNG PEOPLE

On both sides of the Atlantic illicit drug use is strongly linked to age. In Britain, repeated surveys have shown that, although rare during the early teens, use of drugs increases sharply during the next couple of years so that the late teens and early twenties are consistently found to be peak periods of illicit drug use (ISDD, 1994). They have also shown that, for young people, having used an illicit drug can no longer be accurately described as uncommon.

Figure 9.1 summarises the relationship between age and illicit drug use and reveals a number of interesting trends: it shows that illicit drug use is notably more prevalent among young people than older people and it reveals that recency of use is also related to age. Thus, the proportion of ever-users who had not used an illicit substance during the previous month or year increases as one moves up the age scale,

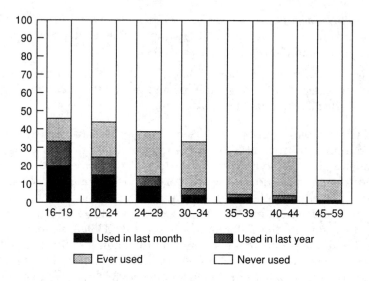

FIGURE 9.1 *Use of illicit drugs in Britain by age (percentages) (Graham and Bowling, 1995)*

indicating an increase in the ratio of ex- to current users. Ostensibly, the data on prevalence and recency lend a certain credence to the normalisation thesis. However, the figure illustrates a *third* trend, and one which is more challenging in this regard. Whilst illicit drug use is clearly more prevalent among the younger than older age groups, this should not blind us to the fact that for none of the categories shown in Figure 9.1 do users outnumber non-users. Even among 16–19-year-olds, the category with the largest proportion of drug users, 54 per cent of respondents had never used an illicit drug at *any* point in their lives. Similarly, the YLS indicates that 64 per cent of 14–25-year-olds had never used an illicit drug (Graham and Bowling, 1995).

The figures quoted above are all based on lifetime measures. That is, they indicate the proportion of people who say they have ever used an illicit drug at any point in their lives. The extent to which such lifetime measures illuminate patterns of drug use is clearly limited. It has, for example, been noted elsewhere (Shiner and Newburn, 1997) that such measures fail to distinguish between current and ex-users. In Britain, estimates of current use have tended to be based on behaviour during the previous year (Graham and Bowling, 1995). Using such a measure, the 1994 BCS indicates that 34 per cent of 16–19-year-olds, and 25 per cent of 20–24-year-olds are current users of illicit drugs. Broadly consistent with this, the YLS points to a level of current use of 24 per cent among the nation's 14–25-year-olds. In contrast to British practice, American researchers have tended to use behaviour during the previous month as the basis for estimates of current use (Gfroerer et al., 1996).

Within this more conservative tradition, the 1994 BCS indicates that 20 per cent of 16–19-year-olds and 15 per cent of 20–24-year-olds are current users. Whichever measure is used, however, apparent levels of current drug use among young people are hardly consistent with a claim of normalisation.[3]

Shifting our focus to America we see reasonably similar patterns. The 1995 MTF indicates that 41 per cent of 15–16-year-old high school students had used an illicit drug at some point in their lives, 33 per cent had done so in the previous year and 20 per cent had done so in the previous month. The equivalent figures for those aged 17–18 are 48, 39 and 24 per cent. Findings from the NHSDA are broadly consistent with those from the MTF survey. Gfroerer et al. (1996) reported that, by 1995, nearly half of those aged 21–25 had tried an illicit drug. They went on to note that levels of current use were highest amongst 16–20-year-olds. Of those aged 16–17, 16 per cent had used an illicit drug during the month before the 1995 NHSDA and this compared with 18 per cent of 18–20-year-olds. Once again, whichever measure is used, the levels of current use uncovered by the MTF survey and the NHSDA do little to support the contention that youthful drug use is a normalised feature of contemporary post-industrial societies.

So far in this discussion we have not made any distinction between different types of drug. This approach obviously simplifies the choices that young people make. If we start to make such distinctions, the picture becomes more complicated. Table 9.1 considers the extent to which cannabis and each of the 'dance' drugs (LSD, amphetamines and Ecstasy) have become an established part of mainstream British youth culture.

Cannabis has been included in the table because of its undoubted status as Britain's most popular illicit drug (ISDD, 1994), and the 'dance' drugs have been included because of their centrality to the normalisation thesis. Parker et al. (1995: 24) suggested that 'the arrival of the "rave" and "pay party" scene in the late 1980s was the watershed whereby drugs moved from subculture status to become part of mainstream youth culture'. A similar, albeit more florid view, was recently expressed by Collin and Godfrey (1997: 264), authors of *Altered State: The Story of Ecstasy Culture and Acid House*:

TABLE 9.1 *Use of cannabis and 'dance' drugs by young people in Britain (percentage of users)*

	16–19-year-olds			14–25-year-olds	
	Ever used	Used in last year	Used in last month	Ever used	Used in last year
Cannabis	36	29	18	33	22
Amphetamines	15	10	6	9	5
LSD	12	8	3	9	5
Ecstasy	8	5	2	7	4

Sources: Ramsay and Percy, 1996: 84–9; Graham and Bowling, 1995: 14

Fifteen years after the first Britons were introduced to MDMA on hedonistic excursions into New York nightlife and a decade after house music emerged from the black gay clubs of Chicago, the synthesis of the two had produced the largest youth cultural phenomenon that Britain had ever seen. Ecstasy culture had become the primary leisure activity for British youth, seamlessly integrated into the fabric of the weekend ritual.

Despite this emphasis on Ecstasy, the 1994 BCS indicates that, in terms of current use, amphetamines are the most popular 'dance' drug and the second most popular of all illicit drugs among young Britons.[4] For those aged 16–19, however, the rate of lifetime amphetamine use is well below half the rate for cannabis use. Shorter time frames point to an even more extreme difference so that, for this age group, current amphetamine use stands at a third of the level of current cannabis use. This pattern holds regardless of which method is used to estimate 'current use'. While use of 'dance' drugs may have increased during the late 1980s and early 1990s (Measham et al., 1993), it tended to do so from a very low baseline (Clements, 1993). Claims that such an activity has become an established part of mainstream British youth culture therefore seem misplaced. The BCS indicates that even the most popular 'dance' drug has only ever been used by one in six people by the time they become 16–19 years old, that only one in ten of this age group have used it during the previous year and only about one in seventeen have done so during the previous month. Furthermore, although cannabis is by far the most widely used illicit drug in Britain, we should recognise that even among young people its use is a minority activity. This is particularly true if we focus on levels of current use. Data from the 1994 BCS concerning patterns of use during the previous year indicate that, despite its status as the nation's favourite illicit drug, less than a third of 16–19-year-olds are current cannabis users. If we employ the more conservative estimate based on use in the previous month then less than a fifth of 16–19-year-olds are defined as current cannabis users. Although this commentary has focused exclusively on the BCS, very similar patterns are evident from the YLS.

Before moving on to the American context it is worth noting that, within Britain, use of what are frequently thought of as 'hard' drugs is very rare. According to the 1994 BCS three in 100 people aged 16–24 have ever used cocaine at some point in their lives, fewer than one in 100 have used heroin, and fewer than one in 200 have used crack. According to the YLS, two in 100 people aged 14–25 have used cocaine, one in 100 have used crack and the same number have used heroin.

Using information from the 1995 MTF survey, Table 9.2 presents prevalence information for the most widely used illicit drugs in America.[5]

For reasons already discussed, we must be careful when making comparisons between Britain and America on the basis of the information that is available to us. Bearing this in mind, however, the data contained in Tables 9.1 and 9.2 point to a number of important similarities

TABLE 9.2 *Use of selected illicit drugs by 17–18-year-old American high school students (percentage of users)*

	Ever used	Used in last year	Used in last month[6]
Cannabis	42	35	21
LSD	12	8	4
Cocaine	6	4	–
Opiates other than heroin	7	5	–
Amphetamines	15	9	–
Sedatives	8	5	–
Tranquillisers	7	4	–

Source: ISR, 1996

between the youth drugs cultures in the two countries.[7] In America, as in Britain, for instance, cannabis is by far the most widely used illicit drug by young people. As in Britain its use, particularly its current use, is a minority activity. Although it appears that there are some similarities between the British and American youth drugs cultures, there also appear to be some notable differences. While use of cocaine is very unusual in Britain, the 1995 MTF survey indicates that approximately one in seventeen American high school students aged 17–18 has used this drug and three out of 100 of them have used it in the form of crack. While barbiturates, tranquillisers and opiates other than heroin are a relatively common part of the American drugs scene there are no equivalent categories in the British surveys with which the levels of use can be compared. Nevertheless, the central messages from the American data are the same as those from the British data: a large proportion of young people have never used an illicit drug; among those who have done so, it is cannabis use that continues to dominate; and, if more subtle measures than 'ever use' are employed, then it becomes very clear that claims that illicit drug use is a normalised feature of postmodern youth culture are clearly exaggerated.

TRENDS IN ILLICIT DRUG USE BY YOUNG PEOPLE

Within the British context, surveys have provided some support for the frequently made claim that youthful drug use is on the increase. Mott and Mirrlees-Black (1993), for instance, noted that the percentage of 16–19-year-olds reporting cannabis use more than doubled between 1983 and 1991. Similarly, a 1992 survey of 15–24-year-olds, which replicated a 1989 survey, reported a virtual doubling of the percentage of respondents admitting drug use (Clements, 1993; Measham et al., 1993). Nevertheless the discussion of trends over time has been hindered by a lack of comprehensive data and it has only been in the 1990s that the British

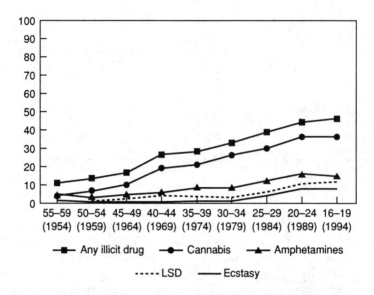

FIGURE 9.2   *Lifetime use of illicit drugs in Britain by age group (percentage of users) (Ramsay and Percy, 1996)*

government has begun to coordinate the systematic and regular collection of detailed data concerning the prevalence of illicit drug use.

In the absence of detailed longitudinal data, cross-sectional data can be used to make some comments about likely changes in the nature of British drug use over the last forty years. Figure 9.2 presents data from the 1994 BCS and shows the proportions of various age groups who reported lifetime use of various illicit drugs.[8] The figures in brackets under the age categories refer to the year in which the respondents of a given age were in their late teens (i.e. 16–19), a period which is generally recognised as being a time of peak drug use (ISDD, 1994). In suggesting that these data can be used to reflect upon trends in young people's drug use we have assumed that for most older drug users their use of illicit substances was restricted to their youth. This is, we would argue, a reasonable assumption. Illicit drug use has been closely associated with youth subcultures since the hippie counter-culture of the 1960s (Young, 1971) and much of what we know points to a situation where drug use is, primarily, a youthful activity. The patterns noted in the discussion following Figure 9.1, for example, whereby the ratio of ex- to current users increases with age is consistent with the suggestion that, for many older 'drug users', illicit drug use is something that was limited to their youth.[9]

Although Figure 9.2 offers some support for the normalisation thesis, it also raises very significant questions. In general terms, it points to a fairly dramatic increase in drug use by British youth during the second half of the twentieth century. More specifically, it charts the emergence and growth of the 'rave' scene and its related drug use, namely the introduction, and growing popularity, of Ecstasy from the early to mid-1980s and the growth of LSD use during the same period. Nonetheless, while the popularity of LSD and Ecstasy appears to have increased reasonably sharply since 1980 the extent to which these drugs have entered the mainstream of British youth culture remains very limited. More important to the argument made here is the point that in terms of overall drug use there is little in Figure 9.2 to indicate any marked or radical break between one period and another. Overall, changing patterns of drug use appear to have taken the form of a fairly steady increase. The trend suggested by Figure 9.2 is one of evolution over an extended period rather than of a sharp, fundamental structural shift. The British data that are available do not support the contention that changes in patterns of drug use since the 1950s are indicative of major epochal change.

The American context enables us to test these ideas further. The MTF survey allows us a certain degree of confidence when considering the ways in which patterns of drug use have evolved over time. This survey has been administered annually since the mid-1970s and Figure 9.3 summarises how levels of reported drug use by 17–18-year-old American high school students have changed since then. In general terms Figure 9.3 is based on the same substances as were included in Table 9.2. In the interests of clarity, however, opiates other than heroin have been omitted,

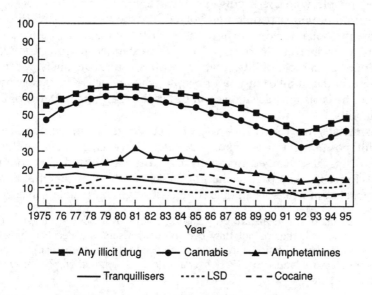

FIGURE 9.3 *Changing patterns of drug use among 17–18-year-old American high school students (percentage of lifetime users) (ISR, 1996)*

as have sedatives. Sedatives have been excluded because the pattern followed, almost identically, that of tranquillisers. Opiates other than heroin have been omitted because, in absolute terms, there was little variability in levels of use: within the period covered by the survey, use of opiates other than heroin peaked in 1977 and 1985 at 10 per cent and hit a low of 6 per cent in 1992.

If the time frame is limited to the period since 1992 then the MTF indicates that there has been an increase in illicit drug use by young Americans. If, however, we take a broader historical perspective then it is clear that this increase is a relatively new phenomenon. The MTF indicates that levels of youthful drug use in the mid-1990s were broadly equivalent to those that existed some twenty years earlier and were notably lower than those that existed in the late 1970s and early 1980s. The downward trend in drug use by young Americans throughout the 1980s undermines the suggestion that increased drug use is a necessary feature of the postmodern condition. Moreover, we should note that this experience of reduced levels of drug use was not limited to America. Silbereisen et al. (1995, 490) found that: 'since 1980, there has been a decrease in the use of both alcohol and drugs among young people in the United States and some European countries, although levels are still far from negligible, and seem to be growing in some areas'.

Following the emphasis of most commentators with an interest in the prevalence of drug use, the discussion presented so far has focused on the proportion of young people who are saying 'yes' to drugs. We also believe, however, that explicit consideration should be given to those young people who are saying 'no'. In America, as we have seen, the proportion of young people uninvolved in drug use increased throughout the previous decade. Turning to the British context, while Figure 9.2 points to an increase in drug use over an extended period, it is worth considering the possibility that there has, simultaneously, been an increase in the number of young people who are actively saying 'no' to drugs. The basis for this suggestion lies in the changing patterns of drug availability.

Historically, the relative scarcity of illicit drugs has made non-use the default position for most young people. However, the availability of illicit drugs has changed markedly over the past two decades (South, 1997). Indeed, a key part of the normalisation thesis is an emphasis on the presence of drugs as an everyday part of young people's lives:

> Adolescents of the 1990s are growing up in and with this new level of drug availability. Whether or not they become drug users is a decision based on personal and peer choice since the availability of drugs is a *normal* part of the leisure-pleasure landscape. (Parker et al., 1995: 25, original emphasis; see also Collison, 1996)

While we have doubts about the appropriateness of the term 'normal' in this context we accept the point that there has, in recent years, been a notable increase in the availability of illicit drugs. A number of things follow from this. Firstly, in the second half of the 1990s, there are relatively few young people who are prevented from using drugs because of their scarcity. Secondly, the vast majority of young people will therefore be presented with a real or active decision about taking drugs. Although the prevalence data reviewed above indicate that a substantial proportion of young people use drugs they also show that most young people still do not use them. These young people, we suggest, are making a *real* and *active* choice.

Related to non-use is the notion of desistance. British and American data indicate that of the young people who have ever used an illicit drug significant proportions are not current or regular users. While, for these young people, there may have been a point in their lives when they used drugs occasionally or even regularly, they may have subsequently and consciously moved to a position of non-use. Further research is needed into the unfolding nature of people's drug careers to shed light on this process (however see Ghate and Chan, 1997).[10]

WHAT DO YOUNG PEOPLE THINK OF ILLICIT DRUG USE?

So far the analysis presented in this chapter has been devoted to patterns of drug use. Within the context of normalisation it is also essential to consider people's attitudes (Shiner and Newburn, 1997). Normalisation refers to a process whereby the meaning of apparently 'deviant' activities is redefined so that 'they are no longer managed as deviant' (Rock, 1973: 84). The extent of this redefinition can vary so that what was once considered deviant can come to be seen as 'normal trouble' (Cavan, 1966: 18) or as 'the standard, taken-for-granted substance and form of acts within the setting' (Rock, 1973: 80). The reaction of the audience is crucial in this process, for as Becker (1963: 8) has noted, deviance is produced through 'the application by others of rules and sanctions to an "offender" '. In order to argue that the status of an act has moved from 'deviant' to 'normal', it is necessary to show that, as well as being widespread, the act has come to be accepted as normal by the relevant audience(s). From this perspective what young people think is at least as relevant as what they do.

Although the link between attitudes and behaviour is, as we know, not necessarily a direct one (Fishbein and Ajzen, 1975; Charlton, 1982; Eiser et al., 1983; Nguyen-Van-Tam and Pearson, 1986), the clear implication of the normalisation thesis is that, in the epoch of postmodernity, youth culture is rebel culture. This was recently made explicit by Collin and Godfrey (1997: 7) when they argued that:

the exponential increase in drug use over the past decade, encouraged and endorsed by the arrival of Ecstasy, predetermined that the mainstream of youth culture became intimately bound up with law-breaking. As drug use became normalised, criminality was democratised. What Irvine Welsh calls the 'chemical generation' is also a generation of outlaws.

Within this formulation young people do not see drug use as problematic. Hirst and McCamley-Finney (1994: 42), for example, have claimed that young people are 'constantly surprised at adults' perceptions of drugs as something dangerous or unusual as, for most of them, they are part of their life'. Such a view was echoed by Coffield and Gofton (1994: 1, 3) who, having sought to 'enter the subjective world of young drug takers', concluded that while drug use is unproblematic for young people it 'is a problem to their uncomprehending parents, to their largely uninformed teachers and to the police'.

This view of the place and meaning of drugs in the lives of young people is, at the very least, guilty of romantic hyperbole. There is clear evidence that the restrictive attitudes to drug use which are held to be characteristic of the adult world are fairly widespread among young people on both sides of the Atlantic. American attitudinal data are far superior to British data and thus provide the starting point for our discussion. The 1995 MTF survey included a range of drug-related attitude measures. Figure 9.4 shows the percentage of 17–18-year-old American high school students who disapproved or strongly disapproved of:

trying cannabis once or twice;
smoking cannabis occasionally;
smoking cannabis regularly;

trying LSD once or twice;
taking LSD regularly;

trying cocaine powder once or twice;
taking cocaine powder occasionally;

trying crack once or twice;
taking crack occasionally.

Reinforcing the point that is evident from young people's patterns of use, Figure 9.4 shows that drugs are generally ordered in some form of hierarchy of disapproval. Thus a notably larger proportion of 17–18-year-old American high school students disapproved of using crack once or twice than disapproved of using cannabis once or twice. Figure 9.4 also indicates that young people's moral judgements concerning drug use vary according to the frequency of use. Hence regular use of cannabis was met with greater disapproval than occasional use. While youthful Americans seem reasonably tolerant of experimental cannabis use, their liberalism has very clear limits. Regular use of cannabis, it would seem, is met with high levels of disapproval as is use of other, 'harder', illicit substances, however tentative this may be.

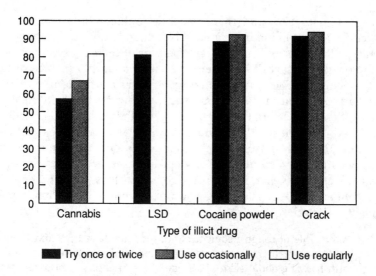

FIGURE 9.4   *Disapproval of drug use among 17–18-year-old American high school students (percentage who disapprove or strongly disapprove) (ISR, 1996)*

Although Britain lacks the quality of survey data that are available in America there is some evidence that British youth, like their American counterparts, tend towards restrictive attitudes. Following their analysis of a representative sample of over 1,000 Britons aged 12 to 15, Dowds and Redfern (1994) reported that two thirds of their respondents considered cannabis use to be a very serious offence. They concluded that among young people in their early to mid-teens, high numbers appear thoroughly convinced of the wrongness of using cannabis and that, within this group as a whole, such an act was viewed as as serious an offence as burglary, shoplifting or stealing cars.

Within Britain there is a growing body of qualitative work which helps to flesh out the nature of young people's attitudes and responses to drug use. Based on our work in the London borough of Newham, we have suggested that restrictive attitudes among young people are based on concerns about the functional, financial and health implications of drug use and, more pertinently in the current context, an association between drug use and other forms of deviant behaviour and a fear that drug use may lead them into general criminality (Shiner and Newburn, 1996, 1997). In general the young people who were interviewed as part of our study viewed drug use with concern and managed it as a problematic, or potentially problematic, activity.

The problematisation of drug use was strongest among respondents who had not used drugs. Familiarity with drugs does not, necessarily, breed enthusiasm about, or tolerance of, their use. Although some of the non-users in our 1996 study had very little contact with drugs, for others, particularly those living in an area of Newham known as Canning Town, contact with drugs and drug users was part of their everyday lives. The nature of this contact did not, however, lead them to embrace drug use or drug culture. The accounts they gave included references to people who had experienced 'bad trips', had become involved in stealing to finance their drug habit, had been chased by the police and arrested, had overdosed, been hospitalised and even died as a result of drug use. A common, although not universal, response among the non-users in the study was the development of strategies, based around peer selection (Coggans and McKellar, 1994), through which they sought to minimise their contact with drugs and drug users. As one young Canning Town resident reflected:

> There's a couple of rough people around, they just take trips and things like that, but I don't really hang around with them kind of people because they're not worth hanging about with . . . if one of my friends . . . bring[s] someone new round, I just say 'is he alright or is he like a bit of a div doing stupid things'. If they say 'divi', I just say don't let him come round here, just keep him away'.[11]

Although strongest among non-users, the view of drug use as a potentially problematic activity was not exclusive to them. Elsewhere we have suggested that the extent to which young drug users are distinct from non-users can be exaggerated (Shiner and Newburn, 1996, 1997). The young people included in our study who had used drugs shared many of the concerns voiced by non-users and they indicated that, in the social milieu within which they operated, drug use was far from being a sanction-free activity. In our view, the principal difference between many young drug users and non-users is the development, by the former, of techniques of neutralisation which temporarily render relevant social controls inoperative and allow them to engage in delinquent activities without abandoning their affiliation to consensus values (Sykes and Matza, 1957; Matza, 1964). The techniques of neutralisation which were evident in our interviews commonly focused on the differences between drugs. Frequently used techniques included claims that the substances being used were not harmful and were not really drugs, and that the user was not consuming enough to get addicted:

> Like [h]ash and weed, what I normally smoke and that, can't really harm you and that . . . like I'm not addicted to like speed or that, so I could give it up any time. The way I do it, I don't get addicted. Weed I don't use it all that often, I don't get addicted to it. Sometimes like I smoke it like seven days in one week but then leave it for a couple of months . . . I don't mind people who take like speed or like a joint now and again or something like that but I don't like the sort of people who take like coke and that . . . because it's a bad drug and that and it could kill you . . . [people who take coke] are putting their lives at risk and that going on coke, but people who smoke ash or take speed and that,

they're not really putting their lives at risk because it takes a lot of speed to kill them . . .

Q: *Say you went round to your sister's tonight and say your sister offered you coke, what would you do?*

I would tell her to fuck off . . . the reason I'm so against that sort of drug and that, because my cousin, he was on it and that and he used to steal like off my auntie and that, like money and her TV and that to get his drugs.

The young drug users included in the study frequently made reference to the rule-governed nature of drug use. They identified that there were clear rules concerning why, where, what and how much it was considered legitimate to use, and that those who broke these rules risked facing sanctions from, and even possible social exclusion by, other users. That young drug users monitor and regulate their own, as well as other people's, consumption is clear from the work of Ghate and Chan (1997). Following a comprehensive review of services for young drug users, they noted that a crisis point such as declining health, death of friends, suicide attempts or relationship breakdown may usher in a decision by an individual to try to terminate or reduce their consumption of drugs. The claim that drug use is viewed by young people as a normal, unproblematic, activity offers little explanation for why some young drug users seek help.

CONCLUSION

In this chapter we have attempted to locate the place and meaning of drug use in post-industrial society. More particularly, we have developed a critique of the increasingly dominant discourse which is reflected in the statements of musicians, policy-makers, police officers, journalists and academics which argues or implies that, for young people, drug use is normalised activity. In our opinion, such a view exaggerates levels of youthful drug use, ignores the level of 'refusal' that must now exist given the relatively ready availability of drugs, and fails to pay sufficient attention to the normative contexts in which youthful drug use occurs. Moreover, by considering the ways in which patterns of drug use have changed over time and by comparing recent experience in Britain and North America we have challenged the view which suggests that current patterns of drug use are indicative of a profound structural and cultural shift in (post)modern society. According to those who have posited a link between postmodernity and patterns of drug use, the postmodern condition is characterised by heightened consumption and a withering and dislocation of moral authority. As part of the process of commodification, illicit drugs are seen to have taken their place in the market place as just another consumable waiting to be devoured by hedonistic youth.

On both sides of the Atlantic it is clear that it is far from unusual for a young person to have used an illicit substance. Despite this, however, it remains the case that the notion of normalisation exaggerates levels of youthful drug use. In Britain, drug use, particularly current use, remains a minority activity and participation in the drug culture of the 'rave' scene is limited to a relatively small proportion of young people. Patterns of youthful drug use in America reveal a number of similarities to those in Britain. Drug use, particularly if we focus on current use and substances other than cannabis, remains a minority activity among young Americans. Any theory relating to the place and meaning of drug use in contemporary youth culture must take account of the fact that many young people do not use, and never have used, an illicit substance.

Despite the similarities in current patterns of youthful drug use in Britain and America, the introduction of a time element to the analysis highlights important differences between the two countries. Although British trends appear to be quite different from American trends both pose a significant challenge to those who would link current patterns of drug use to global changes in the social structure. While British data do point to increases in youthful drug use this trend appears to date back to the middle of the century and has taken the form of a relatively steady increase rather than a radical or sudden shift from one era to another. The posited link between postmodernity and contemporary patterns of drug use is further weakened by the trends that have been observed in America and some European countries. The 1980s saw a consistent fall in the proportion of youthful Americans who were involved in drug use. Although the 1990s have witnessed a reversal of this trend, the American experience undermines the claim that increased drug use is an inevitable product of global changes in the structure of post-industrial societies. It follows from this that changes in patterns of drug use in Britain reflect particular historical and national conditions and are not the simple reflection of broad global processes.

Although drugs researchers, particularly those in Britain, have focused on young people's behaviour it is equally important to consider their attitudes. Claims that drug use has become normalised ignore evidence that, on both sides of the Atlantic, restrictive attitudes are widespread among young people and that drug use continues to be heavily rule governed. Furthermore, the view that, for young people, drug use is unproblematic fails to make sense of the suggestion that they carefully monitor and regulate their own, and other people's, drug use. That drug use is managed as a potentially problematic activity by young people is evident in the sanctions imposed on users who break the rules and in the decisions made by those young drug users who seek help.

Claims for normalisation which pay insufficient attention to the distinctions that young people make between different illicit substances and which take insufficient account of the recency or normative context of behaviour run the risk of feeding 'respectable fears'. Much of what is currently being said about young people and drugs, including a great deal of academic discourse, has simply reinforced adult concerns about the problematic nature of youth. Though significant changes are occurring, there remain considerable continuities with the past. As Pearson has argued, the unhelpful, historical amnesia which tends to characterise the youth question means that 'youth cultures and youth crime assume the appearance of ever-increasing outrage and perpetual novelty' (1994: 1168). Academics and policy-makers need to develop new ways of talking and thinking about young people's drug use. We need to develop a set of ideas, and a way of expressing them, which is sensitive to changes in patterns of drug use and to differences between youth subcultures, but which also takes seriously the non-user and the concerns that many young people continue to have about illicit drug use.

NOTES

1. In late 1995 Leah Betts, an Essex schoolgirl, fell into a coma and died after taking an Ecstasy tablet on her eighteenth birthday. Although there has been a suggestion that the cause of the tragedy was water intoxication, Leah's death sparked an avalanche of media coverage and has become inextricably linked to Ecstasy in the public psyche (see Sharkey, 1996).
2. The figures and tables presented in this chapter are taken from aggregated data published by various authors. This restricted the ways that we could present the data as there were certain gaps and inconsistencies in the published data. It also meant that we had to present the data using the classifications generated by the various authors.
3. Graham and Bowling (1995) did not report patterns of use during the previous month.
4. This statement holds regardless of whether current use is measured at the level of the previous year or the previous month.
5. In the original tables for the MTF the term 'marijuana' was used. The authors of this chapter have used cannabis as their preferred term. Similarly, while the original tables include the term 'stimulants' the footnotes indicate that this term is interchangeable with that of amphetamines. The latter has been used throughout this chapter as the authors' preferred term.
6. The monthly figures for substances other than cannabis and LSD were not available from the source that was used (ISR, 1996).
7. The levels of cannabis and amphetamine use reported by 17–18-year-old Americans in response to the MTF survey are remarkably similar to those disclosed by British youths aged 16–19 in response to the BCS.
8. We are very grateful to the Research and Statistics Directorate at the Home Office and, in particular, to Andrew Percy for providing a more detailed age breakdown than was published in Ramsay and Percy (1996).
9. In this context the term 'drug user' has been used to describe people who have *ever* used an illicit drug.
10. Ghate and Chan's (1997) work is reviewed more fully later on in this chapter. It shows how young people adapt their drug use in response to

changing circumstances and, how, for example, a crisis point such as declining health, death of friends, suicide attempts or relationship break-down may usher in a decision by an individual to try to terminate or reduce their consumption of drugs.

11. The terms 'div' and 'divi' mean idiot or fool.

REFERENCES

Beck, U. (1992) *Risk Society: Towards a New Modernity.* London: Sage.

Beck, U., Giddens, A. and Lash, S. (1994) *Reflexive Modernisation.* Cambridge: Polity Press.

Becker, H. (1963) *Outsiders: Studies in the Sociology of Deviance.* London: Macmillan.

Cavan, S. (1966) *Liquor License.* Chicago: Aldine.

Charlton, A. (1982) 'Lung cancer: the ultimate smoking deterrent for young people?' *Journal of the Institute of Health Education,* 20 (1): 5–12.

Clements, I. (1993) 'Too hot to handle', *Druglink: The Journal on Drug Misuse in Britain,* 8: 10–12, London: Institute for the Study of Drug Dependence.

Coffield, F. and Gofton, L. (1994) *Drugs and Young People.* London: Institute for Public Policy Research.

Coggans, N. and McKellar, S. (1994) 'Peer pressure: a convenient explanation', *Druglink: The Journal on Drug Misuse in Britain,* 9: 16–18, London: Institute for the Study of Drug Dependence.

Collin, M. and Godfrey, J. (1997) *Altered State: The Story of Ecstasy Culture and Acid House.* London: Serpent's Tail.

Dowds, L. and Redfern, J. (1994) *Drug Education amongst Teenagers: a 1992 British Crime Survey Analysis.* London: Home Office.

Eiser, R., Vander Pligt, J. and Friend, P. (1983) 'Adolescents' arguments for and against smoking', *Journal of the Institute of Health Education,* 21 (3): 73–8.

Fishbein, M. and Ajzen, I. (1975) *Belief, Attitude, Intervention and Behaviour: An Introduction to Theory and Research.* Reading, MA: Addison-Wesley.

Gfroerer, J., Wright, D., Gustin, J., Rivero, M. and Cottone, T. (1996) *Preliminary Estimates from the 1995 National Household Survey on Drug Abuse* (Advanced Report 18).

Ghate, D. and Chan, L. (1997) *The Effectiveness of Services for Young Drug Users.* London: MORI.

Giddens, A. (1990) *The Consequences of Modernity.* Cambridge: Polity Press.

Giddens, A. (1991) *Modernity and Self-Identity.* Cambridge: Polity Press.

Graham, J. and Bowling, B. (1995) *Young People and Crime.* London: Home Office.

Hirst, J. and McCamley-Finney, A. (1994) *The Place and Meaning of Drugs in the Lives of Young People.* Sheffield: Health Research Institute, Sheffield Hallam University.

Huxley, A. (1932) *Brave New World.* London: Flamingo.

ISDD (1994) *Drug Misuse in Britain 1994.* London: Institute for the Study of Drug Dependence.

ISR (1996) *Monitoring the Future: A Continuing Study of American Youth.* Michigan: Institute for Social Research, University of Michigan.

Kumar, K. (1995) *From Post-Industrial to Post-Modern Society.* Oxford: Basil Blackwell.

Lash, S. and Urry, J. (1987) *The End of Organised Capitalism.* Cambridge: Polity Press.

Lyotard, J.F. (1984) *The Postmodern Condition.* Manchester: Manchester University Press.

Matza, D. (1964) *Delinquency and Drift.* New York: John Wiley.

Measham, F., Newcombe, R. and Parker, H. (1993) 'The post-heroin generation', *Druglink: The Journal on Drug Misuse in Britain*, 8: 16–17, London: Institute for the Study of Drug Dependence.

Measham, F., Newcombe, R. and Parker. H. (1994) 'The normalization of recreational drug use amongst young people in North-West England', *British Journal of Sociology*, 45: 287–312.

Mott, J. and Mirrlees-Black, C. (1993) *Self-reported Drug Misuse in England and Wales from the 1992 British Crime Survey.* London: Home Office Research and Statistics Department.

Nguyen-Van-Tam, J. and Pearson, J. (1986) 'Teenagers and motorcycles: knowledge and perception of risks', *Journal of the Institute of Health Education*, 24 (1): 32–9.

Paphides, P. (1997) 'Rave new world', *Time Out*, 11–18 June: 12.

Parker, H., Measham, F. and Aldridge, J. (1995) *Drugs Futures: Changing Patterns of Drug Use amongst English Youth.* London: Institute for the Study of Drug Dependence.

Pearson, G. (1983) *Hooligan: A History of Respectable Fears.* London: Macmillan.

Ramsay, M. and Percy, A. (1996) *Drug Misuse Declared: Results of the 1994 British Crime Survey.* London: Home Office.

Rock, P. (1973) *Deviant Behaviour.* London: Hutchinson.

Sharkey, A. (1996) 'Sorted or distorted', *Guardian*, 26 January: G2, 2.

Shiner, M. and Newburn, T. (1996) *The Youth Awareness Programme: An Evaluation of a Peer Education Drugs Project.* London: Central Drugs Prevention Unit, Home Office.

Shiner, M. and Newburn, T. (1997) 'Definitely, maybe not: the normalisation of recreational drug use amongst young people', *Sociology*, 31 (3): 1–19.

Silbereisen, R.K., Robins, R. and Rutter, M. (1995) 'Secular trends in substance use: concepts and data on the impact of social change on alcohol and drug abuse', in M. Rutter and D. Smith (eds), *Psychosocial Disorders in Young People: Time Trends and Their Causes.* Chichester: Wiley.

South, N. (1997) 'Drugs: use, crime, and control', in M. Maguire, R. Morgan and R. Reiner (eds), *The Oxford Handbook of Criminology*, 2nd edn. Oxford: Clarendon Press.

Sykes, G. and Matza, D. (1957) 'Techniques of neutralization', *American Sociological Review*, 22.

INDEX